Pay Yourself Back

ARE you tired? It is getting close to the time of year when people talk of feeling "all tired out" and there is much discussion of spring tonics. If you are fatigued and there is nothing organically wrong, the tonic you need and prob-

rest. If hard physical work is making you feel "all in" you may require more hours of sleep than usual even though this m⁓⁓ mean temporar⁓ ily giving up some form of ar⁓ you are not eating the right

Wear and Rest

Rest

This graph shows what happens when more energy is used by wear and tear than is paid back by rest.

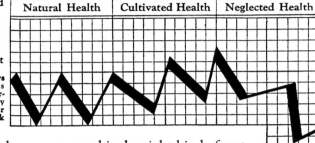

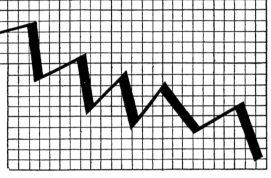

Natural Health	Cultivated Health	Neglected Health	Impaired Health	Bro

Normal Energy

Healthy Fatigue

Excessive Fatigue

Break-down

ably the only one you need is the right kind of rest to restore your energy.

To one person, rest may mean sleep; to another, physical exercise; to a third, recreation.

While it is true that few of us work up to our full capacity, and much so-called fatigue is imagined or just pure laziness—yet it is also true that many people work far beyond their strength without realizing the danger.

A certain amount of fatigue after exertion is natu-ral, but excessive fatigue is Nature's safety-device for warning that rest is needed. When you are over-tired, your powers of resistance are lowered and you are more susceptible to disease.

What brings about excessive fatigue? Usually over-strain—either physical or mental—and insufficient rest. Because your activity is both of the body and the mind, and one reacts on the other, your fatigue is a close interlacing of physical and mental weari-ness. Neither can be relieved separately. Emotional disturbances—worry, fear, resentment, discon-tent and depression also cause fatigue. The tired man is often a worried man, and the worried man is usually a tired man.

If you are over-tired, find the reason and then try to plan your time so that you will have sufficient

making food. If you are a mental worker the kind of rest you probably need is exercise in fresh air. If excessive emotion is making you tired, the right kind of recreation probably will help you.

Remember that excessive fatigue is not a thing to be lightly shrugged away. There is often a direct connection between the first neglected signs of fatigue and a serious breakdown from which re-covery is a slow, disheartening process.

If you tire too easily and if rest does not put you back in good condition, it is more than likely that your health is affected and needs attention.

Workers—take warning! Pay back the energy that you take out of yourself. As the years mount up, longer and longer periods of rest are necessary to make restoration. The "spring tonic" that you need most likely is just a rearrangement of your hours of work, play and rest, and not medicine.

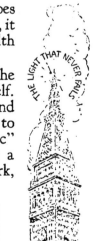

THE LIGHT THAT NEVER FAILS

Published by

METROPOLITAN LIFE INSURANCE COMPANY—NEW YORK

Biggest in the World, More Assets, More Policyholders, More Insurance in force, More new Insurance each year

(In answering this advertisement please mention THE SURVEY. It helps us, it identifies you.)

622

NATIONAL URBAN LEAGUE

FOR SOCIAL SERVICE AMONG NEGROES

127 EAST 23RD STREET ROOMS 31-33-34 NEW YORK CITY

TELEPHONE: GRAMERCY 3978

EUGENE KINCKLE JONES
EXECUTIVE SECRETARY

March 1, 1925.

Dear Survey Reader:-

The National Urban League seeks to improve the living conditions of Negroes in cities, making a specialty of opening new avenues of employment to Negroes and encouraging them in their efforts to become more efficient.

There are forty Urban Leagues, twenty-six with offices and staffs. Eighteen are included in community chests, receiving the endorsement that this connection entails. Colored social workers are trained through fellowships provided by the League at leading schools of social work. All League Boards, national and local, are composed of leading white and colored citizens, thus guaranteeing the best inter-racial thought on our common community problems growing out of race contacts.

Our Department of Research makes careful surveys of social conditions preparatory to launching programs of improvement. We provide facts on the Negro for lecturers, writers and students. We publish "OPPORTUNITY" magazine - a journal of Negro life, and our local organizations conduct programs in health, housing, recreation or general community welfare in accordance with the local need and demand.

Our budget for 1925 is $57,000, including $9,000 for the new Industrial Department which we hope will help take the color line out of industry. We invite you to $10 membership in the League or a contribution towards the $1,500 balance needed to complete our special industrial budget.

Sincerely yours,

EKJ/PWJ

Eugene Kinckle Jones
Eugene Kinckle Jones,
Executive Secretary.

Social Studies

Conducted by

Joseph K. Hart

What Shall We Do with the Facts?

THIS is no easy matter. The old white overseer of a Southern plantation took the employer's son to town with him one August day. He stopped at the grocery to get some provisions. When the grocer had taken down the order he suggested that the overseer take the small boy down to the ice plant to see them make ice. After protesting that the grocer must be "fooling," since anybody knew there "couldn't be ice in August," he reluctantly consented to the adventure. The two of them arrived at the plant just in time to see the workers turning out a number of great transparent cakes, which were undeniably ice. The overseer gazed in terror for a few moments; then seizing the boy by the hand, he ran down the steps and down the street for several blocks before he stopped. Out of breath at last, he turned and, shaking his finger in the small boy's face until he had recovered his breath, he finally said:

"It aint so; and if it is so, it aint right, and I'm going to have the preacher preach agin it next Sunday."

Here, also, are facts. What's to be done about them? Well, it must be confessed that America is, on the whole, in little mood for facts, just now. We prefer fancies more than facts; and we like our fancies to be tinged with fearsomeness.

It cheers us mightily to be afeared. It makes us appreciate our homes and schools and churches. The fate of the Child Labor Amendment shows America at our saddest and best. Facts are dull things. Bed-time stories, with bears growling in the woods and lions under the beds, make our beds feel wonderfully downy and comforting. We are going to take care of our own children: we are not going to let some ogre state, probably taking its cues from Russia, tell us what to do with our children. When we have eaten fearsome fancies long enough we shall become noble; perhaps even become handsome.

There are scientists who say, with that folly that is so characteristic of the scientist: "You'd best be careful how you fool with facts—they are sometimes loaded!" But that sort of talk is just the professional salesman trying to dispose of his own wares. Facts can be evaded—out of hand. We can legislate evolution out of existence. We can turn the scientist out of his chair and restore our old fanciful traditions. We can feed our minds on folly—and grow fat—of mind.

What shall we do with facts? Some people face them— but that gets them into trouble. Perhaps we'd best continue to do as we have always done, praise them and ignore them!

Analytic Index of This Issue

1. Child Welfare:

    Negro children in Harlem, p. 691

2. Family Welfare:

    Negro family life, p. 690
    Fate of the Harlem family, p. 698

3. Law and Lawbreakers:

    Bootlegging in Harlem, p. 694f

4. Conquest of Disease:

    Fate of the old stock, p. 641
    Nursing services in Harlem, p. 699
    The Negro and the doctor, p. 713

5. Promotion of Health:

    Health of the Negro, p. 714
    Health Work in Michigan, p. 700

6. Mental Hygiene:

    Race prejudice in New York City, p. 680f
    The Negro woman's fight for freedom, p. 689f
    Gambling amongst Negroes, p. 692f

7. Organizing Social Forces:

    The Negro's group life, p. 634; 648f
    Group patterns in Harlem, p. 677f
    Social work in Harlem, p. 698

8. Town Planning:

    Building a city on prejudice, p. 682f
    Planning the city church, p. 695f

9. City Communities:

    The meaning of cities to races, p. 630
    How Harlem came to be, p. 635f
    Effects of city life, p. 641
    City patterns, p. 676f
    How the city treats the Negro, p. 692f

10. Country Communities:

    The old South in the city, p. 644f

11. Immigration and Race Relations:

    The new Negro, p. 631f
    From many lands, p. 648f
    Race prejudice amongst Negroes, p. 650
    Youth and the race, p. 659f

12. School and Community:

    Education in Harlem, p. 646
    Books by Negroes, p. 703ff

13. Education outside the School:

    How races change, p. 631f
    The origins of jazz, p. 635
    How the city educates, p. 642
    Negro folk music, p. 655ff

14. Industrial Conditions:

    Negro property owners in Harlem, p. 638
    The Negro worker, p. 643

15. Industrial Relations:

    The gang laborer, p. 639
    The Negro woman worker, p. 689f
    The Negro in industry, p. 719f

16. Social Invention in Industry:

    End of the Canadian Industrial Disputes Investigation act, p. 700
    Status of minimum wage legislation, p. 700

17. Peace and International Relations:

    International relations in Harlem, p. 677f
    Problems of opium control, p. 701

18. Motives and Ideals:

    Hopes for democracy, p. 629
    What the Negro wants, p. 631f
    Religion in Harlem, p. 644f
    Types of personality, p. 651ff
    Origins of culture, p. 655f
    What is jazz? p. 665f
    The arts of the Negro, p. 668f
    Spiritual origins of the American Negro, p. 670f
    The inner life of Harlem, p. 679

A Glimpse Ahead!

KIPLING gave us the high road of India in "Kim." Sinclair Lewis set down America on "Main Street." But that contrast is not the whole story of East and West.

We have no hesitancy in saying that here in the Northern cities of the United States, of which New York is arch type, is going forward something which will take its place in the great pageant of humanity.

But Harlem does not tell the whole story of the Negro in America. It is a fresh approach to an old story. It is a coat cut of city cloth—with the seams of social problems which underlie it, the cultural pattern which surfaces it. In the months ahead Survey Graphic will bring out articles which will throw light on other factors in race relations.

Hampton, Tuskegee and Points North

DR. ROBERT R. MOTON, *Principal, Tuskegee Institute.*

Thousands of countrysides have felt the yeast of the leadership of Armstrong and Frissell, Washington and Moton. Now comes the northward migration. How are the values which have been wrought out in an educational program, which is slowly revolutionizing the economy of the cotton states, to be conserved in the new situation?

A Southern Negro's Impression of Harlem

JOHN HOPE, *President, Morehouse College, Atlanta.*

President Hope, who is throwing open the sciences as never before to the youth of his race, will give his keen and outspoken observations of the Harlem scene.

The School of the Home-Acres

ROSSA B. COOLEY, *Principal, Penn School, St. Helena Island, South Carolina.*

Here on a sea island off South Carolina is carried forward what Professor Hart has called the most interesting experiment in elementary education in the United States today; where the farms have been brought

to school, and then the school spread out on the Island until school and community are coterminous.

Southern Experience in Its Bearing on the Northern City

WILL W. ALEXANDER, *Director, Commission on Interracial Cooperation, Atlanta.*

In many Southern communities a new method which has promise has come in with the rise and spread of the inter-racial councils. When the human history of the South is written this movement may come to be looked back upon as ushering in a new epoch. What has this constructive Southern experience to offer the North?

Where East Africa Borders the Future

JAMES H. DILLARD, *President, The Slater Fund, Charlottesville, Va.*

We would have to go back to Stanley if not to Marco Polo to find a counterpart of the educational expeditions sent out by the Phelps Stokes Fund. Dr. Dillard was a member of the East African Commission which reports this spring.

The Regional Community

IN late April a world conference on Town City and Regional Planning will be held in New York. As their special contribution to the exchange of ideas which will then take place, a small imaginative group of planners who call themselves the Regional Planning Association of America have collaborated with the editors of The Survey in gathering for our May Graphic a series of articles, maps, diagrams and sketches which will throw a fresh light on the enormous quandary in which city-dwellers and city-planners find themselves and on the promise of a new approach to the city, with the region as a base. Among those collaborating:

Governor Alfred E. Smith	Alexander M. Bing
Clarence E. Stein	Benton Mackaye
Lewis Mumford	Stuart Chase
Art Young	Henry Wright
Frederick L. Ackerman	Joseph K. Hart
Frederick Bigger	Robert W. Bruére

THE Survey Graphic is maintained mutually by 1700 reader-members of Survey Associates to engage in just such pieces of social interpretation as this.

If you are a professional man or woman and want to know of the living contributions of other professions where they overlap yours in the realm of the common welfare; if you are a lawyer who wants to know of the big advances in health, a physician alive to the cross-fires of psychology and education—a business man aware of the upward thrust of labor—

If you want to know Who and How and Whither—the Survey Graphic is for you.

SURVEY ASSOCIATES.
112 East 19th Street, New York.

Put me down for a six-months trial subscription to Survey Graphic, monthly, beginning with the current issue and send me a bill for $1.00 (one year $3.00)

Name ....

Address ....

SURVEY ASSOCIATES, INC.
PUBLISHERS
THE SURVEY—Twice-a-month—$5.00 a year
SURVEY GRAPHIC—Monthly—$3.00 a year
ROBERT W. deFOREST, *President*
JULIAN W. MACK, V. EVERIT MACY, *Vice-Presidents*
ANN REED BRENNER, *Secretary*
ARTHUR KELLOGG, *Treasurer*

PAUL U. KELLOGG, *Editor*
Associate Editors

JOSEPH K. HART	HAVEN EMERSON, M.D.
ROBERT W. BRUÈRE	MARY ROSS
MARTHA BENSLEY BRUÈRE	SARA MERRILL

LEON WHIPPLE
GEDDES SMITH, *Managing Editor*
Contributing Editors

EDWARD T. DEVINE	GRAHAM TAYLOR
JANE ADDAMS	FLORENCE KELLEY

ARTHUR KELLOGG, *Manager*
JOHN D. KENDERDINE, *Extension Manager*
MARY R. ANDERSON, *Advertising*

112 East 19 Street, New York

SURVEY GRAPHIC

Vol. VI, No. 6   March, 1925

CONTENTS

I. The Greatest Negro Community in the World

HARLEM 629
ENTER THE NEW NEGRO . . *Alain Locke* 631
THE MAKING OF HARLEM . *James W. Johnson* 635
BLACK WORKERS AND THE CITY . . . .
                 Charles S. Johnson 641
THE SOUTH LINGERS ON . . *Rudolph Fisher* 644
THE TROPICS IN NEW YORK . *W. A. Domingo* 648

II. The Negro Expresses Himself

HARLEM TYPES . . . . . . *Winold Reiss* 651
THE BLACK MAN BRINGS HIS GIFTS . . .
                 W. E. B. DuBois 655
YOUTH SPEAKS, Poems . *Countée Cullen, Anne
  Spencer, Angelina Grimke, Claude McKay, Jean
  Toomer and Langston Hughes* 659
JAZZ AT HOME . . . . . *J. A. Rogers* 665
NEGRO ART AND AMERICA . *Albert C. Barnes* 668
THE NEGRO DIGS UP HIS PAST . *A. Schomburg* 670
THE ART OF THE ANCESTORS 673
HERITAGE . . . . . . *Countée Cullen* 674

III. Black and White—Studies in Race Contacts

THE DILEMMA OF SOCIAL PATTERN . . . .
                 Melville J. Herskovits 677
THE RHYTHM OF HARLEM . *Konrad Bercovici* 679
COLOR LINES . . . . . . *Walter F. White* 680
HARVEST OF RACE PREJUDICE . *Kelly Miller* 682
BREAKING THROUGH . *Eunice Roberta Hunton* 684
PORTRAITS OF NEGRO WOMEN . *Winold Reiss* 685
THE DOUBLE TASK . *Elise Johnson McDougald* 689
AMBUSHED IN THE CITY . *Winthrop D. Lane* 692
THE CHURCH AND THE NEGRO SPIRIT . .
                 George E. Haynes 695
EDITORIALS 698
BOOKS 702

The Gist of It

THE Survey is seeking, month by month and year by year to follow the subtle traces of race growth and interaction through the shifting outline of social organization and by the flickering light of individual achievement. There are times when these forces that work so slowly and so delicately seem suddenly to flower—and we become aware that the curtain has lifted on a new act in the drama of part or all of us. Such, we believe, was the case with Ireland on the threshold of political emancipation, and the New Ireland spoke for itself in our issue of November 1921; with the New Russia which was to some degree interpreted in March 1923; and with the newly awakened Mexico, in May 1924. If The Survey reads the signs aright, such a dramatic flowering of a new race-spirit is taking place close at home—among American Negroes, and the stage of that new episode is Harlem.

FOR the concept of this issue, for painstaking collaboration in its preparation, for the full-length study of The New Negro (p. 631) and for many smaller pieces in the mosaic of this number, The Survey is indebted to Alain Locke, a graduate of Harvard, Oxford and Berlin, now professor of philosophy at Harvard University, and himself a brilliant exemplar of that poise and insight which are happy omens for the Negro's future.

THE Making of Harlem is recounted by James Weldon Johnson (p. 635). This journalist, editor, poet, publicist is executive secretary of the National Association for the Advancement of Colored People, editor of the Book of American Negro Poetry, and author of Fifty Years and After, and The Autobiography of an Ex-Colored Man.

CHARLES S. JOHNSON, who studies Black Workers and the City (p. 641) is director of publicity and research for the National Urban League and the editor of its organ, Opportunity; a Journal of Negro Life. A social survey expert, he was assistant secretary of the Chicago Commission on Race Relations. Rudolph Fisher, who sketches some Southern strains in the city (p. 644) is a young short-story writer of distinctive achievement. A West Indian, a journalist and author, W. A. Domingo writes of The Tropics in New York (p. 648).

WINOLD REISS'S studies of Mexican types will be vividly remembered by readers of the Mexican Number.

THE versatile editor of The Crisis, author of Souls of Black Folk, Darkwater, The Gift of Black Folk W. E. B. DuBois presents the Negro bringing gifts (p. 655). For the courtesy of permitting the republication of a number of poems, in addition to those here published for the first time, The Survey's thanks go to the authors and publishers mentioned. J. A. Rogers, who characterizes Jazz at Home (p. 665) is the author of From Superman to Man.

WHAT the Negro's creative temperament may mean to America (p. 668) is the theme of Albert C. Barnes, a connoisseur whose galleries at Merion, Pennsylvania, house a distinguished collection. Arthur A. Schomburg (The Negro Digs Up His Past, p. 670), is a member of the American Negro Academy.

TURNING from art expression to sociological fact and social problem—Melville J. Herskovits, an anthropologist engaged in an extended study of the problem of variability under racial crossing, opens the third section of the issue with a study of The Dilemma of Social Pattern (p. 676), to which Konrad Bercovici, with the intuitive vigor which characterized his Around the World in New York, offers an intriguing companion-piece in The Rhythm of Harlem.

WALTER F. WHITE, whose The Fire in the Flint was an outstanding novel of 1924, is assistant secretary of the National Association for the Advancement of Colored People. He studies the personal effects of prejudice in Color Lines (p. 680), while Dean Kelly Miller of the Junior College of Howard University, a leader in the Negro Sanhedrin, discusses its social aspects (p. 682). A further sidelight on segregation is carried by Eunice Hunton's Breaking Through (p. 684). Miss Hunton, a recent Smith graduate, is a social worker and writer.

A vocational expert, social worker, leader in women's work, recently appointed assistant principal of Public School No. 89, in Harlem, Mrs. McDougald tells of the double task of Negro women (p. 689). The grim facts of exploitation which must be reckoned with in Harlem are tersely summarized by Winthrop D. Lane (p. 692) a contributing editor of The Survey.

GEORGE E. HAYNES, secretary of the Commission on Church and Race Relations of the Federal Council of Churches of Christ in America, tells of the churches in Harlem (p. 695).

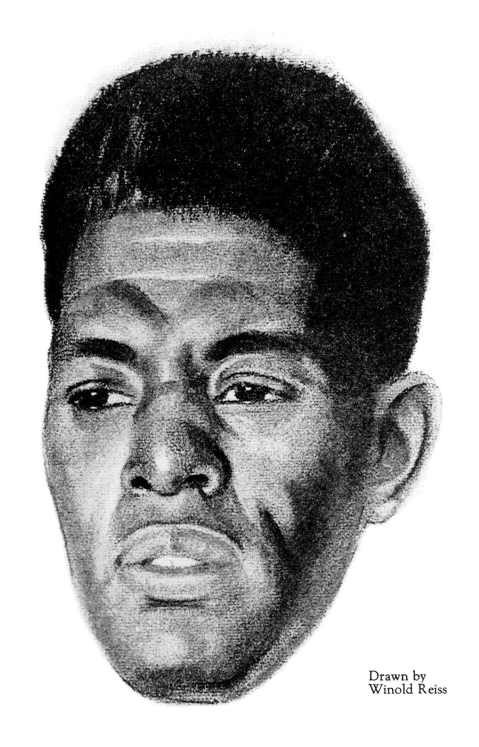

Drawn by
Winold Reiss

ROLAND HAYES

Whose achievement as a singer symbolizes the promise of the younger generation

SURVEY GRAPHIC

MARCH
1925

Volume VI
No. 6

Harlem

IF we were to offer a symbol of what Harlem has come to mean in the short span of twenty years it would be another statue of liberty on the landward side of New York. It stands for a folk-movement which in human significance can be compared only with the pushing back of the western frontier in the first half of the last century, or the waves of immigration which have swept in from overseas in the last half. Numerically far smaller than either of these movements, the volume of migration is such none the less that Harlem has become the greatest Negro community the world has known—without counterpart in the South or in Africa. But beyond this, Harlem represents the Negro's latest thrust towards Democracy.

The special significance that today stamps it as the sign and center of the renaissance of a people lies, however, layers deep under the Harlem that many know but few have begun to understand. Physically Harlem is little more than a note of sharper color in the kaleidoscope of New York. The metropolis pays little heed to the shifting crystallizations of its own heterogeneous millions. Never having experienced permanence, it has watched, without emotion or even curiosity, Irish, Jew, Italian, Negro, a score of other races drift in and out of the same colorless tenements.

So Harlem has come into being and grasped its destiny with little heed from New York. And to the herded thousands who shoot beneath it twice a day on the subway, or the comparatively few whose daily travel takes them within sight of its fringes or down its main arteries, it is a black belt and nothing more. The pattern of delicatessen store and cigar shop and restaurant and undertaker's shop which repeats itself a thousand times on each of New York's long avenues is unbroken through Harlem. Its apartments, churches and storefronts antedated the Negroes and, for all New York knows, may outlast them there. For most of New York, Harlem is merely a rough rectangle of commonplace city blocks, lying between and to east and west of Lenox and Seventh Avenues, stretching nearly a mile north and south—and unaccountably full of Negroes.

Another Harlem is savored by the few—a Harlem of racy music and racier dancing, of cabarets famous or notorious according to their kind, of amusement in which abandon and sophistication are cheek by jowl—a Harlem which draws the connoisseur in diversion as well as the undiscriminating sightseer. This Harlem is the fertile source of the "shufflin'" and "rollin'" and "runnin' wild" revues that establish themselves season after season in "downtown" theaters. It is part of the exotic fringe of the metropolis.

Beneath this lies again the Harlem of the newspapers—a Harlem of monster parades and political flummery, a Harlem swept by revolutionary oratory or draped about the mysterious figures of Negro "millionaires," a Harlem preoccupied with naive adjustments to a white world—a Harlem, in short, grotesque with the distortions of journalism.

YET in final analysis, Harlem is neither slum, ghetto, resort or colony, though it is in part all of them. It is—or promises at least to be—a race capital. Europe seething in a dozen centers with emergent nationalities, Palestine full of a renascent Judaism—these are no more alive with the spirit of a racial awakening than Harlem; culturally and spiritually it focuses a people. Negro life is not only founding new centers, but finding a new soul. The tide of Negro migration, northward and city-ward, is not to be fully explained as a blind flood started by the demands of war industry coupled with the shutting off of foreign migration, or by the pressure of poor crops coupled with increased social terrorism in certain sections of the South and Southwest. Neither labor demand, the boll-weevil nor the Ku Klux Klan is a basic factor, however contributory any or all of them may have been. The wash and rush of this human tide on the beach line of the northern city centers is to be explained primarily in terms of a new vision of opportunity, of social and economic freedom, of a spirit to seize, even in the face of an extortionate and heavy toll, a chance for the improvement of conditions. With each successive wave of it, the movement of the Negro migrant becomes more and more like that of the European waves at their crests, a mass movement toward the larger and the more democratic chance—in the Negro's case a deliberate flight not only from countryside to city, but from mediaeval America to modern.

The secret lies close to what distinguishes Harlem from the ghettos with which it is sometimes compared. The ghetto picture is that of a slowly dissolving mass, bound by ties of custom and culture and association, in the midst of a freer and more varied society. From the racial standpoint, our Harlems are themselves crucibles. Here in Manhattan is not merely the largest Negro community in the world, but the first concentration in history of so many diverse elements of Negro life. It has attracted the African, the West Indian, the Negro American; has brought together the Negro of the North and the Negro of the South; the man from the city and the man from the town and village; the peasant, the student, the business man, the professional man, artist, poet, musician, adventurer and worker, preacher and criminal, exploiter and social outcast. Each group has come with its own separate motives and for its own special ends, but their greatest experience has been the finding of one another. Proscription and prejudice have thrown these dissimilar elements into a common area of contact and interaction. Within this area, race sympathy and unity have determined a further fusing of sentiment and experience. So what began in terms of segregation becomes more and more, as its elements mix and react, the laboratory of a great race-welding. Hitherto, it must be admitted that American Negroes have been a race more in name than in fact, or to be exact, more in sentiment than in experience. The chief bond between them has been that of a common condition rather than a common consciousness; a problem in common rather than a life in common. In Harlem, Negro life is seizing upon its first chances for group expression and self-determination. That is why our comparison is taken with those nascent centers of folk-expression and self-determination which are playing a creative part in the world today. Without pretense to their political significance, Harlem has the same role to play for the New Negro as Dublin has had for the New Ireland or Prague for the New Czechoslovakia.

It is true the formidable centers of our race life, educational, industrial, financial, are not in Harlem, yet here, nevertheless, are the forces that make a group known and felt in the world. The reformers, the fighting advocates, the inner spokesmen, the poets, artists and social prophets are here, and pouring in toward them are the fluid ambitious youth and pressing in upon them the migrant masses. The professional observers, and the enveloping communities as well, are conscious of the physics of this stir and movement, of the cruder and more obvious facts of a ferment and a migration. But they are as yet largely unaware of the psychology of it, of the galvanizing shocks and reactions, which mark the social awakening and internal reorganization which are making a race out of its own disunited elements.

A railroad ticket and a suitcase, like a Bagdad carpet, transport the Negro peasant from the cotton-field and farm to the heart of the most complex urban civilization. Here, in the mass, he must and does survive a jump of two generations in social economy and of a century and more in civilization. Meanwhile the Negro poet, student, artist, thinker, by the very move that normally would take him off at a tangent from the masses, finds himself in their midst, in a situation concentrating the racial side of his experience and heightening his race-consciousness. These moving, half-awakened newcomers provide an exceptional seed-bed for the germinating contacts of the enlightened minority. And that is why statistics are out of joint with fact in Harlem, and will be for a generation or so.

HARLEM, I grant you, isn't typical—but it is significant, it is prophetic. No sane observer, however sympathetic to the new trend, would contend that the great masses are articulate as yet, but they stir, they move, they are more than physically restless. The challenge of the new intellectuals among them is clear enough—the "race radicals" and realists who have broken with the old epoch of philanthropic guidance, sentimental appeal and protest. But are we after all only reading into the stirrings of a sleeping giant the dreams of an agitator? The answer is in the migrating peasant. It is the "man farthest down" who is most active in getting up. One of the most characteristic symptoms of this is the professional man himself migrating to recapture his constituency after a vain effort to maintain in some Southern corner what for years back seemed an established living and clientele. The clergyman following his errant flock, the physician or lawyer trailing his clients, supply the true clues. In a real sense it is the rank and file who are leading, and the leaders who are following. A transformed and transforming psychology permeates the masses.

When the racial leaders of twenty years ago spoke of developing race-pride and stimulating race-consciousness, and of the desirability of race solidarity, they could not in any accurate degree have anticipated the abrupt feeling that has surged up and now pervades the awakened centers. Some of the recognized Negro leaders and a powerful section of white opinion identified with "race work" of the older order have indeed attempted to discount this feeling as a "passing phase," an attack of "race nerves," so to speak, an "aftermath of the war," and the like. It has not abated, however, if we are to gage by the present tone and temper of the Negro press, or by the shift in popular support from the officially recognized and orthodox spokesmen to those of the independent, popular, and often radical type who are unmistakable symptoms of a new order. It is a social disservice to blunt the fact that the Negro of the Northern centers has reached a stage where tutelage, even of the most interested and well-intentioned sort, must give place to new relationships, where positive self-direction must be reckoned with in ever increasing measure.

As a service to this new understanding, the contributors to this Harlem number have been asked, not merely to describe Harlem as a city of migrants and as a race center, but to voice these new aspirations of a people, to read the clear message of the new conditions, and to discuss some of the new relationships and contacts they involve. First, we shall look at Harlem, with its kindred centers in the Northern and Mid-Western cities, as the way mark of a momentous folk movement; then as the center of a gripping struggle for an industrial and urban foothold. But more significant than either of these, we shall also view it as the stage of the pageant of contemporary Negro life. In the drama of its new and progressive aspects, we may be witnessing the resurgence of a race; with our eyes focussed on the Harlem scene we may dramatically glimpse the New Negro.

A. L.

Enter the New Negro

By ALAIN LOCKE

IN the last decade something beyond the watch and guard of statistics has happened in the life of the American Negro and the three norns who have traditionally presided over the Negro problem have a changeling in their laps. The Sociologist, The Philanthropist, the Race-leader are not unaware of the New Negro, but they are at a loss to account for him. He simply cannot be swathed in their formulae. For the younger generation is vibrant with a new psychology; the new spirit is awake in the masses, and under the very eyes of the professional observers is transforming what has been a perennial problem into the progressive phases of contemporary Negro life.

Could such a metamorphosis have taken place as suddenly as it has appeared to? The answer is no; not because the New Negro is not here, but because the Old Negro had long become more of a myth than a man. The Old Negro, we must remember, was a creature of moral debate and historical controversy. His has been a stock figure perpetuated as an historical fiction partly in innocent sentimentalism, partly in deliberate reactionism. The Negro himself has contributed his share to this through a sort of protective social mimicry forced upon him by the adverse circumstances of dependence. So for generations in the mind of America, the Negro has been more of a formula than a human being—a something to be argued about, condemned or defended, to be "kept down," or "in his place," or "helped up," to be worried with or worried over, harassed or patronized, a social bogey or a social burden. The thinking Negro even has been induced to share this same general attitude, to focus his attention on controversial issues, to see himself in the distorted perspective of a social problem. His shadow, so to speak, has been more real to him than his personality. Through having had to appeal from the unjust stereotypes of his oppressors and traducers to those of his liberators, friends and benefactors he has subscribed to the traditional positions from which his case has been viewed. Little true social or self-understanding has or could come from such a situation.

But while the minds of most of us, black and white, have thus burrowed in the trenches of the Civil War and Reconstruction, the actual march of development has simply flanked these positions, necessitating a sudden reorientation of view. We have not been watching in the right direction; set North and South on a sectional axis, we have not noticed the East till the sun has us blinking.

Recall how suddenly the Negro spirituals revealed themselves; suppressed for generations under the stereotypes of Wesleyan hymn harmony, secretive, half-ashamed, until the courage of being natural brought them out—and behold, there was folk-music. Similarly the mind of the Negro seems suddenly to have slipped from under the tyranny of social intimidation and to be shaking off the psychology of imitation and implied inferiority. By shedding the old chrysalis of the Negro problem we are achieving something like a spiritual emancipation. Until recently, lacking self-understanding, we have been almost as much of a problem to ourselves as we still are to others. But the decade that found us with a problem has left us with only a task. The multitude perhaps feels as yet only a strange relief and a new vague urge, but the thinking few know that in the reaction the vital inner grip of prejudice has been broken.

With this renewed self-respect and self-dependence, the life of the Negro community is bound to enter a new dynamic phase, the buoyancy from within compensating for whatever pressure there may be of conditions from without. The migrant masses, shifting from countryside to city, hurdle several generations of experience at a leap, but more important, the same thing happens spiritually in the life-attitudes and self-expression of the Young Negro, in his poetry, his art, his education and his new outlook, with the additional advantage, of course, of the poise and greater certainty of knowing what it is all about. From this comes the promise and warrant of a new leadership. As one of them has discerningly put it:

> We have tomorrow   Yesterday, a night-gone thing
> Bright before us   A sun-down name.
> Like a flame.
>
> And dawn today
> Broad arch above the road we came.
> We march!

This is what, even more than any "most creditable record of fifty years of freedom," requires that the Negro of today be seen through other than the dusty spectacles of past controversy. The day of "aunties," "uncles" and "mammies" is equally gone. Uncle Tom and Sambo have passed on, and even the "Colonel" and "George" play barnstorm roles from which they escape with relief when the public spotlight is off. The popular melodrama has about played itself out, and it is time to scrap the fictions, garret the bogeys and settle down to a realistic facing of facts.

FIRST we must observe some of the changes which since the traditional lines of opinion were drawn have rendered these quite obsolete. A main change has been, of course, that shifting of the Negro population which has made the Negro problem no longer exclusively or even predominantly Southern. Why should our minds remain sectionalized, when the problem itself no longer is? Then the trend of migration has not only been toward the North and the Central Midwest, but city-ward and to the great centers of industry—the problems of adjustment are new, practical, local and not peculiarly racial. Rather they are an integral part of the large industrial and social problems of our present-day democracy. And finally, with the Negro rapidly in process of class differentiation, if it ever was warrantable to regard and treat the Negro en masse it is becoming with every day less possible, more unjust and more ridiculous.

The Negro too, for his part, has idols of the tribe to

smash. If on the one hand the white man has erred in making the Negro appear to be that which would excuse or extenuate his treatment of him, the Negro, in turn, has too often unnecessarily excused himself because of the way he has been treated. The intelligent Negro of today is resolved not to make discrimination an extenuation for his shortcomings in performance, individual or collective; he is trying to hold himself at par, neither inflated by sentimental allowances nor depreciated by current social discounts. For this he must know himself and be known for precisely what he is, and for that reason he welcomes the new scientific rather than the old sentimental interest. Sentimental interest in the Negro has ebbed. We used to lament this as the falling off of our friends; now we rejoice and pray to be delivered both from self-pity and condescension. The mind of each racial group has had a bitter weaning, apathy or hatred on one side matching disillusionment or resentment on the other; but they face each other today with the possibility at least of entirely new mutual attitudes.

It does not follow that if the Negro were better known, he would be better liked or better treated. But mutual understanding is basic for any subsequent cooperation and adjustment. The effort toward this will at least have the effect of remedying in large part what has been the most unsatisfactory feature of our present stage of race relationships in America, namely the fact that the more intelligent and representative elements of the two race groups have at so many points got quite out of vital touch with one another.

The fiction is that the life of the races is separate, and increasingly so. The fact is that they have touched too closely at the unfavorable and too lightly at the favorable levels.

While inter-racial councils have sprung up in the South, drawing on forward elements of both races, in the Northern cities manual laborers may brush elbows in their everyday work, but the community and business leaders have experienced no such interplay or far too little of it. These segments must achieve contact or the race situation in America becomes desperate. Fortunately this is happening. There is a growing realization that in social effort the cooperative basis must supplant long-distance philanthropy, and that the only safeguard for mass relations in the future must be provided in the carefully maintained contacts of the enlightened minorities of both race groups. In the intellectual realm a renewed and keen curiosity is replacing the recent apathy; the Negro is being carefully studied, not just talked about and discussed. In art and letters, instead of being wholly caricatured, he is being seriously portrayed and painted.

To all of this the New Negro is keenly responsive as an augury of a new democracy in American culture. He is contributing his share to the new social understanding. But the desire to be understood would never in itself have been sufficient to have opened so completely the protectively closed portals of the thinking Negro's mind. There is still too much possibility of being snubbed or patronized for that. It was rather the necessity for fuller, truer, self-expression, the realization of the unwisdom of allowing social discrimination to segregate him mentally, and a counter-attitude to cramp and fetter his own living—and so the "spite-wall" that the intellectuals built over the "color-line" has happily been taken down. Much of this reopening of intellectual contacts has centered in New York and has been richly

fruitful not merely in the enlarging of personal experience, but in the definite enrichment of American art and letters and in the clarifying of our common vision of the social tasks ahead.

The particular significance in the reestablishment of contact between the more advanced and representative classes is that it promises to offset some of the unfavorable reactions of the past, or at least to re-surface race contacts somewhat for the future. Subtly the conditions that are moulding a New Negro are moulding a new American attitude.

However, this new phase of things is delicate; it will call for less charity but more justice; less help, but infinitely closer understanding. This is indeed a critical stage of race relationships because of the likelihood, if the new temper is not understood, of engendering sharp group antagonism and a second crop of more calculated prejudice. In some quarters, it has already done so. Having weaned the Negro, public opinion cannot continue to paternalize. The Negro today is inevitably moving forward under the control largely of his own objectives. What are these objectives? Those of his outer life are happily already well and finally formulated, for they are none other than the ideals of American institutions and democracy. Those of his inner life are yet in process of formation, for the new psychology at present is more of a consensus of feeling than of opinion, of attitude rather than of program. Still some points seem to have crystallized.

UP to the present one may adequately describe the Negro's "inner objectives" as an attempt to repair a damaged group psychology and reshape a warped social perspective. Their realization has required a new mentality for the American Negro. And as it matures we begin to see its effects; at first, negative, iconoclastic, and then positive and constructive. In this new group psychology we note the lapse of sentimental appeal, then the development of a more positive self-respect and self-reliance; the repudiation of social dependence, and then the gradual recovery from hyper-sensitiveness and "touchy" nerves, the repudiation of the double standard of judgment with its special philanthropic allowances and then the sturdier desire for objective and scientific appraisal; and finally the rise from social disillusionment to race pride, from the sense of social debt to the responsibilities of social contribution, and offsetting the necessary working and commonsense acceptance of restricted conditions, the belief in ultimate esteem and recognition. Therefore the Negro today wishes to be known for what he is, even in his faults and shortcomings, and scorns a craven and precarious survival at the price of seeming to be what he is not. He resents being spoken for as a social ward or minor, even by his own, and to being regarded a chronic patient for the sociological clinic, the sick man of American Democracy. For the same reasons, he himself is through with those social nostrums and panaceas, the so-called "solutions" of his "problem," with which he and the country have been so liberally dosed in the past. Religion, freedom, education, money—in turn, he has ardently hoped for and peculiarly trusted these things; he still believes in them, but not in blind trust that they alone will solve his life-problem.

Each generation, however, will have its creed and that of the present is the belief in the efficacy of collective effort, in race cooperation. This deep feeling of race is at present the mainspring of Negro life. It seems to be the outcome of the reaction to proscription and prejudice; an attempt, fairly successful on the whole, to convert a defensive into an offensive position, a handicap into an incentive. It is radical in tone, but not in purpose and only the most stupid forms of opposition, misunderstanding or persecution could make it otherwise. Of course, the thinking Negro has shifted a little toward the left with the world-trend, and there is an increasing group who affiliate with radical and liberal movements. But fundamentally for the present the Negro is radical on race matters, conservative on others, in other words, a "forced radical," a social protestant rather than a genuine radical. Yet under further pressure and injustice iconoclastic thought and motives will inevitably increase. Harlem's quixotic radicalisms call for their ounce of democracy today lest tomorrow they be beyond cure.

The Negro mind reaches out as yet to nothing but American wants, American ideas. But this forced attempt to build his Americanism on race values is a unique social experiment, and its ultimate success is impossible except through the fullest sharing of American culture and institutions. There should be no delusion about this. American nerves in sections unstrung with race hysteria are often fed the opiate that the trend of Negro advance is wholly separatist, and that the effect of its operation will be to encyst the Negro as a benign foreign body in the body politic. This cannot be—even if it were desirable. The racialism of the Negro is no limitation or reservation with respect to American life; it is only a constructive effort to build the obstructions in the stream of his progress into an efficient dam of social energy and power. Democracy itself is obstructed and stagnated to the extent that any of its channels are closed. Indeed they cannot be selectively closed. So the choice is not between one way for the Negro and another way for the rest, but between American institutions frustrated on the one hand and American ideals progressively fulfilled and realized on the other.

There is, of course, a warrantably comfortable feeling in being on the right side of the country's professed ideals. We realize that we cannot be undone without America's undoing. It is within the gamut of this attitude that the thinking Negro faces America, but the variations of mood in connection with it are if anything more significant than the attitude itself. Sometimes we have it taken with the defiant ironic challenge of McKay:

Mine is the future grinding down today
Like a great landslip moving to the sea,
Bearing its freight of debris far away
Where the green hungry waters restlessly
Heave mammoth pyramids and break and roar
Their eerie challenge to the crumbling shore.

Sometimes, perhaps more frequently as yet, in the fervent and almost filial appeal and counsel of Weldon Johnson's:

O Southland, dear Southland!
Then why do you still cling
To an idle age and a musty page,
To a dead and useless thing.

But between defiance and appeal, midway almost between cynicism and hope, the prevailing mind stands in the mood of the same author's To America, an attitude of sober query and stoical challenge:

How would you have us, as we are?
Or sinking 'neath the load we bear,

Our eyes fixed forward on a star,
Or gazing empty at despair?

Rising or falling? Men or things?
With dragging pace or footsteps fleet?
Strong, willing sinews in your wings,
Or tightening chains about your feet?

More and more, however, an intelligent realization of the great discrepancy between the American social creed and the American social practice forces upon the Negro the taking of the moral advantage that is his. Only the steadying and sobering effect of a truly characteristic gentleness of spirit prevents the rapid rise of a definite cynicism and counter-hate and a defiant superiority feeling. Human as this reaction would be, the majority still deprecate its advent, and would gladly see it forestalled by the speedy amelioration of its causes. We wish our race pride to be a healthier, more positive achievement than a feeling based upon a realization of the shortcomings of others. But all paths toward the attainment of a sound social attitude have been difficult; only a relatively few enlightened minds have been able as the phrase puts it "to rise above" prejudice. The ordinary man has had until recently only a hard choice between the alternatives of supine and humiliating submission and stimulating but hurtful counter-prejudice. Fortunately from some inner, desperate resourcefulness has recently sprung up the simple expedient of fighting prejudice by mental passive resistance, in other words by trying to ignore it. For the few, this manna may perhaps be effective, but the masses cannot thrive on it.

FORTUNATELY there are constructive channels opening out into which the balked social feelings of the American Negro can flow freely.

Without them there would be much more pressure and danger than there is. These compensating interests are racial but in a new and enlarged way. One is the consciousness of acting as the advance-guard of the African peoples in their contact with Twentieth Century civilization; the other, the sense of a mission of rehabilitating the race in world esteem from that loss of prestige for which the fate and conditions of slavery have so largely been responsible. Harlem, as we shall see, is the center of both these movements; she is the home of the Negro's "Zionism." The pulse of the Negro world has begun to beat in Harlem. A Negro newspaper carrying news material in English, French and Spanish, gathered from all quarters of America, the West Indies and Africa has maintained itself in Harlem for over five years. Two important magazines, both edited from New York, maintain their news and circulation consistently on a cosmopolitan scale. Under American auspices and backing, three pan-African congresses have been held abroad for the discussion of common interests, colonial questions and the future cooperative development of Africa. In terms of the race question as a world problem, the Negro mind has leapt, so to speak, upon the parapets of prejudice and extended its cramped horizons. In so doing it has linked up with the growing group consciousness of the dark-peoples and is gradually learning their common interests. As one of our writers has recently put it: "It is imperative that we understand the white world in its relations to the non-white world." As with the Jew, persecution is making the Negro international.

As a world phenomenon this wider race consciousness is

a different thing from the much asserted rising tide of color. Its inevitable causes are not of our making. The consequences are not necessarily damaging to the best interests of civilization. Whether it actually brings into being new Armadas of conflict or argosies of cultural exchange and enlightenment can only be decided by the attitude of the dominant races in an era of critical change. With the American Negro his new internationalism is primarily an effort to recapture contact with the scattered peoples of African derivation. Garveyism may be a transient, if spectacular, phenomenon, but the possible role of the American Negro in the future development of Africa is one of the most constructive and universally helpful missions that any modern people can lay claim to.

Constructive participation in such causes cannot help giving the Negro valuable group incentives, as well as increased prestige at home and abroad. Our greatest rehabilitation may possibly come through such channels, but for the present, more immediate hope rests in the revaluation by white and black alike of the Negro in terms of his artistic endowments and cultural contributions, past and prospective. It must be increasingly recognized that the Negro has already made very substantial contributions, not only in his folk-art, music especially, which has always found appreciation, but in larger, though humbler and less acknowledged ways. For generations the Negro has been the peasant matrix of that section of America which has most undervalued him, and here he has contributed not only materially in labor and in social patience, but spiritually as well. The South has unconsciously absorbed the gift of his folk-temperament. In less than half a generation it will be easier to recognize this, but the fact remains that a leaven of humor, sentiment, imagination and tropic nonchalance has gone into the making of the South from a humble, unacknowledged source. A second crop of the Negro's gifts promises still more largely. He now becomes a conscious contributor and lays aside the status of a beneficiary and ward for that of a collaborator and participant in American civilization. The great social gain in this is the releasing of our talented group from the arid fields of controversy and debate to the productive fields of creative expression. The especially cultural recognition they win should in turn prove the key to that revaluation of the Negro which must precede or accompany any considerable further betterment of race relationships. But whatever the general effect, the present generation will have added the motives of self-expression and spiritual development to the old and still unfinished task of making material headway and progress. No one who understandingly faces the situation with its substantial accomplishment or views the new scene with its still more abundant promise can be entirely without hope. And certainly, if in our lifetime the Negro should not be able to celebrate his full initiation into American democracy, he can at least, on the warrant of these things, celebrate the attainment of a significant and satisfying new phase of group development, and with it a spiritual Coming of Age.

Drawn by Walter Von Ruckteschell

YOUNG AFRICA

The Making of Harlem

By JAMES WELDON JOHNSON

IN the history of New York, the significance of the name Harlem has changed from Dutch to Irish to Jewish to Negro. Of these changes, the last has come most swiftly. Throughout colored America, from Massachusetts to Mississippi, and across the continent to Los Angeles and Seattle, its name, which as late as fifteen years ago had scarcely been heard, now stands for the Negro metropolis. Harlem is indeed the great Mecca for the sight-seer, the pleasure-seeker, the curious, the adventurous, the enterprising, the ambitious and the talented of the whole Negro world; for the lure of it has reached down to every island of the Carib Sea and has penetrated even into Africa.

In the make-up of New York, Harlem is not merely a Negro colony or community, it is a city within a city, the greatest Negro city in the world. It is not a slum or a fringe, it is located in the heart of Manhattan and occupies one of the most beautiful and healthful sections of the city. It is not a "quarter" of dilapidated tenements, but is made up of new-law apartments and handsome dwellings, with well-paved and well-lighted streets. It has its own churches, social and civic centers, shops, theatres and other places of amusement. And it contains more Negroes to the square mile than any other spot on earth. A stranger who rides up magnificent Seventh Avenue on a bus or in an automobile must be struck with surprise at the transformation which takes place after he crosses One Hundred and Twenty-fifth Street. Beginning there, the population suddenly darkens and he rides through twenty-five solid blocks where the passers-by, the shoppers, those sitting in restaurants, coming out of theatres, standing in doorways and looking out of windows are practically all Negroes; and then he emerges where the population as suddenly becomes white again. There is nothing just like it in any other city in the country, for there is no preparation for it; no change in the character of the houses and streets; no change, indeed, in the appearance of the people, except their color.

NEGRO Harlem is practically a development of the past decade, but the story behind it goes back a long way. There have always been colored people in New York. In the middle of the last century they lived in the vicinity of Lispenard, Broome and Spring Streets. When Washington Square and lower Fifth Avenue was the center of aristocratic life, the colored people, whose chief occupation was domestic service in the homes of the rich, lived in a fringe and were scattered in nests to the south, east and west of the square. As late as the 80's the major part of the colored population lived in Sullivan, Thompson, Bleecker, Grove, Minetta Lane and adjacent streets. It is curious to note that some of these nests still persist. In a number of the blocks of Greenwich Village and Little Italy may be found small groups of Negroes who have never lived in any other section of the city. By about 1890 the center of colored population had shifted to the upper Twenties and lower Thirties west of Sixth Avenue. Ten years later another considerable shift northward had been made to West Fifty-third Street.

The West Fifty-third Street settlement deserves some special mention because it ushered in a new phase of life among colored New Yorkers. Three rather well appointed hotels were opened in the street and they quickly became the centers of a sort of fashionable life that hitherto had not existed. On Sunday evenings these hotels served dinner to music and attracted crowds of well-dressed diners. One of these hotels, The Marshall, became famous as the headquarters of Negro talent. There gathered the actors, the musicians, the composers, the writers, the singers, dancers and vaudevillians. There one went to get a close-up of Williams and Walker, Cole and Johnson, Ernest Hogan, Will Marion Cook, Jim Europe, Aida Overton, and of others equally and less known. Paul Laurence Dunbar was frequently there whenever he was in New York. Numbers of those who love to shine by the light reflected from celebrities were always to be found. The first modern jazz band ever heard in New York, or, perhaps anywhere, was organized at The Marshall. It was a playing-singing-dancing orchestra, making the first dominant use of banjos, saxophones, clarinets and trap drums in combination, and was called The Memphis Students. Jim Europe was a member of that band, and out of it grew the famous Clef Club, of which he was the noted leader, and which for a long time monopolized the business of "entertaining" private parties and furnishing music for the new dance craze. Also in the Clef Club was "Buddy" Gilmore who originated trap drumming as it is now practiced, and set hundreds of white men to juggling their sticks and doing acrobatic stunts while they manipulated a dozen other noise-making devices aside from their drums. A good many well-known white performers frequented The Marshall and for seven or eight years the place was one of the sights of New York.

THE move to Fifty-third Street was the result of the opportunity to get into newer and better houses. About 1900 the move to Harlem began, and for the same reason. Harlem had been overbuilt with large, new-law apartment houses, but rapid transportation to that section was very inadequate—the Lenox Avenue Subway had not yet been built—and landlords were finding difficulty in keeping houses on the east side of the section filled. Residents along and near Seventh Avenue were fairly well served by the Eighth Avenue Elevated. A colored man, in the real estate business at this time, Philip A. Payton, approached several of these landlords with the proposition that he would fill their empty or partially empty houses with steady colored tenants. The suggestion was accepted, and one or two houses on One Hundred and Thirty-fourth Street east of Lenox Avenue were taken over. Gradually other houses were filled. The whites paid little attention to the movement until it began to spread west of Lenox Avenue; they then took steps to check it. They proposed through a financial organization, the Hudson Realty Company, to buy in all properties occupied by colored people and evict the tenants. The Negroes countered by similar methods. Payton formed the Afro-American Realty Company, a Negro corporation organized for the purpose of buying and leasing houses for occupancy by colored people. Under this counter stroke the opposition subsided for several years.

But the continually increasing pressure of colored people to the west over the Lenox Avenue dead line caused the opposition to break out again, but in a new and more menacing form. Several white men undertook to organize all the white people of the community for the purpose of inducing financial institutions not to lend money or renew mortgages on properties occupied by colored people. In this effort they had considerable success, and created a situation which has not yet been completely overcome, a situation which is one of the hardest and most unjustifiable the Negro property owner in Harlem has to contend with. The Afro-American Realty Company was now defunct, but two or three colored men of means stepped into the breach. Philip A. Payton and J. C. Thomas bought two five-story apartments, dispossessed the white tenants and put in colored. J. B. Nail bought a row of five apartments and did the same thing. St. Philip's Church bought a row of thirteen apartment houses on One Hundred and Thirty-fifth Street, running from Seventh Avenue almost to Lenox.

The situation now resolved itself into an actual contest. Negroes not only continued to occupy available apartment houses, but began to purchase private dwellings between Lenox and Seventh Avenues. Then the whole movement, in the eyes of the whites, took on the aspect of an "invasion"; they became panic stricken and began fleeing as from a plague. The presence of one colored family in a block, no matter how well bred and orderly, was sufficient to precipitate a flight. House after house and block after block was actually deserted. It was a great demonstration of human beings running amuck. None of them stopped to reason why they were doing it or what would happen if they didn't. The banks and lending companies holding mortgages on these deserted houses were compelled to take them over. For some time they held these houses vacant, preferring to do that and carry the charges than to rent or sell them to colored people. But values dropped and continued to drop until at the outbreak of the war in Europe property in the northern part of Harlem had reached the nadir.

IN the meantime the Negro colony was becoming more stable; the churches were being moved from the lower part of the city; social and civic centers were being formed; and gradually a community was being evolved. Following the outbreak of the war in Europe Negro Harlem received a new and tremendous impetus. Because of the war thousands of aliens in the United States rushed back to their native lands to join the colors and immigration practically ceased. The result was a critical shortage in labor. This shortage was rapidly increased as the United States went more and more largely into the business of furnishing munitions and supplies to the warring countries. To help meet this shortage of common labor Negroes were brought up from the South. The government itself took the first steps, following the practice in vogue in Germany of shifting labor according to the supply and demand in various parts of the country. The example of the government was promptly taken up by the big industrial concerns, which sent hundreds, perhaps thousands, of labor agents into the South who recruited Negroes by wholesale. I was in Jacksonville, Fla., for a while at that time, and I sat one day and watched the stream of migrants passing to take the train. For hours they passed steadily, carrying flimsy suit cases,

Photograph by Paul Thompson

Rush hour at the corner of 135th Street and Lenox Avenue, the subway station in the heart of Harlem. Though the original settlement of Negroes in Harlem came about indirectly because of lack of transit facilities, it is now served by the best New York has to offer, including a branch of the Fifth Avenue bus lines

new and shiny, rusty old ones, bursting at the seams, boxes and bundles and impedimenta of all sorts, including banjos, guitars, birds in cages and what not. Similar scenes were being enacted in cities and towns all over that region. The first wave of the great exodus of Negroes from the South was on. Great numbers of these migrants headed for New York or eventually got there, and naturally the majority went up into Harlem. But the Negro population of Harlem was not swollen by migrants from the South alone; the opportunity for Negro labor exerted its pull upon the Negroes of the West Indies, and those islanders in the course of time poured into Harlem to the number of twenty-five thousand or more.

These new-comers did not have to look for work; work looked for them, and at wages of which they had never even dreamed. And here is where the unlooked for, the unprecedented, the miraculous happened. According to all preconceived notions, these Negroes suddenly earning large sums of money for the first time in their lives should have had their heads turned; they should have squandered it in the most silly and absurd manners imaginable. Later, after the United States had entered the war and even Negroes in the South were making money fast, many stories in accord with the tradition came out of that section. There was the one about the colored man who went into a general store and on hearing a phonograph for the first time promptly ordered six of them, one for each child in the house. I shall not stop to discuss whether Negroes in the South did that sort of thing or not, but I do know that those who got to New York didn't. The Negroes of Harlem, for the greater part, worked and saved their money. Nobody knew how much they had saved until congestion made expansion necessary for tenants and ownership profitable for landlords, and they began to buy property. Persons who would never be suspected of having money bought property. The Rev. W. W. Brown, pastor of the Metropolitan Baptist Church, repeatedly made "Buy propery" the text of his sermons. A large part of his congregation carried out the injunction. The church itself set an example by purchasing a magnificent brown stone church building on Seventh Avenue from a white congregation. Buying property be-

Photograph by Paul Thompson

Sadly as Harlem lacks space to play outdoors, there is no lack of the play spirit either inside Harlem's crowded homes or on the broad avenues that cut through it. Parades are almost of daily occurrence —whether the occasion be the arrival of a vaudeville troupe, the patriotic enthusiasm of a new organization, or a funeral

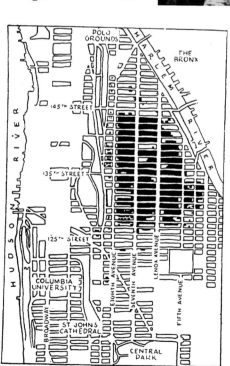

This sketch map shows approximately where Negroes live in Harlem, according to a housing survey made in 1924 by the New York Urban League. The fringe of houses in which both Negro and white tenants live is not indicated. The first houses occupied by Negroes were on 134th Street east of Lenox Avenue

came a fever. At the height of this activity, that is, 1920-21, it was not an uncommon thing for a colored washerwoman or cook to go into a real estate office and lay down from one thousand to five thousand dollars on a house. "Pig Foot Mary" is a character in Harlem. Everybody who knows the corner of Lenox Avenue and One Hundred and Thirty-fifth Street knows "Mary" and her stand and has been tempted by the smell of her pigsfeet, fried chicken and hot corn, even if he has not been a customer. "Mary," whose real name is Mrs. Mary Dean, bought the five-story apartment house at the corner of Seventh Avenue and One Hundred and Thirty-seventh Street at a price of $42,000. Later she sold it to the Y. W. C. A. for dormitory purposes. The Y. W. C. A. sold it recently to Adolph Howell, a leading colored undertaker, the price given being $72,000. Often companies of a half dozen men combined to buy a house—these combinations were and still are generally made up of West Indians—and would produce five or ten thousand dollars to put through the deal.

When the buying activity began to make itself

felt, the lending companies that had been holding vacant the handsome dwellings on and abutting Seventh Avenue decided to put them on the market. The values on these houses had dropped to the lowest mark possible and they were put up at astonishingly low prices. Houses that had been bought at from $15,000 to $20,000 were sold at one-third those figures. They were quickly gobbled up. The Equitable Life Assurance Company held 106 model private houses that were designed by Stanford White. They are built with courts running straight through the block and closed off by wrought iron gates. Every one of these houses was sold within eleven months at an aggregate price of about two million dollars. Today they are probably worth about 100 per cent more. And not only have private dwellings and similar apartments been bought but big elevator apartments have been taken over. Corporations have been organized for this purpose. Two of these, The Antillian Realty Company, composed of West Indian Negroes, and the Sphinx Securities Company, composed of American and West Indian Negroes, represent holdings amounting to approximately $750,000. Individual Negroes and companies in the South have invested in Harlem real estate. About two years ago a Negro institution of Savannah, Ga., bought a parcel for $115,000 which it sold a month or so ago at a profit of $110,000.

I am informed by John E. Nail, a successful colored real estate dealer of Harlem and a reliable authority, that the total value of property in Harlem owned and controlled by colored people would at a conservative estimate amount to more than sixty million dollars. These figures are amazing, especially when we take into account the short time in which they have been piled up. Twenty years ago Negroes were begging for the privilege of renting a flat in

Gateway and court in the block designed as a unit by Stanford White before the Negroes moved to Harlem—a block which has few rivals in the city for distinction of line and mass and its air of quiet dignity

Harlem. Fifteen years ago barely a half dozen colored men owned real property in all Manhattan. And down to ten years ago the amount that had been acquired in Harlem was comparatively negligible. Today Negro Harlem is practically owned by Negroes.

The question naturally arises, "Are the Negroes going to be able to hold Harlem?" If they have been steadily driven northward for the past hundred years and out of less desirable sections, can they hold this choice bit of Manhattan Island? It is hardly probable that Negroes will hold Harlem indefinitely, but when they are forced out it will not be for the same reasons that forced them out of former quarters in New York City. The situation is entirely different and without precedent. When colored people do leave Harlem, their homes, their churches, their investments and their businesses, it will be because the land has become so valuable they can no longer afford to live on it. But the date of another move northward is very far in the future. What will Harlem be and become in the meantime? Is there danger that the Negro may lose his economic status in New York and be unable to hold his property? Will Harlem become merely a famous ghetto,

Drawn by M. Gray Johnson

The back of the houses on "Strivers' Row," as the de luxe block on West 139th St. between Seventh and Eighth Avenues is called by dwellers in less beautiful streets

or will it be a center of intellectual, cultural and economic forces exerting an influence throughout the world, especially upon Negro peoples? Will it become a point of friction between the races in New York?

I think there is less danger to the Negroes of New York of losing out economically and industrially than to the Negroes of any large city in the North. In most of the big industrial centers Negroes are engaged in gang labor. They are employed by thousands in the stock yards in Chicago, by thousands in the automobile plants in Detroit; and in those cities they are likely to be the first to be let go, and in thousands, with every business depression. In New York there is hardly such a thing as gang labor among Negroes, except among the longshoremen, and it is in the longshoremen's unions, above all others, that Negroes stand on an equal footing. Employment among Negroes in New York is highly diversified; in the main they are employed more as individuals than as non-integral parts of a gang. Furthermore, Harlem is gradually becoming more and more a self-supporting community. Negroes there are steadily branching out into new businesses and enterprises in which Negroes are employed. So the danger of great numbers of Negroes being thrown out of work at once, with a resulting economic crisis among them, is less in New York than in most of the large cities of the North to which Southern migrants have come.

These facts have an effect which goes beyond the economic and industrial situation. They have a direct bearing on the future character of Harlem and on the question as to whether Harlem will be a point of friction between

Looking toward the Lafayette theatre on Seventh Avenue

the races in New York. It is true that Harlem is a Negro community, well defined and stable; anchored to its fixed homes, churches, institutions, business and amusement places; having its own working, business and professional classes. It is experiencing a constant growth of group consciousness and community feeling. Harlem is therefore, in many respects, typically Negro. It has many unique characteristics. It has movement, color, gaiety, singing, dancing, boisterous laughter and loud talk. One of its outstanding features is brass band parades. Hardly a Sunday passes but that there are several of these parades of which many are gorgeous with regalia and insignia. Almost any excuse will do—the death of an humble member of the Elks, the laying of a corner stone, the "turning out" of the order of this or that. In many of these characteristics it is similar to the Italian colony. But withal, Harlem grows more metropolitan and more a part of New York all the while. Why is it then that its tendency is not to become a mere "quarter"?

Harlem doorway

I shall give three reasons that seem to me to be important in their order. First, the language of Harlem is not alien; it is not Italian or Yiddish; it is English. Harlem talks American, reads American, thinks American. Second, Harlem is not physically a "quarter." It is not a section cut off. It is merely a zone through which four main arteries of the city run. Third, the fact that there is little or no gang labor gives Harlem Negroes the opportunity for individual expansion and individual contacts with the life and spirit of New York. A thousand Negroes from Mississippi put to work as a gang in a Pittsburgh steel mill will for a long time remain a thousand Negroes from Mississippi. Under the conditions that prevail in New York they would all within six months become New Yorkers. The rapidity with which Negroes become good New Yorkers is one of the marvels to observers.

These three reasons form a single reason why there is small probability that Harlem will ever be a point of race friction between the races in New York. One of the prin-

cipal factors in the race riot in Chicago in 1919 was the fact that at that time there were 12,000 Negroes employed in gangs in the stock yards. There was considerable race feeling in Harlem at the time of the hegira of white residents due to the "invasion," but that feeling, of course, is no more. Indeed, a number of the old white residents who didn't go or could not get away before the housing shortage struck New York are now living peacefully side by side with colored residents. In fact, in some cases white and colored tenants occupy apartments in the same house. Many white merchants still do business in thickest Harlem. On the whole, I know of no place in the country where the feeling between the races is so cordial and at the same time so matter-of-fact and taken for granted. One of the surest safeguards against an outbreak in New York such as took place in so many Northern cities in the summer of 1919 is the large proportion of Negro police on duty in Harlem.

To my mind, Harlem is more than a Negro community; it is a large scale laboratory experiment in the race problem. The statement has often been made that if Negroes were transported to the North in large numbers the race problem with all of its acuteness and with new aspects would be transferred with them. Well, 175,000 Negroes live closely together in Harlem, in the heart of New York, 75,000 more than live in any Southern city, and do so without any race friction. Nor is there any unusual record of crime. I once heard a captain of the 38th Police Precinct (the Harlem precinct) say that on the whole it was the most law-abiding precinct in the city. New York guarantees its Negro citizens the fundamental rights of American citizenship and protects them in the exercise of those rights. In return the Negro loves New York and is proud of it, and contributes in his way to its greatness. He still meets with discriminations, but possessing the basic rights, he knows that these discriminations will be abolished.

I believe that the Negro's advantages and opportunities are greater in Harlem than in any other place in the country, and that Harlem will become the intellectual, the cultural and the financial center for Negroes of the United States, and will exert a vital influence upon all Negro peoples.

Drawn by Mahonri Young

THE LABORER

Black Workers and the City

By CHARLES S. JOHNSON

From bayou and island and Southern hamlet they have come—the black masses, beckoned by that "new Statue of Liberty on the landward side of New York." What strain and stress of adjustment have they met? What have they found to do in the shifting life of the city? What handicaps reappear? What new opportunities have they won?

THE glamorous city is draining the open spaces; it draws upon the human opulence of Europe; it threatens now to drain the black belt of the South. It makes no difference that New York is fast becoming unlivable, a "great shop in which people barter and sell, get rich quick and die early" —there are millions of others eager to offer themselves. The dull monotony of rural life, the high wages, the gaiety, the unoppressive anonymity, the prestige of the city with its crowds and exitement set in motion years ago a trek to New York which knew no color line. How has the Negro fared in this drift to the city?

It is a strange fact that in the cities of the North, the native born Negro population, as if in biological revolt against its environment, barely perpetuates itself. For whatever reason, there is lacking that lusty vigor of increase which has nearly trebled the Negro population as a whole. Within the past sixty years the natural increase of this old Northern stock —apart from migrations—has been negligible. And its status has been shifting. Time was when that small cluster of descendants of the benevolent old Dutch masters and of the free Negroes moved with freedom and complacent importance about the intimate fringe of the city's active life. These Negroes were the barbers, caterers, bakers, restauranteurs, coachmen—all highly elaborated personal service positions. The crafts permitted them wide freedom: they were skilled artisans. They owned businesses which were independent of Negro patronage. This group is passing, its splendor shorn. The rapid evolution of business, blind to the amenities on which they flourished, has devoured their establishments, unsupported and weak in capital resources; the incoming hordes of Europeans have edged them out of their inheritance of personal service businesses, clashed with them in competition for the rough muscle jobs and driven them back into the obscurity of individual personal service.

For forty years, moreover, there have been dribbling in from the South, the West Indies and South America, small increments of population which through imperceptible gradations have changed the whole complexion and outlook of the Negro New Yorker. New blood and diverse cultures these brought—and each a separate problem of assimilation. As the years passed the old migrants have "rubbed off the green," adopted the slang and sophistication of the city, mingled and married, and their children are now the native-born New Yorkers. For fifty years scattered families have been uniting in the hectic metropolis from every state in the union and every province of the West Indies. There have always been undigested colonies—the Sons and Daughters of North Carolina, the Virginia Society, the Southern Bene-

ficial League—these are survivals of self-conscious, intimate bodies. But the mass is in the melting pot of the city.

There were in New York City in 1920, by the census count, 152,467 Negroes. Of these 39,233 are reported as born in New York State, 30,436 in foreign countries, principally the West Indies, and 78,242 in other states, principally the South. Since 1920 about 50,000 more Southerners have been added to the population, bulging the narrow strip of Harlem in which it had lived and spilling over the old boundaries. There are no less than 25,000 Virginians in New York City, more than 20,000 North and South Carolinians, and 10,000 Georgians. Every Southern state has contributed its quota to a heterogeneity which matches that of cosmopolitan New York. If the present Negro New Yorker were analyzed he would be found to be composed of one part native, one part West Indian and about three parts Southern. If the tests of the army psychologists could work with the precision and certainty with which they are accredited, the Negroes who make up the present population of New York City would be declared to represent different races, for the differences between South and North by actual measurement are greater than the differences between whites and Negroes.

II

THE city creates its own types. The Jew, for example, is by every aptitude and economic attachment a city dweller. Modern students of human behavior are discovering in his neurotic constitution, now assumed as a clearly recognizable racial characteristic, a definite connection not only with the emotional strain of peculiar racial status but also with the terrific pressure of city life.

The Negro by tradition, and probably by temperament, represents the exact contrast. His metier is agriculture. To this economy his mental and social habits have been adjusted. No elaborate equipment is necessary for the work of the farm. Life is organized on a simple plan looking to a minimum of wants and a rigid economy of means. The incomplex gestures of unskilled manual labor and even domestic service; the broad, dully sensitive touch of body and hands trained to groom and nurse the soil, develop distinctive physical habits and a musculature appropriate to simple processes. Add to this groundwork of occupational habits the social structure in which the Southern rural Negro is cast, his inhibitions, repressions and cultural poverty, and the present city Negro becomes more intelligible. It is a motley group which is now in the ascendency in the city. The picturesqueness of the South, the memory of pain, the warped lives, the ghostly shadows of fear, crudeness, ignorance and

641

unsophistication, are laid upon the surface of the city in a curious pattern.

The students of human behavior who with such quick comprehension attribute the nervousness of the Jew and the growing nervous disorders of city dwellers in general to the tension of city life overlook the play of tremendous factors in the life of the Negroes who are transplanted from one culture to another.

The city Negro is only now in evolution. In the change old moorings have been abandoned, personal relations, in which "individuals are in contact at practically all points of their lives" are replaced by group relations "in which they are in contact at only one or two points of their lives." The old controls no longer operate. Whether it is apparent or not, the newcomers are forced to reorganize their lives—to enter a new status and adjust to it that eager restlessness which prompted them to leave home. It is not inconceivable that the conduct of these individuals which seems so strange and at times so primitive and reckless, is the result of just this disorientation. And the conduct so often construed as unbearable arrogance is definitely nothing more than a compensation for the lack of self-respect, which fate through the medium of the social system of the South has denied them. The naive reaction of a migrant, as expressed in a letter to his friend in the South, illustrates the point:

Dear Partner: ... I am all fixed now and living well. I don't have to work hard. Don't have to mister every little boy comes along. I haven't heard a white man call a colored a nigger you know how—since I been here. I can ride in the street or steam car anywhere I get a seat. I don't care to mix with white what I mean I am not crazy about being with white folks, but if I have to pay the same fare I have learn to want the same acomidation and if you are first in a place here shoping you don't have to wait till all the white folks get thro tradeing yet amid all this I love the good old south and am praying that God may give every well wisher a chance to be a man regardless of his color. ...

If the Negroes in Harlem show at times less courtesy toward white visitors than is required by the canons of good taste, this is bad, but understandable. It was remarked shortly after the first migration that the newcomers on boarding street cars invariably strode to the front even if there were seats in the rear. This is, perhaps, a mild example of tendencies expressed more strikingly in other directions, for with but few exceptions they are forced to sit in the rear of street cars throughout the South.

The dislocation shows itself in other ways. In the South one dominant agency of social control is the church. It is the center for "face-to-face" relations. The pastor is the leader. The role of the pastor and the social utility of the church are obvious in this letter sent home:

Dear pastor: I find it my duty to write you my whereabouts, also family. ... I shall send my church money in a few days. I am trying to influence our members here to do the same. I received notice printed in a R. R. car (Get right with God) O, I had nothing so striking as the above mottoe. Let me no how is our church I am so anxious to no. My wife always talking about her seat in the church want to no who occupying it. Yours in Christ.

Religion affords an outlet for the emotional energies thwarted in other directions. The psychologists will find rich material for speculation on the emotional nature of some of the Negroes set into the New York pattern in this confession:

I got here in time to attend one of the greatest revivals in the history of my life—over 500 people join the church. We had a Holy Ghost shower. You know I like to have run wild.

In the new environment there are many and varied substitutes which answer more or less directly the myriad desires indiscriminately comprehended by the church. The complaint of the ministers that these "emancipated" souls "stray away from God" when they reach the city is perhaps warranted on the basis of the fixed status of the church in the South, but it is not an accurate interpretation of what has happened. When the old ties are broken new satisfactions are sought. Sometimes the Young Mens' Christian Association functions. This has in some cities made rivalry between the churches and the Associations. More often the demands of the young exceed the "sterilized" amusements of Christian organizations. It is not uncommon to find groups who faithfully attend church Sunday evenings and as as faithfully seek further stimulation in a cabaret afterwards. Many have been helped to find themselves, no doubt, by having their old churches and pastors reappear in the new home and resume control. But too often, as with European immigrants, the family loses control over the children who become assimilated more rapidly than their parents. Tragic evidences of this appear coldly detailed in the records of delinquency.

Living in the city means more than mental adjustment. Harlem is one of the most densely peopled spots in the world. The narrow strip between 114th and 145th Streets, Fifth and Eighth Avenues, which once held 50,000 Negroes and was regarded as crowded, now pretends to accomodate nearer 150,000. Some of the consequences of this painful overcrowding are presented in other pages of this number. Not the least important is its effect on health. The physical environment of the city registered a disconcerting toll in deaths and disease until the social agencies forsook the old dogma of the racial scientists that the physical constitution of the Negro was inherently weak, and set about controlling it. Notable advances have been made, but the glamor of the city still casts grim shadows.

III

CITIES have personalities. Their chief industries are likely to determine not only respective characters, but the type of persons they attract and hold. Detroit manufactures automobiles, Chicago slaughters cattle, Pittsburgh smelts iron and steel—these three communities draw different types of workers whose industrial habits are interlaced with correspondingly different cultural backgrounds. One might look to this factor as having significance in the selection of Negro workers and indeed in the relations of the Negro population with the community. The technical intricacy of the automobile industry, like the army intelligence tests, sifts out the heavy-handed worker who fits admirably into the economy of the steel industries where 80 per cent of the operations are unskilled. A temperamental equipment easily adapted to the knife-play and stench of killing and preserving cattle is not readily interchangeable either with the elaborated technique of the factory or the sheer muscle play and endurance required by the mill. These communities draw different types of workers. Perhaps to these subtle shades of difference may be attributed—at least in part—this fact: Chicago's industries drew from the current of northward migration a Negro increase of 154 per cent and out of the consequent fermentation grew a race riot which took a terrific toll in life and property. Detroit's industries, just a short space removed, drew an increase of 611.3 per cent, and nothing has happened to break the rhythm of working and living relations. Moreover, in both cities the Negro population by the increase became precisely 4.1 per cent of the whole.

Similar differences between cities account for the curiously varied types of Negroes who manage to maintain themselves in New York. They defy racial classification. The Negro worker can no more become a fixed racial concept than can the white worker. Conceived in terms either of capacity or opportunity, the employment of Negroes gives rise to the most perplexing paradoxes. If it is a question of what a Negro is mentally and physically able to do, there are as many affirmations of competence as denials of it. Employers disagree. Some find Negroes equal to whites, some find them slow and stodgy; some regard them as temperamental and "snippy," some find them genial and loyal. What has not been taken into account is the difference between the Negro groups already referred to and between the stages of their orientation.

The Negro worker facing a job confronts the cankered traditions of centuries built upon racial dogma, founded upon beliefs long upset. Racial orthodoxy seems to demand that the respective status of the white and Negro races be maintained as nearly intact as the interests of industry will permit. Study the distribution of Negro workers in New York City: they are by all odds the most available class for personal service positions—"blind alley" jobs which lead to nothing beyond the merit of long and faithful service. They are the porters, waiters, messengers, elevator tenders, chauffeurs and janitors. In these jobs 24,528 Negro men, by the last census count, found employment. And this number represented nearly half of all the Negro men at work in New York. The work is not difficult, the pay is fair and in lieu of anything better they drift into it. On the other hand employers know that with the normal outlets blocked for superior Negro workers, the chances favor their getting better Negro workers than white for the wages paid. None of the Horatio Alger ascensions from messenger to manager or from porter to president need be counted into the labor turnover where Negroes are concerned. Once a porter, barring the phenomenal, always a porter.

We might take another aspect of this economic picture: Negro workers, it will be found, are freely employed in certain jobs requiring strength and bodily agility, but little skill. A good example of this is longshore work. This is irregular and fitful, combining long periods of rest with sudden and sustained physical exertion. Employment of this type also leads nowhere but to worn bodies and retirement to less arduous tasks. The largest single group of Negro workers are longshoremen. There were 5,387 in 1920: 14 per cent of all the longshoremen in the city and 9 per cent of all the Negro men at work.

Negro women are freely employed as laundresses and servants. Though they are in fierce competition with the women of other races, 24,438 or 60 per cent of all the Negro women working in New York are either laundresses or servants.

In work requiring a period of apprenticeship Negroes are rarely employed. This limits the skilled workers and the number of Negroes eligible on this basis for membership in certain trade unions. There were only 56 Negro ap-

prentices in the 9,561 counted in the census of 1920.

In work requiring contact with the public in the capacity of salesman or representative, Negroes are infrequently employed (if they are known to be Negroes) except in Negro businesses.

In work requiring supervision over white workers they are rarely employed, though there are a few striking exceptions.

In skilled work requiring membership in unions they are employed only in small numbers, and membership is rarely encouraged unless the union is threatened. Since the apprentice-recruits for these jobs are discouraged, and the numbers sparse, the safety of the union is rarely threatened by an unorganized Negro minority. In certain responsible skilled positions, such as locomotive engineers, street car and subway motormen, Negroes are never employed.

The distinctions are irrational. A Negro worker may not be a street or subway conductor because of the possibility of public objection to contact—but he may be a ticket chopper. He may not be a money changer in a subway station because honesty is required—yet he may be entrusted, as a messenger, with thousands of dollars daily. He may not sell goods over a counter—but he may deliver the goods after they have been sold. He may be a porter in charge of a sleeping car without a conductor, but never a conductor; he may be a policeman but not a fireman; a linotyper, but not a motion picture operator; a glass annealer, but not a glass blower; a deck hand, but not a sailor. The list could be continued indefinitely.

For those who might think, however, that this reflects the range of the Negroes' industrial capacity, it is recorded that of 321 specific occupations in New York City listed in the 1920 Census, there were one or more Negroes in 316 of them. In 175 of these occupations over 50 Negroes were employed. This wide range of employment is one of the surface indications of a deeper revolution. The sudden thinning out of recruits for the bottom places in industry following the declaration of war and the restricted immigration of South European laborers, has broken during the past ten years many of the traditions which held the Negro workers with their faces to the wall. New positions in industry have been opened up and gradually Negro men, at least, are abandoning personal service for the greater pay of industrial work.

This can be illustrated by a few significant increases. Shortly after labor unions became active throughout the country Negro artisans threatened to disappear. In 1910 there were but 268 Negro carpenters in New York City. But in 1920 in New York the number had increased to 737. Chauffeurs who numbered 490 in 1910 were 2,195 in 1920. Ten years ago there were no known clothing workers, but now there are over 6,000. The same applies to workers in textile industries who numbered at the last count 2,685. Electricians, machinists and musicians have increased over a hundred per cent. The number of shoemakers jumped from 14 to 581, stationery firemen from 249 to 1,076, mechanics from practically none to 462 and real estate agents from 89 to 247.

One feels tempted to inquire of the "workers' friend," the unions, why those trades in which these unions are well organized have not shown equivalent increases in Negro workers. Ten years added but 18 brick masons, 81 painters, 16 plasterers and 42 plumbers.

The number of elevator (Continued on page 718)

The South Lingers On

By RUDOLPH FISHER

Photograph by Lewis W. Hine

EZEKIEL TAYLOR, preacher of the gospel of Jesus Christ, walked slowly along One Hundred and Thirty-Third Street, conspicuously alien. He was little and old and bent. A short, bushy white beard framed his shiny black face and his tieless celluloid collar. A long, greasy, green-black Prince Albert, with lapels frayed and buttons worn through to their metal hung loosely from his shoulders. His trousers were big and baggy and limp, yet not enough so to hide the dejected bend of his knees.

A little boy noted the beard and gibed, "Hey, Santa Claus! 'Tain't Chris'mas yet!" And the little boy's playmates chorused, "Haw, haw! Lookit the colored Santa Claus!"

"For of such is the kingdom of heaven," mused Ezekiel Taylor. No. The kingdom of Harlem. Children turned into mockers. Satan in the hearts of infants. Harlem—city of the devil—outpost of hell.

Darkness settled, like the gloom in the old preacher's heart; darkness an hour late, for these sinners even tinkered with God's time, substituting their "daylight-saving." Wicked, yes. But sad too, as though they were desperately warding off the inescapable night of sorrow in which they must suffer for their sins. Harlem. What a field! What numberless souls to save!—These very taunting children who knew not even the simplest of the commandments—

But he was old and alone and defeated. The world had called to his best. It had offered money, and they had gone; first the young men whom he had fathered, whom he had brought up from infancy in his little Southern church; then their wives and children, whom they eventually sent for; and finally their parents, loath to leave their shepherd and their dear, decrepit shacks, but dependent and without choice.

"Whyn't y' come to New York?" old Deacon Gassoway had insisted. "Martin and Eli and Jim Lee and his fambly's all up da' now an' doin' fine. We'll all git together an' start a chu'ch of our own, an' you'll still be pastor an' it'll be jes' same as 'twas hyeh." Full of that hope, he had come. But where were they? He had captained his little ship till it sank; he had clung to a splint and been tossed ashore; but the shore was cold, gray, hard and rock-strewn.

He had been in barren places before but God had been there too. Was Harlem then past hope? Was the connection between this place and heaven broken, so that the servant of God went hungry while little children ridiculed? Into his mind, like a reply, crept an old familiar hymn, and he found himself humming it softly:

> The Lord will provide,
> The Lord will provide,
> In some way or 'nother,
> The Lord will provide.
> It may not be in your way,
> It may not be in mine,
> But yet in His own way
> The Lord will provide.

Then suddenly, astonished, he stopped, listening. He had not been singing alone—a chorus of voices somewhere near had caught up his hymn. Its volume was gradually increasing. He looked about for a church. There was none. He covered his deaf ear so that it might not handicap his good one. The song seemed to issue from one of the private houses a little way down the street.

He approached with eager apprehension and stood wonderingly before a long flight of brownstone steps leading to an open entrance. The high first floor of the house, that to which the steps led, was brightly lighted, and the three front windows had their panes covered with colored tissue-paper designed to resemble church windows. Strongly, cheeringly the song came out to the listener:

> The Lord will provide,
> The Lord will provide,
> In some way or 'nother,
> The Lord will provide.

Ezekiel Taylor hesitated an incredulous moment, then smiling, he mounted the steps and went in.

The Reverend Shackleton Ealey had been inspired to preach the gospel by the draft laws of 1917. He remained in the profession not out of gratitude to its having kept him out of war, but because he found it a far less precarious mode of living than that devoted to poker, blackjack and dice. He was stocky and flat-faced and yellow, with many black freckles and the eyes of a dogfish. And he was clever enough not to conceal his origin, but to make capital out of his conversion from gambler to preacher and to confine himself to those less enlightened groups that thoroughly believed in the possibility of so sudden and complete a transformation.

The inflow of rural folk from the South was therefore

fortune, and Reverend Shackleton Ealey spent hours in Pennsylvania station greeting newly arrived migrants, urging them to visit his meeting-place and promising them the satisfaction of "that old-time religion." Many had come—and contributed.

This was prayer-meeting night. Reverend Ealey had his seat on a low platform at the distant end of the double room originally designed for a "parlor." From behind a pulpit-stand improvised out of soap-boxes and covered with calico he counted his congregation and estimated his profit.

A stranger entered uncertainly, looked about a moment, and took a seat near the door. Reverend Shackleton Ealey appraised him: a little bent-over old man with a bushy white beard and a long Prince Albert coat. Perfect type—fertile soil. He must greet this stranger at the close of the meeting and effusively make him welcome.

But Sister Gassoway was already by the stranger's side, shaking his hand vigorously and with unmistakable joy; and during the next hymn she came over to old man Gassoway and whispered in his ear, whereupon he jumped up wide-eyed, looked around, and made broadly smiling toward the newcomer. Others turned to see, and many, on seeing, began to whisper excitedly into their neighbor's ear and turned to see again. The stranger was occasioning altogether too great a stir. Reverend Ealey decided to pray.

His prayer was a masterpiece. It besought of God protection for His people in a strange and wicked land; it called down His damnation upon those dens of iniquity, the dance halls, the theatres, the cabarets; it berated the poker-sharp, the blackjack player, the dice-roller; it denounced the drunkard, the bootlegger, the dope-peddler; and it ended in a sweeping tirade against the wolf-in-sheep's-clothing, whatever his motive might be.

Another hymn and the meeting came to a close.

The stranger was surrounded before Reverend Ealey could reach him. When finally he approached the old preacher with extended hand and hollow-hearted smile, old man Gassoway was saying:

"Yas, suh, Rev'n Taylor, dass jes' whut we goin' do. Start makin' 'rangements tomorrer. Martin an' Jim Lee's over to Ebeneezer, but dey doan like it 'tall. Says hit's too hifalutin for 'em, de way dese Harlem cullud folks wushup; Ain' got no Holy Ghos' in 'em, dass whut. Jes' come in an' set down an' git up an' go out. Never moans, never shouts, never even says 'amen.' Most of us is hyeh, an' we gonna git together an' start us a ch'ch of our own, wid you f' pastor, like we said. Yas, suh. Hyeh's Brother Ealey now. Brother Ealey, dis hyeh's our old preacher Rev'n Taylor. We was jes' tellin him—"

The Reverend Shackleton Ealey had at last a genuine revelation—that the better-yielding half of his flock was on the wing. An old oath of frustration leaped to his lips—"God—" but he managed to bite it in the middle—"bless you, my brother," he growled.

II

"WHAT makes you think you can cook?"
"Why, brother, I been in the neighborhood o' grub all my life!"
"Humph! Fly bird, you are."
"Pretty near all birds fly, friend."
"Yes—even black birds."
The applicant for the cook's job lost his joviality. "All

right. I'm a black bird. You're a half-yaller hound. Step out in the air an' I'll fly down your dam' throat, so I can see if your insides is yaller, too!"

The clerk grinned. "You must do your cooking on the top of your head. Turn around and fly out that door there and see if the Hundred and Thirty-Fifth Street breeze won't cool you off some. We want a fireless cooker."

With an unmistakable suggestion as to how the clerk might dispose of his job the applicant rolled cloudily out of the employment office. The clerk called "Next!" and Jake Crinshaw, still convulsed with astonishment, nearly lost his turn.

"What kind of work are you looking for, buddy?"
"No purtickler kin', suh. Jes' work, dass all."
"Well, what can you do?"
"Mos' anything, I reckon."
"Drive a car?"
"No suh. Never done dat."
"Wait table?"
"Well, I never is."
"Run elevator?"
"No, suh."
"What have you been doing?"
"Farmin'."
"Farming? Where?"
"Jennin's Landin', Virginia. 'At's wha' all my folks is fum."
"How long you been here?"
"Ain' been hyeh a week yit. Still huntin' work." Jake answered rather apologetically. The question had been almost hostile.

"Oh—migrant." In the clerk's tone were patronization, some contempt, a little cynical amusement and complete comprehension. "Migrant" meant nothing to Jake; to the clerk it explained everything.

"M-hm. Did you try the office up above—between here and Seventh Avenue? They wanted two dozen laborers for a railroad camp upstate—pay your transportation, board and everything."

"Yas, suh—up there yestiddy, but de man say dey had all dey need. Tole me to try y'all down hyeh."

"M-hm. Well, I'm sorry, but we haven't anything for you this morning. Come in later in the week. Something may turn up."

"Yas, suh. Thank y' suh."

Jake made his discouraged way to the sidewalk and stood contemplating. His blue jumpers were clean and spotless—they had been his Sunday-go-to-meeting ones at home. He wore big, broad, yellow shoes and a shapeless tan felt hat, beneath whose brim the hair was close cut, the neck shaved bare. He was very much dressed up.

The applicant who had preceded him approached. "What'd that yaller dog tell you, bud?"

"Tole me come in later."

"Huh! That's what they all say. Only way for a guy with guts to get anything in this town is to be a bigger crook 'n the next one." He pointed to two well-dressed young men idling on the curb. "See them two? They used to wait on a job where I was chef. Now look at 'em —prosperous! An' how 'd they get that way? Hmph! That one's a pimp an' th' other's a pickpocket. Take your choice." And the cynic departed.

But Jake had greater faith in Harlem. Its praises had been sounded too highly—there must be something.

He turned and looked at the signboard that had led him to enter the employment office. It was a wooden blackboard, on which was written in chalk: "Help wanted. All sorts of jobs. If we haven't it, leave your name and we'll find it." The clerk hadn't asked Jake *his* name.

A clanging, shrieking fire engine appeared from nowhere and swept terrifyingly past. It frightened Jake like the first locomotive he had seen as a child. He shrank back against the building. Another engine passed. No more. He felt better. No one minded the engines. No one noticed that he did. Harlem itself was a fire engine.

Jake could read the signs on the buildings across the street: "Harlem Commercial and Savings Bank"—"Hale and Clark, Real Estate"—"Restaurant and Delicatessen, J. W. Jackson, proprietor"—"The Music Shop"—"John Gilmore, Tonsorial Parlor." He looked up at the buildings. They were menacingly big and tall and close. There were no trees. No ground for trees to grow from. Sidewalks overflowing with children. Streets crammed full of street-cars and automobiles. Noise, hurry, bustle—fire engines.

Jake looked again at the signboard. Help wanted—all sorts. After a while he heaved a great sigh, turned slowly, and slouched wearily on, hoping to catch sight of another employment office with a signboard out front.

III

IT was eleven o'clock at night. Majutah knew that Harry would be waiting on the doorstep downstairs. He knew better than to ring the bell so late—she had warned him. And there was no telephone. Grandmother wouldn't consent to having a telephone in the flat—she thought it would draw lightning. As if every other flat in the house didn't have one, as if lightning would strike all the others and leave theirs unharmed! Grandmother was such a nuisance with her old fogeyisms. If it weren't for her down-home ideas there'd be no trouble getting out now to go to the cabaret with Harry. As it was, Majutah would have to steal down the hall past Grandmother's room in the hope that she would be asleep.

Majutah looked to her attire. The bright red sandals and scarlet stockings, she fancied, made her feet look smaller and her legs bigger. This was desirable, since her black crepe dress, losing in width what style had added to its length, would not permit her to sit comfortably and cross her knees without occasioning ample display of everything below them. Her vanity-case mirror revealed how exactly the long pendant earrings matched her red coral beads and how perfectly becoming the new close bob was, and assured her for the tenth time that Egyptian rouge made her skin look lighter. She was ready.

Into the narrow hallways she tipped, steadying herself against the walls, and slowly approached the outside door at the end. Grandmother's room was the last off the hallway. Majutah reached it, slipped successfully past, and started silently to open the door to freedom.

"Jutie?"

How she hated to be called Jutie! Why couldn't the meddlesome old thing say Madge like everyone else?

"Ma'am?"

"Wha' you goin' dis time o' night?"

"Just downstairs to mail a letter."

"You easin' out mighty quiet, if dat's all you goin' do. Come 'eh. Lemme look at you."

Majutah slipped off her pendants and beads and laid them on the floor. She entered her grandmother's room, standing where the foot of the bed would hide her gay shoes and stockings. Useless precautions. The shrewd old woman inspected her grandaughter a minute in disapproving silence, then asked:

"Well, wha's de letter?"

"Hello, Madge," said Harry. "What held you up? You look mad enough to bite bricks."

"I am. Grandmother, of course. She's a pest. Always nosing and meddling. I'm grown, and the money I make supports both of us, and I'm sick of acting like a kid just to please her."

"How'd you manage?"

"I didn't manage. I just gave her a piece of my mind and came on out."

"Mustn't hurt the old lady's feelings. It's just her way of looking out for you."

"I don't need any looking out for—or advice either!"

"Excuse me. Which way—Happy's or Edmonds'?"

"Edmonds'—darn it!"

"Right."

It was two o'clock in the morning. Majutah's grandmother closed her Bible and turned down the oil lamp by which she preferred to read it. For a long time she sat thinking of Jutie—and of Harlem, this city of Satan. It was Harlem that had changed Jutie—this great, noisy, heartless, crowded place where you lived under the same roof with a hundred people you never knew; where night was alive and morning dead. It was Harlem—those brazen women with whom Jutie sewed, who swore and shimmied and laughed at the suggestion of going to church. Jutie wore red stockings. Jutie wore dresses that looked like nightgowns. Jutie painted her face and straightened her hair, instead of leaving it as God intended. Jutie—lied—often.

And while Madge laughed at a wanton song, her grandmother knelt by her bed and through the sinful babel of the airshaft, through her own silent tears, prayed to God in heaven for Jutie's lost soul.

IV

"TOO much learnin' ain' good f' nobody. When I was her age I couldn' write my own name."

"You can't write much mo' 'n that now. Too much learnin'! Whoever heard o' sich a thing!"

Anna's father, disregarding experience in arguing with his wife, pressed his point. "Sho they's sich a thing as too much learnin'! 'At gal's gittin' so she don't b'lieve nuthin'!"

"Hmph! Didn't she jes' tell me las' night she didn' b'lieve they ever was any Adam an' Eve?"

"Well, I ain' so sho they ever was any myself! An' one thing is certain: If that gal o' mine wants to keep on studyin' an' go up there to that City College an' learn how to teach school an' be somebody, I'll work my fingers to the bone to help her do it! Now!"

"That ain' what I'm talkin' 'bout. You ain' worked no harder 'n I is to help her git this far. Hyeh she is ready to graduate from high school. Think of it—high school! When we come along they didn' even *have* no high schools. Fus' thing y' know she be so far above us we can't reach her with a fence-rail. Then you'll wish you'd a listened to me. What I says is, she done gone far enough."

"Ain' no sich thing as far enough when you wants to go farther. 'Tain' as if it was gonna cost a whole lot. That's the trouble with you cullud folks now. Git so far an' stop—set down—through—don't want no mo'." Her disgust was boundless. "Y' got too much cotton field in you, that's what!"

The father grinned. "They sho' ain' no cotton field in yo' mouth, honey."

"No they ain'. An' they ain' no need o' all this arguin' either, 'cause all that gal's got to do is come in hyeh right now an' put her arms 'roun' yo' neck, an' you'd send her to Europe if she wanted to go!"

"Well, all I says is, when dey gits to denyin' de Bible hit's time to stop 'em."

"Well all I says is, if Cousin Sukie an' yo' no 'count brother, Jonathan, can send their gal all the way from Athens to them Howard's an' pay car-fare an' boa'd an' ev'ything, we can send our gal—"

She broke off as a door slammed. There was a rush, a delightful squeal, and both parents were being smothered in a cyclone of embraces by a wildly jubilant daughter.

"Mummy! Daddy! I won it! I won it!"

"What under the sun—?"

"The scholarship, Mummy! The scholarship!"

"No!"

"Yes I did! I can go to Columbia! I can go to Teacher's College! Isn't it great?"

Anna's mother turned triumphantly to her husband; but he was beaming at his daughter.

"You sho' is yo' daddy's chile. Teacher's College! Why that's wha' I been wantin' you to go all along!"

V

RARE sight in a close-built, topheavy city—space. A wide open lot, extending along One Hundred and Thirty-Eighth Street almost from Lenox to Seventh Avenue; baring the mangy backs of a long row of One Hundred and Thirty-Ninth Street houses; disclosing their gaping, gasping windows, their shameless strings of half-laundered rags, which gulp up what little air the windows seek to inhale. Occupying the Lenox Avenue end of the lot, the so-called Garvey tabernacle, wide, low, squat, with its stingy little entrance; occupying the other, the church tent where summer camp meetings are held.

Pete and his buddy, Lucky, left their head-to-head game of coon-can as darkness came on. Time to go out—had to save gas. Pete went to the window and looked down at the tent across the street.

"Looks like the side show of a circus. Ever been in?"

"Not me. I'm a preacher's son—got enough o' that stuff when I was a kid and couldn't protect myself."

"Ought to be a pretty good show when some o' them old-time sisters get happy. Too early for the cabarets; let's go in a while, just for the hell of it."

"You sure are hard up for somethin' to do."

"Aw, come on. Somethin' funny's bound to happen. You might even get religion, you dam' bootlegger."

Luck grinned. "Might meet some o' my customers, you mean."

Through the thick, musty heat imprisoned by the canvas shelter a man's voice rose, leading a spiritual. Other voices chimed eagerly in, some high, clear, sweet; some low, mellow, full,—all swelling, rounding out the refrain till it filled the place, so that it seemed the flimsy walls and roof must soon be torn from their moorings and swept aloft with the song:

Where you running, sinner?
Where you running, I say?
Running from the fire—
You can't cross here!

The preacher stood waiting for the song to melt away. There was a moment of abysmal silence, into which the thousand blasphemies filtering in from outside dropped unheeded.

The preacher was talking in deep, impressive tones. One old patriarch was already supplementing each statement with a matter-of-fact "amen!" of approval.

The preacher was describing hell. He was enumerating without exception the horrors that befall the damned: maddening thirst for the drunkard; for the gambler, insatiable flame, his own greed devouring his soul. The preacher's voice no longer talked—it sang; mournfully at first, monotonously up and down, up and down—a chant in minor mode; then more intensely, more excitedly; now fairly strident.

The amens of approval were no longer matter-of-fact, perfunctory. They were quick, spontaneous, escaping the lips of their own accord; they were frequent and loud and began to come from the edges of the assembly instead of just the front rows. The old men cried, "Help him, Lord!" "Preach the word!" "Glory!" taking no apparent heed of the awfulness of the description, and the old women continuously moaned aloud, nodding their bonneted heads, or swaying rhythmically forward and back in their seats.

Suddenly the preacher stopped, leaving the old men and old women still noisy with spiritual momentum. He stood motionless till the last echo of approbation subsided, then repeated the text from which his discourse had taken origin; repeated it in a whisper, lugubrious, hoarse, almost inaudible; "'In—hell—'"—paused, then without warning wildly shrieked, "'In hell—'" stopped—returned to his hoarse whisper—"'he lifted up his eyes. . . .'"

"What the hell you want to leave for?" Pete complained when he and Lucky reached the sidewalk. That old bird would 'a' coughed up his gizzard in two more minutes. What's the idea?"

"Aw hell—I don't know.—You think that stuff's funny. You laugh at it. I don't, that's all." Lucky hesitated. The urge to speak outweighed the fear of being ridiculed. "Dam' 'f I know what it is—maybe because it makes me think of the old folks or somethin'—but—hell—it just sorter—gets me—"

Lucky turned abruptly away and started off. Pete watched him for a moment with a look that should have been astonished, outraged, incredulous—but wasn't. He overtook him, put an arm about his shoulders, and because he had to say something as they walked on, muttered reassuringly:

"Well—if you ain't the damnedest fool—"

The Tropics in New York

By W. A. DOMINGO

WITHIN Harlem's seventy or eighty blocks, for the first time in their lives, colored people of Spanish, French, Dutch, Arabian, Danish, Portuguese, British and native African ancestry or nationality meet and move together.

A dusky tribe of destiny seekers, these brown and black and yellow folk, eyes filled with visions of their heritage—palm fringed sea shores, murmuring streams, luxuriant hills and vales—have made their epical march from the far corners of the earth to Harlem. They bring with them vestiges of their folk life—their lean, sunburnt faces, their quiet, halting speech, fortified by a graceful insouciance, their light, loose-fitting clothes of ancient cut telling the story of a dogged, romantic pilgrimage to the El Dorado of their dreams.

Here they have their first contact with each other, with large numbers of American Negroes, and with the American brand of race prejudice. Divided by tradition, culture, historical background and group perspective, these diverse peoples are gradually hammered into a loose unit by the impersonal force of congested residential segregation. Unlike others of the foreign-born, black immigrants find it impossible to segregate themselves into colonies; too dark of complexion to pose as Cubans or some other Negroid but alien-tongued foreigners, they are inevitably swallowed up in black Harlem. Their situation requires an adjustment unlike that of any other class of the immigrant population; and but for the assistance of their kinsfolk they would be capsized almost on the very shores of their haven.

According to the census for 1920 there were in the United States 73,803 foreign-born Negroes; of that number 36,613, or approximately 50 per cent lived in New York City, 28,184 of them in the Borough of Manhattan. They formed slightly less than 20 per cent of the total Negro population of New York.

From 1920 to 1923 the foreign-born Negro population

The Tropics in New York
By CLAUDE McKAY

Bananas ripe and green, and ginger root,
  Cocoa in pods and alligator pears,
And tangerines and mangoes and grape fruit,
  Fit for the highest prize at parish fairs.

Set in the window, bringing memories
  Of fruit-trees laden by low-singing rills,
And dewy dawns, and mystical blue skies
  In benediction over nun-like hills.

My eyes grew dim, and I could no more gaze;
  A wave of longing through my body swept,
And, hungry for the old familiar ways,
  I turned aside and bowed my head and wept.
        —From Harlem Shadows, Harcourt, Brace & Co.

of the United States was increased nearly 40 per cent through the entry of 30,849 Africans (black). In 1921 the high-water mark of 9,873 was registered. This increase was not permanent, for in 1923 there was an exit of 1,525 against an entry of 7,554. If the 20 per cent that left that year is an index of the proportion leaving annually, it is safe to estimate a net increase of about 24,000 between 1920 and 1923. If the newcomers are distributed throughout the country in the same proportion as their predecessors, the present foreign-born Negro population of Harlem is about 35,000. These people are, therefore, a formidable minority whose presence cannot be ignored or discounted. It is this large body of foreign born who contribute those qualities that make New York so unlike Pittsburgh, Washington, Chicago and other cities with large aggregations of American Negroes.

The largest number came from the British West Indies and were attracted to New York by purely economic reasons. The next largest group consists of Spanish-speaking Negroes from Latin America. Distinct because of their language, and sufficiently numerous to maintain themselves as a cultural unit, the Spanish element has but little contact with the English speaking majority. For the most part they keep to themselves and follow in the main certain definite occupational lines. A smaller group, French-speaking, have emigrated from Haiti and the French West Indies. There are also a few Africans, a batch of voluntary pilgrims over the old track of the slave-traders.

Among the English-speaking West Indian population of Harlem are some 8,000 natives of the American Virgin Islands. A considerable part of these people were forced to migrate to the mainland as a consequence of the operation of the Volstead Act which destroyed the lucrative rum industry and helped to reduce the number of foreign vessels that used to call at the former free port of Charlotte Amelia for various stores. Despite their long Danish connection these people are culturally and linguistically English, rather than Danish. Unlike the British Negroes in New York, the Virgin Islanders take an intelligent and aggressive interest in the affairs of their former home and are organized to cooperate with their brothers there who are valiantly struggling to substitute civil government for the present naval administration of the islands.

To the average American Negro all English-speaking black foreigners are West Indians, and by that is usually meant British subjects. There is a general assumption that there is everything in common among West Indians, though nothing can be further from the truth. West Indians regard themselves as Antiguans or Jamaicans as the case might be, and a glance at the map will quickly reveal the physical obstacles that militate against homogeneity of population; separations of many sorts, geographical, political and cultural tend everywhere to make and crystallize local characteristics.

This undiscriminating attitude on the part of native Negroes, as well as the friction generated from contact between the two groups, has created an artificial and defensive unity among the islanders which reveals itself in an instinctive closing of their ranks when attacked by outsiders; but among themselves organization along insular lines is the general rule. Their social grouping, however, does not follow insular precedents. Social gradation is determined in the islands by family connections, education, wealth and position. As each island is a complete society in itself, Negroes occupy from the lowliest to the most exalted positions. The barrier separating the colored aristocrat from the laboring class of the same color is as difficult to surmount as a similar barrier between Englishmen. Most of the islanders in New York are from the middle, artisan and laboring classes. Arriving in a country whose every influence is calculated to democratize their race and destroy the distinctions they had been accustomed to, even those West Indians whose stations in life have been of the lowest soon lose whatever servility they brought with them. In its place they substitute all of the self-assertiveness of the classes they formerly paid deference to.

West Indians have been coming to the United States for over a century. The part they have played in Negro progress is conceded to be important. As early as 1827 a Jamaican, John Brown Russwurm, one of the founders of Liberia, was the first colored man to be graduated from an American college and to publish a newspaper in this country; sixteen years later his fellow countryman, Peter Ogden, organized in New York City the first Odd-Fellows Lodge for Negroes. Prior to the Civil War, West Indian contribution to American Negro life was so great that Dr. W. E. B. DuBois, in his Souls of Black Folk, credits them with main responsibility for the manhood program presented by the race in the early decades of the last century. Indicative of their tendency to blaze new paths is the achievement of John W. A. Shaw of Antigua who, in the early 90's of the last century, passed the civil service tests and became deputy commissioner of taxes for the County of Queens.

It is probably not realized, indeed, to what extent West Indian Negroes have contributed to the wealth, power and prestige of the United States. Major-General Goethals, chief engineer and builder of the Panama Canal, has testified in glowing language to the fact that when all other labor was tried and failed it was the black men of the Caribbean whose intelligence, skill, muscle and endurance made the union of the Pacific and the Atlantic a reality.

Coming to the United States from countries in which they had experienced no legalized social or occupational disabilities, West Indians very naturally have found it difficult to adapt themselves to the tasks that are, by custom, reserved for Negroes in the North. Skilled at various trades and having a contempt for body service and menial work, many of the immigrants apply for positions that the average American Negro has been schooled to regard as restricted to white men only with the result that through their persistence and doggedness in fighting white labor, West Indians have in many cases been pioneers and shock troops to open a way for Negroes into new fields of employment.

This freedom from spiritual inertia characterizes the women no less than the men, for it is largely through them that the occupational field has been broadened for colored women in New York. By their determination, sometimes reinforced by a dexterous use of their hatpins, these women have made it possible for members of their race to enter the needle trades freely.

It is safe to say that West Indian representation in the skilled trades is relatively large; this is also true of the professions, especially medicine and dentistry. Like the Jew, they are forever launching out in business, and such retail businesses as are in the hands of Negroes in Harlem are largely in the control of the foreign-born. While American Negroes predominate in forms of business like barber shops and pool rooms in which there is no competition from white men, West Indians turn their efforts almost invariably to fields like grocery stores, tailor shops, jewelry stores and fruit vending in which they meet the fiercest kind of competition. In some of these fields they are the pioneers or the only surviving competitors of white business concerns. In more ambitious business enterprises like real estate and insurance they are relatively numerous. The only Casino and moving picture theatre operated by Negroes in Harlem is in the hands of a native of one of the small islands. On Seventh Avenue a West Indian woman conducts a millinery store that would be a credit to Fifth Avenue.

The analogy between the West Indian and the Jew may be carried farther; they are both ambitious, eager for education, willing to engage in business, argumentative, aggressive and possessed of great proselytizing zeal for any cause they espouse. West Indians are great contenders for their rights and because of their respect for law are inclined to be litigious. In addition, they are, as a whole, home-loving, hard-working and frugal. Like their English exemplars they are fond of sport, lack a sense of humor (yet the greatest black comedian of America, Bert Williams, was from the Bahamas) and are very serious and intense in their attitude toward life. Always mindful of their folk in the homeland, they save their earnings and are an important factor in the establishment of the record that the Money Order and Postal Savings Departments of College Station Post Office have for being among the busiest in the country.

Ten years ago it was possible to distinguish the West Indian in Harlem especially during the summer months. Accustomed to wearing cool, light-colored garments in the tropics,

Subway Wind
By CLAUDE McKAY

Far down, down through the city's great, gaunt gut
  The gray train rushing bears the weary wind;
In the packed cars the fans the crowd's breath cut,
  Leaving the sick and heavy air behind.
And pale-cheeked children seek the upper door
  To give their summer jackets to the breeze;
Their laugh is swallowed in the deafening roar
  Of captive wind that moans for fields and seas;
Seas cooling warm where native schooners drift
  Through sleepy waters, while gulls wheel and sweep,
Waiting for windy waves the keels to lift
  Lightly among the islands of the deep;
Islands of lofty palm trees blooming white
  That lend their perfume to the tropic sea,
Where fields lie idle in the dew drenched night,
  And the Trades float above them fresh and free.
                    —From Harlem Shadows, Harcourt, Brace & Co.

he would stroll along Lenox Avenue on a hot day resplendent in white shoes and flannel pants, the butt of many a jest from his American brothers who, today, have adopted the styles that they formerly derided. This trait of non-conformity manifested by the foreign-born has irritated American Negroes, who resent the implied self-sufficiency, and as a result there is a considerable amount of prejudice against West Indians. It is claimed that they are proud and arrogant; that they think themselves superior to the natives. And although educated Negroes of New York are loudest in publicly decrying the hostility between the two groups, it is nevertheless true that feelings against West Indians is strongest among members of that class. This is explainable on the ground of professional jealousy and competition for leadership. As the islanders press forward and upward they meet the same kind of opposition from the native Negro that the Jew and other ambitious white aliens receive from white Americans. Naturalized West Indians have found from experience that American Negroes are reluctant to concede them the right to political leadership even when qualified intellectually. Unlike their American brothers the islanders are free from those traditions that bind them to any party and, as a consequence are independent to the point of being radical. Indeed, it is they who largely compose the few political and economic radicals in Harlem; without them the genuinely radical movement among New York Negroes would be unworthy of attention.

There is a diametrical difference between American and West Indian Negroes in their worship. While large sections of the former are inclined to indulge in displays of emotionalism that border on hysteria, the latter, in their Wesleyan Methodist and Baptist churches maintain in the face of the assumption that people from the tropics are necessarily emotional, all the punctilious emotional restraint characteristic of their English background. In religious radicalism the foreign-born are again pioneers and propagandists. The only modernist church among the thousands of Negroes in New York (and perhaps the country) is led by a West Indian, Rev. E. Ethelred Brown, an ordained Unitarian minister, and is largely supported by his fellow-islanders.

In facing the problem of race prejudice, foreign born Negroes, and West Indians in particular, are forced to undergo considerable adjustment. Forming a racial majority in their own countries and not being accustomed to discrimination expressly felt as racial, they rebel against the "color line" as they find it in America. For while color and caste lines tend to converge in the islands, it is nevertheless true that because of the ratio of population, historical background and traditions of rebellions before and since their emancipation, West Indians of color do not have their activities, social, occupational and otherwise, determined by their race. Color plays a part but it is not the prime determinant of advancement; hence, the deep feeling of resentment when the "color line," legal or customary, is met and found to be a barrier to individual progress. For this reason the West Indian has thrown himself whole-heartedly into the fight against lynching, discrimination and the other disabilities from which Negroes in America suffer.

It must be remembered that the foreign-born black men and women, more so even than other groups of immigrants, are the hardiest and most venturesome of their folk. They were dissatisfied at home, and it is to be expected that they

would not be altogether satisfied with limitation of opportunity here when they have staked so much to gain enlargement of opportunity. They do not suffer from the local anesthesia of custom and pride which makes otherwise intolerable situations bearable for the home-staying majorities.

Just as the West Indian has been a sort of leaven in the American loaf, so the American Negro is beginning to play a reciprocal role in the life of the foreign Negro communities, as for instance, the recent championing of the rights of Haiti and Liberia and the Virgin Islands, as well as the growing resentment at the treatment of natives in the African colonial dependencies. This world-wide reaction of the darker races to their common as well as local grievances is one of the most significant facts of recent development. Exchange of views and extension of race organization beyond American boundaries is likely to develop on a considerable scale in the near future, in terms principally of educational and economical projects. Former ties have been almost solely the medium of church missionary enterprises.

It has been asserted that the movement headed by the most-advertised of all West Indians, Marcus Garvey, absentee "president" of the continent of Africa, represents the attempt of West Indian peasants to solve the American race problem. This is no more true than it would be to say that the editorial attitude of The Crisis during the war reflected the spirit of American Negroes respecting their grievances or that the late Booker T. Washington successfully delimited the educational aspirations of his people. The support given Garvey by a certain type of his countrymen is partly explained by their group reaction to attacks made upon him because of his nationality. On the other hand the earliest and most persistent exposures of Garvey's multitudinous schemes were initiated by West Indians in New York like Cyril Briggs and the writer.

Prejudice against West Indians is in direct ratio to their number; hence its strength in New York where they are heavily concentrated. It is not unlike the hostility between Englishmen and Americans of the same racial stock. It is to be expected that the feeling will always be more or less present between the immigrant and the native born. However it does not extend to the children of the two groups, as they are subject to the same environment and develop identity of speech and psychology. Then, too, there has been an appreciable amount of intermarriage, especially between foreign born men and native women. Not to be ignored is the fact that congestion in Harlem has forced both groups to be less discriminating in accepting lodgers, thus making for reconciling contacts.

The outstanding contribution of West Indians to American Negro life is the insistent assertion of their manhood in an environment that demands too much servility and unprotesting acquiescence from men of African blood. This unwillingness to conform and be standardized, to accept tamely an inferior status and abdicate their humanity, finds an open expression in the activities of the foreign-born Negro in America.

Their dominant characteristic is that of blazing new paths, breaking the bonds that would fetter the feet of a virile people—a spirit eloquently expressed in the defiant lines of the Jamaican poet, Claude McKay:

> Like men we'll face the murderous, cowardly pack,
> Pressed to the wall, dying, but fighting back.

Congo : a familiar of the New York studios

Harlem Types

PORTRAITS BY WINOLD REISS

HERE and elsewhere throughout this number, Winold Reiss presents us a graphic interpretation of Negro life, freshly conceived after its own patterns. Concretely in his portrait sketches, abstractly in his symbolic designs, he has aimed to portray the soul and spirit of a people. And by the simple but rare process of not setting up petty canons in the face of nature's own creative artistry, Winold Reiss has achieved what amounts to a revealing discovery of the significance, human and artistic, of one of the great dialects of human physiognomy, of some of the little understood but powerful idioms of nature's speech. Harlem, or any Negro community, spreads a rich and novel palette for the serious artist. It needs but enlightenment of mind and eye to make its intriguing problems and promising resources available for the stimulation and enrichment of American art.

Mother and child

CONVENTIONS stand doubly in the way of artistic portrayal of Negro folk; certain narrowly arbitrary conventions of physical beauty, and as well, that inevitable inscrutability of things seen but not understood. Caricature has put upon the countenance of the Negro the mask of the comic and the grotesque, whereas in deeper truth and comprehension, nature or experience have put there the stamp of the very opposite, the serious, the tragic, the wistful. At times, too, there is a quality of soul that can only be called brooding and mystical. Here they are to be seen as we know them to be in fact. While it is a revealing interpretation for all, for the Negro artist, still for the most part confronting timidly his own material, there is certainly a particular stimulus and inspiration in this redeeming vision. Through it in all likelihood must come his best development in the field of the pictorial arts, for his capacity to express beauty depends vitally upon the capacity to see it in his own life and to generate it out of his own experience.

Young America: native-born

WINOLD REISS, son of Fritz Reiss, the landscape painter, pupil of Franz von Stuck of Munich, has become a master delineator of folk character by wide experience and definite specialization. With ever-ripening skill, he has studied and drawn the folk-types of Sweden, Holland, of the Black Forest and his own native Tyrol, and in America, the Black Foot Indians, the Pueblo people, the Mexicans, and now, the American Negro. His art owes its peculiar success as much to the philosophy of his approach as to his technical skill. He is a folk-lorist of the brush and palette, seeking always the folk character back of the individual, the psychology behind the physiognomy. In design also he looks not merely for decorative elements, but for the pattern of the culture from which it sprang. Without loss of naturalistic accuracy and individuality, he somehow subtly expresses the type, and without being any the less human, captures the racial and local. What Gauguin and his followers have done for the Far East, and the work of Ufer and Blumenschein and the Taos school for the Pueblo and Indian, seems about to be done for the Negro and Africa: in short, painting, the most local of arts, in terms of its own limitations even, is achieving universality.

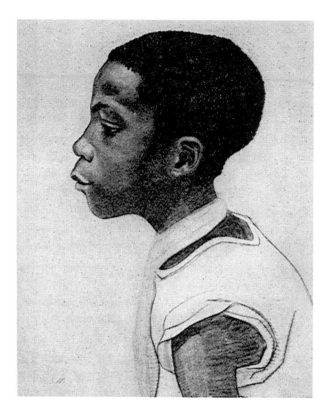

A Boy Scout

A woman lawyer

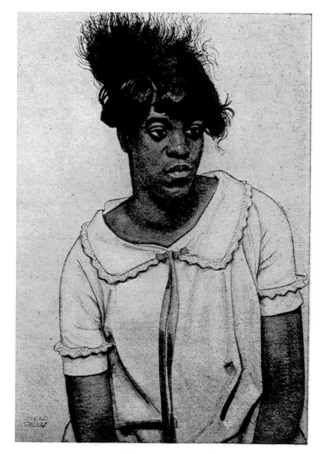

Girl in the white blouse

A college lad

The Black Man Brings His Gifts

By W. E. BURGHARDT DU BOIS

E'VE got a pretty fine town out here in middle Indiana. We claim fifty thousand inhabitants although the census cheats us out of nearly half. You can't depend on those guys in Washington. The new Pennsylvania station has just gone up and looks big and clean although a bit empty on account of the new antiloafing ordinance. There is a White Way extending down through the business section which makes us quite gay at night. Of course, we have Rotary, Kiwanis, the Chamber of Commerce and the Federation of Women's Clubs. There are six churches, not counting the colored folks.

Well, last year somebody suggested we have an America's Making pageant just like New York. You see, we need something to sort of bring us together after the war. We had a lot of Germans here and near-Germans and we had to pull them up pretty stiff. In all, we had seven or eight races or nations, not counting the colored people. We salute the flag and many of us can sing The Star Spangled Banner without books. But we really need Americanization; a sort of wholesome getting together.

So, as I have said, last year the Federation of Women's Clubs started the matter and got a committee appointed. They appointed me and Birdie; Mrs. Cadwalader Lee (who is an awfully aristocratic Southern lady); Bill Graves, who runs the biggest store; the editor of the daily paper and the Methodist preacher, who has the biggest church. They made me secretary but Birdie suggested that we needed an impartial chairman who knew something about the subject, for, says she, "What with the Germans, Poles, Scandinavians and Italians, everybody will claim so much that there'll be nothing left for the real Americans." We met and considered the idea favorably and wrote to the state university. They sent us down a professor with a funny name and any number of degrees. It seems that he taught sociology and "applied ethics," whatever that may be.

"I'll bet he's a Jew," said Birdie as soon as she looked at him. "I've got nothing against Jews but I just don't like them. They're too pushing."

First thing off the bat, this professor, who wore a cloak and spoke exceedingly proper and too low for anybody to hear unless they were listening, asked if the colored people ought not to be represented. That took us a bit by surprise as we hadn't thought of them at all. Mrs. Cadwalader Lee said she thought it might be best to have a small auxiliary colored committee and that she would ask her cook to get one up.

"WELL," says I, after we had gotten nicely settled for our first real meeting, "what is the first thing that's gone to making America and who did it?" I had my own mind on music and painting and I know that Birdie is daft on architecture; but before we either of us could speak, Bill Graves grinned and said, "hard work."

The chairman nodded and said, "Quite true, labor."

I didn't know just what to say but I whispered to Birdie that it seemed to me that we ought to stress some of the higher things. The chairman must have heard me because he said that all higher things rested on the foundation of human toil.

"But, whose labor?" asked the editor. "Since we are all descended from working people, isn't labor a sort of common contribution which, as it comes from everybody, need not be counted?"

"I should hardly consent to that statement," said Mrs. Cadwalader Lee, who is said to be descended from a governor and a lord.

"At any rate," said the chairman, "the Negroes were America's first great labor force."

"Negroes!" shrilled Birdie, "but we can't have them!"

"I should think," said Mrs. Cadwalader Lee, softly, "that we might have a very interesting darky scene. Negroes hoeing cotton and that sort of thing." We all were thankful to Mrs. Lee and immediately saw that that would be rather good; Mrs. Lee again said she would consult her cook, a very intelligent and exemplary person.

"Next," I said firmly, "comes music."

"Folk songs," said the Methodist preacher.

"Yes," I continued. "There would be Italian and German and—"

"But I thought this was to be American," said the chairman.

"Sure," I answered, "German-American and Italian-American and so forth."

"There ain't no such animal," says Birdie, but Mrs. Cadwalader Lee reminded us of Foster's work and thought we might have a chorus to sing Old Folks at Home, Old Kentucky Home and Nelly Was a Lady. Here the editor pulled out a book on American folk songs by Krehbiel or some such German name and read an extract. (I had to copy it for the minutes.) It said:

The only considerable body of songs which has come into existence in the territory now compassed by the United States, I might even say in North America, excepting the primitive songs of the Indians (which present an entirely different aspect), are the songs of the former black slaves. In Canada the songs of the people, or that portion of the people that can be said still to sing from impulse, are predominantly French, not only in language but in subject. They were for the greater part transferred to this continent with the bodily integrity which they now possess. Only a small portion show an admixture of Indian elements; but the songs of the black slaves of the South are original and native products. They contain idioms which were transplanted from Africa, but as songs they are the product of American institutions; of the social, political and geographical environment within which their creators were placed in America; of the influences to which they were subjected in America; of the joys, sorrows and experiences which fell to their lot in America.

Nowhere save on the plantations of the South could the emotional life which is essential to the development of true folksong be developed; nowhere else was there the necessary meeting of the spiritual cause and the simple agent and vehicle. The white inhabitants of the continent have never been in the state of cultural ingenuousness which prompts spontaneous emotional utterances in music.

This rather took our breath and the chairman suggested that the auxiliary colored committee might attend to this. Mrs. Cadwalader Lee was very nice about it. (She has such lovely manners and gets her dresses direct from New York.) She said that she was sure it could all be worked out satisfactorily. We would need a number of servants and helpers. Well, under the leadership of that gifted cook, we'd have a cotton-hoeing scene to represent labor and while hoeing they would sing Negro ditties; afterward they could serve the food and clean up.

That was fine, but I didn't propose to be sidetracked.

"But," I says, "we don't want to confine ourselves to folk songs. There is a lot of splendid American music like that of Victor Herbert and Irving Berlin."

The editor grinned. But the chairman was real nice and he mentioned several folks I never heard of—Paine, Buck, Chadwick and DeKoven. And, of course, I know of Nevin and McDowell. Still that editor grinned and said, "Yes, and Harry Burleigh and W. C. Handy and Nathaniel Dett."

Here the preacher spoke up. "I especially like that man, Dett. Our choir sang his Listen to the Lambs last Christmas."

"Oh, yes," said Mrs. Cadwalader Lee, "and Burleigh's Young Warrior was one of the greatest of our war songs."

"I am sure," said the Methodist preacher, "that our choir will be glad to furnish the music."

"But are they colored?" asked the chairman, who had been silent.

"Colored?" we gasped.

"Well, you see, each race was to furnish its own contribution."

"Yes," we chorused, "but this is white American music."

"Not on your life," said the editor, who is awfully slangy. "Of course you know Burleigh and Dett and Handy are all Negroes."

"I think you're mistaken," said Mrs. Cadwalader Lee, getting a bit red in the face.

But sure enough, the chairman said they were and we did not dare dispute him. He even said that Foster's melodies were based on Negro musical themes.

"Well," said the preacher, "I am sure there are no Negroes in town who could sing Listen to the Lambs," and the editor added, "And I hardly think your choir could render The Memphis Blues just as it ought to be." We looked at each other dubiously and I saw right then and there that America's Making had a small chance of being put on in our town. Somebody said that there was a choir in one of the colored churches that could sing this music, but Mrs. Cadwalader Lee reminded us that there would be insuperable difficulties if we tried to bring in obstreperous and high-brow Negroes who demanded social equality. It seems that one of these churches had hired a new social worker—a most objectionable colored person who complained when Mrs. Lee called her by her first name.

"THAT editor is just lugging the Negroes in," said I to Birdie.

"The Negroes seem to be lugging us in," she replied, and she launched us into architecture. From architecture we went to painting. There were Sargent and Whistler and Abbey. Birdie had seen Tanner's Raising of Lazarus in the Luxembourg and suggested a tableau.

"We might get him to help," said the editor. "He's having an exhibit in New York." We were thrilled, all except Mrs. Lee. "I understand he has Negro blood," she said coldly, "and besides, I do not think much of his work." We dropped that and hurried to inventions.

Here, of course, America is preeminent and we must pick and choose. First the preacher asked what kinds of inventions we ought to stress since America was so very inventive. Bill Graves wanted to stress those which had made big money, while the preacher wanted to emphasize those which had "made for righteousness." Birdie said she was strong for those which were really helpful and the chairman suggested the telephone, things that had helped travel, labor-saving devices, etc.

Well, we named over a number of things and especially stressed the telephone. The editor mentioned Granville Wood as one who had helped to perfect the telephone but we didn't listen. I'm sure he was a Negro. But in spite of all, the chairman spoke up again.

"Shoes," he said.

"Well," said I, "I didn't know we invented shoes. I thought they were pretty common before America was discovered."

"But American shoes are the best in the world," said the editor, and then the chairman told us of the United Shoe Machinery Company and how they made shoes.

"And," he added, "that lasting machine which is at the bottom of their success was invented by a Negro."

"I don't believe it," said Birdie flatly, looking at Mrs. Cadwalader Lee. Mrs. Lee got pale this time.

"Of course," she said, "if you are just going to drag in the Negro by the ears—"

"Still," said the editor, "we are after the truth, ain't we? And it is certainly true that Matzeliger invented the lasting machine and you wouldn't want your sister to marry Matzeliger, now would you?"

"Ain't he dead?" asked Birdie, and Mrs. Cadwalader Lee doubted if we ought to be interested in anything as common as shoes.

"I should think automobiles and locomotives would express our genius better."

"Only, we didn't invent them," said the editor.

"But we did invent a method of oiling them while in motion," said the chairman.

"And I'll bet a colored man did that," said Birdie.

"Quite true," answered the chairman. "His name was Elijah McCoy. He is still living in Detroit and I talked with him the other day."

"MIGHT I ask," said Mrs. Cadwalader Lee, looking the chairman full in the face, "if you yourself are of pure white blood?" We all started and we looked the chairman over. He was of dark complexion and his hair was none too straight. He had big black eyes that did not smile much; and yet there couldn't be any doubt about his being white. Wasn't he a professor in the state university and would they hire a colored man no matter how much he knew? The chairman answered.

"I do not know about the purity of my blood although I have usually been called white. Still, one never knows," and he looked solemnly at Mrs. Cadwalader Lee.

Of course, I rushed in, angels being afraid, and cried,

"Dancing—we haven't provided for dancing and we ought to have a lot of that."

"Lovely," says Birdie, "I know a Mexican girl who can do a tango and we could have folk-dancing for the Irish and Scotch."

"The Negroes invented the tango as well as the cake walk and the whole modern dance craze is theirs," said the editor.

This time the preacher saved us. "I'm afraid," said he, "that I could not countenance public dancing. I am aware that our church has changed its traditional attitude somewhat, but I am old-fashioned. If you are to have dancing—" We hastened to reassure him unanimously. We would have no dancing. We dropped it then and there.

Mrs. Lee now spoke up. "It seems to me," she said, "that the real greatness of America lies in her literature. Not only the great writers like Poe and Lanier but in our folk-lore. There are the lovely legends of the mountain whites and, of course, the Uncle Remus tales. I sometimes used to recite them and would not be unwilling to give my services to this pageant.

"Negro dialect, aren't they?" asked the editor, with vast innocence.

"Yes," said Mrs. Lee, "but I am quite familiar with the dialect."

"But oughtn't they to be given by a Negro?" persisted the editor.

"Certainly not; they were written by a white man, Joel Chandler Harris."

"Yes," added the chairman, "he set them down, but the Negroes originated them—they are thoroughly African."

Mrs. Cadwalader Lee actually sniffed. "I am sorry," she said, "but it seems to me that this matter has taken a turn quite different from our original purpose and I'm afraid I may not be able to take part." This would kill the thing, to my mind, but Birdie was not sure.

"Oh, I don't know," she whispered, "she is too high-brow anyway and this thing ought to be a matter of the common people. I don't mind having a few colored people take part so long as they don't want to sit and eat with us; but I do draw the line on Jews."

Well, we took up education next and before we got through, in popped Booker T. Washington. And then came democracy and it looked like everybody had had a hand in that, even the Germans and Italians. The chairman also said that two hundred thousand Negroes had fought for their own liberty in the Civil War and in the war to make the world safe for democracy. But that didn't impress Mrs. Lee or any of the rest of us and we concluded to leave the Negro out of democracy.

"First thing you know you'll have us eating with Negroes," said Birdie, and the chairman said that he'd eaten with Republicans and sinners. I suppose he meant to slur Democrats and Socialists but it was a funny way to do it. Somehow I couldn't just figure out that chairman. I kept watching him.

Then up pops that editor with a lot of notes and papers. "What about exploration?" he asks. Well, we had forgotten that, but naturally the Italians could stage a good stunt with Columbus.

"And the French and Spanish," said Birdie, "only there are none of them in town, thank God!"

"But there are colored folk!" said that chairman. I just gave him a withering look.

"Were they Columbus' cooks?" I asked.

"Probably," said the chairman, "but the one I have in mind discovered New Mexico and Arizona. But I'm afraid," he added slowly, "that we're getting nowhere."

"We've already got there," said Birdie. But the chairman continued: "How could we when we're talking for people and not letting them express themselves?"

"But aren't we the committee?" I asked.

"Yes, and by our own appointment."

"But we represent all the races," I insisted, "except, well—except the Negroes."

"Just so," replied the chairman, "and while I may seem to you to be unduly stressing the work of Negroes, that is simply because they are not represented here. I promise to say nothing further on the matter if you will indulge me a few minutes. In the next room, a colored woman is waiting. She is that social worker at the colored church and she is here by my invitation, I had hoped to have her invited to sit on this committee. As that does not seem possible, may she say just a word?"

He looked at me. I looked at Birdie and Birdie stared at Mrs. Cadwalader Lee. Mrs. Lee arose.

"Certainly—oh, certainly," she said sweetly. "Don't let me interfere. But, of course, you will understand that we Lees must draw the line somewhere," and out she sailed.

I KNEW the whole thing was dead as a door nail and I was just about to tell Birdie so when in marched that Negro before we'd had a chance to talk about her. She had on a tailor-made gown that cost fifty dollars if a cent, a smart toque and (would you believe it?) she was a graduate of the University of Chicago! If there's anything I hate it's a college woman. And here was a black one at that. I didn't know just how to treat her so I sort of half turned my shoulder to her and looked out the window. She began with an essay. It had a lot of long words which sounded right even if they weren't. What she seemed to be driving at was this:

Who made this big country? Not the millionaires, the ministers and the "know-alls," but laborers and drudges and slaves. And she said that we had no business to forget this and pretend that we were all descended from the nobility and gentry and college graduates. She even went so far as to say that cranks and prostitutes and plain fools had a hand in making this republic, and that the real glory of America was what it proved as to the possibilities of common-place people and that the hope of the future lay right in these every-day people.

It was the truth and I knew it and so did all of us, but, of course, we didn't dare to let on to each other, much less to her. So I just kept staring out the window and she laid aside her essay and began to talk. She handed to the Negro, music, painting, sculpture, drama, dancing, poetry and letters. She named a lot of people I never heard of; and others like Dunbar and Braithwaite and Chesnutt, but I had always thought they were white. She reminded us of Bert Williams and told us of some fellows named Aldridge and Gilpin.

And then she got on our nerves. She said all this writing and doing beautiful things hurt. That it was born of suffering. That sometimes the pain blurred the message, but that the blood and crying (*Continued on page* 710)

By Winold Reiss

PAUL   ROBESON

Youth Speaks

WE might know the future but for our chronic tendency to turn to age rather than to youth for the forecast. And when youth speaks, the future listens, however the present may shut its ears. Here we have Negro youth, foretelling in the mirror of art what we must see and recognize in the streets of reality tomorrow.

Primarily, of course, it is youth that speaks in the voice of Negro youth, but the overtones are distinctive; Negro youth speaks out of an unique experience and with a particular representativeness. All classes of a people under social pressure are permeated with a common experience; they are emotionally welded as others cannot be. With them, even ordinary living has epic depth and lyric intensity, and this, their material handicap, is their spiritual advantage. So, in a day when art has run to classes, cliques and coteries, and life lacks more and more a vital common background, the Negro artist, out of the depths of his group and personal experience, has to his hand almost the conditions of a classical art.

Negro genius today relies upon the race-gift as a vast spiritual endowment from which our best developments have come and must come. Racial expression as a conscious motive, it is true, is fading out of our latest art, but just as surely the age of truer, finer group expression is coming in—for race expression does not need to be deliberate to be vital. Indeed at its best it never is. This was the case with our instinctive and quite matchless folk-art, and begins to be the same again as we approach cultural maturity in a phase of art that promises now to be fully representative. The interval between has been an awkward age, where from the anxious desire and attempt to be representative much that was really unrepresentative has come; we have lately had an art that was stiltedly self-conscious, and racially rhetorical rather than racially expressive. Our poets have now stopped speaking for the Negro—they speak as Negroes. Where formerly they spoke to others and tried to interpret, they now speak to their own and try to express. They have stopped posing, being nearer to the attainment of poise.

The younger generation has thus achieved an objective attitude toward life. Race for them is but an idiom of experience, a sort of added enriching adventure and discipline, giving subtler overtones to life, making it more beautiful and interesting, even if more poignantly so. So experienced, it affords a deepening rather than a narrowing of social vision. The artistic problem of the Young Negro has not been so much that of acquiring the outer mastery of form and technique as that of achieving an inner mastery of mood and spirit. That accomplished, there has come the happy release from self-consciousness, rhetoric, bombast, and the hampering habit of setting artistic values with primary regard for moral effect—all those pathetic over-compensations of a group inferiority complex which our social dilemmas inflicted upon several unhappy generations. Our poets no longer have the hard choice between an over-assertive and and appealing attitude. By the same effort, they have shaken themselves free from the minstrel tradition and the fowling-nets of dialect, and through acquiring ease and simplicity in serious expression, have carried the folk-gift to the altitudes of art. There they seek and find art's intrinsic values and satisfactions—and if America were deaf, they would still sing.

But America listens—perhaps in curiosity at first; later, we may be sure, in understanding. But—a moment of patience. The generation now in the artistic vanguard inherits the fine and dearly bought achievement of another generation of creative workmen who have been pioneers and path-breakers in the cultural development and recognition of the Negro in the arts. Though still in their prime, as veterans of a hard struggle, they must have the praise and gratitude that is due them. We have had, in fiction, Chestnutt and Burghardt Du Bois; in drama, Du Bois again and Angelina Grimke; in poetry Dunbar, James Weldon Johnson, Fenton and Charles Bertram Johnson, Everett Hawkins, Lucien Watkins, Cotter, Jameson; and in another file of poets, Miss Grimke, Anne Spencer, and Georgia Douglas Johnson; in criticism and *belles lettres,* Braithwaite and Dr. Du Bois; in painting, Tanner and Scott; in sculpture, Meta Warrick and May Jackson; in acting Gilpin and Robeson; in music, Burleigh. Nor must the fine collaboration of white American artists be omitted; the work of Ridgeley Torrence and Eugene O'Neill in drama, of Stribling, and Shands and Clement Wood in fiction, all of which has helped in the bringing of the materials of Negro life out of the shambles of conventional polemics, cheap romance and journalism into the domain of pure and unbiassed art. Then, rich in this legacy, but richer still, I think, in their own endowment of talent, comes the youngest generation of our Afro-American culture: in music, Diton, Dett, Grant Still, and Roland Hayes; in fiction, Jessie Fauset, Walter White, Claude McKay (a forthcoming book); in drama, Willis Richardson; in the field of the short story, Jean Toomer, Eric Walrond, Rudolf Fisher; and finally a vivid galaxy of young Negro poets, McKay, Jean Toomer, Langston Hughes and Countée Cullen.

These constitute a new generation not because of years only, but because of a new aesthetic and a new philosophy of life. They have all swung above the horizon in the last three years, and we can say without disparagement of the past that in that short space of time they have gained collectively from publishers, editors, critics and the general public more recognition than has ever before come to Negro creative artists in an entire working lifetime. First novels of unquestioned distinction, first acceptances by premier journals whose pages are the ambition of veteran craftsmen, international acclaim, the conquest for us of new provinces of art, the development for the first time among us of literary coteries and channels for the contact of creative minds, and most important of all, a spiritual quickening and racial leavening such as no generation has yet felt and known. It has been their achievement also to bring the artistic advance of the Negro sharply into stepping alignment with contemporary artistic thought, mood and style. They are thoroughly modern, some of them ultra-modern, and Negro thoughts now wear the uniform of the age.

But for all that, the heart beats a little differently. Toomer gives a folk-lilt and ecstasy to the prose of the American modernists. McKay adds Aesop and irony to the social novel and a peasant clarity and naïveté to lyric thought, Fisher adds Uncle Remus to the art of Maupassant and O. Henry. Hughes puts Biblical fervor into free verse, Hayes carries the gush and depth of folk-song to the old masters, Cullen blends the simple with the sophisticated and puts the vineyards themselves into his crystal goblets. There is in all the marriage of a fresh emotional endowment with the finest niceties of art. Here for the enrichment of American and modern art, among our contemporaries, in a people who still have the ancient key, are some of the things we thought culture had forever lost. Art cannot disdain the gift of a natural irony, of a transfiguring imagination, of rhapsodic Biblical speech, of dynamic musical swing, of cosmic emotion such as only the gifted pagans knew, of a return to nature, not by way of the forced and worn formula of Romanticism, but through the closeness of an imagination that has never broken kinship with nature. Art must accept such gifts, and revaluate the giver.

Not all the new art is in the field of pure art values. There is poetry of sturdy social protest, and fiction of calm, dispassionate social analysis. But reason and realism have cured us of sentimentality: instead of the wail and appeal, there is challenge and indictment. Satire is just beneath the surface of our latest prose, and tonic irony has come into our poetic wells. These are good medicines for the common mind, for us they are necessary antidotes against social poison. Their influence means that at least for us the worst symptoms of the social distemper are passing. And so the social promise of our recent art is as great as the artistic. It has brought with it, first of all, that wholesome, welcome virtue of finding beauty in oneself; the younger generation can no longer be twitted as "cultural nondescripts" or accused of "being out of love with their own nativity." They have instinctive love and pride of race, and, spiritually compensating for the present lacks of America, ardent respect and love for Africa, the motherland. Gradually too under some spiritualizing reaction, the brands and wounds of social persecution are becoming the proud stigmata of spiritual immunity and moral victory. Already enough progress has been made in this direction so that it is no longer true that the Negro mind is too engulfed in its own social dilemmas for control of the necessary perspective of art, or too depressed to attain the full horizons of self and social criticism. Indeed, by the evidence and promise of the cultured few, we are at last spiritually free, and offer through art an emancipating vision to America. But it is a presumption to speak further for those who have spoken and can speak so adequately for themselves.   A. L.

Harlem Life

Seven Poems by COUNTÉE CULLEN

Harlem Wine

This is not water running here,
These thick rebellious streams
That hurtle flesh and bone past fear
Down alleyways of dreams.

This is a wine that must flow on
Not caring how or where,
So it has ways to flow upon
Where song is in the air.

So it can woo an artful flute
With loose, elastic lips,
Its measurement of joy compute
With blithe, ecstatic hips.

To a Brown Girl

What if his glance is bold and free,
His mouth the lash of whips?
So should the eyes of lovers be,
And so a lovers lips.

What if no puritanic strain
Confines him to the nice?
He will not pass this way again
Nor hunger for you twice.

Since in the end consort together
Magdalen and Mary,
Youth is the time for careless weather;
Later, lass, be wary.

Tableau

Locked arm in arm they cross the way,
The black boy and the white,
The golden splendor of the day,
The sable pride of night.

From lowered blinds the dark folk stare
And here the fair folk talk,
Indignant that these two should dare
In unison to walk.

Oblivious to look and word
They pass, and see no wonder
That lightning brilliant as a sword
Should blaze the path of thunder.

To a Brown Boy

That brown girl's swagger gives a twitch
To beauty like a queen;
Lad, never dam your body's itch
When loveliness is seen.

For there is ample room for bliss
In pride in clean, brown limbs,
And lips know better how to kiss
Than how to raise white hymns.

And when your body's death gives birth
To soil for spring to crown,
Men will not ask if that rare earth
Was white flesh once, or brown.

—From The Bookman

She of the Dancing Feet Sings

And what would I do in heaven, pray,
Me with my dancing feet,
And limbs like apple boughs that sway
When the gusty rain winds beat?

And how would I thrive in a perfect plac
Where dancing would be sin,
With not a man to love my face,
Nor an arm to hold me in?

The seraphs and the cherubim
Would be too proud to bend
To sing the faery tunes that brim
My heart from end to end.

The wistful angels down in hell
Will smile to see my face,
And understand, because they fell
From that all-perfect place.

In Memory of Col. Charles Young

Along the shore the tall, thin grass
That fringes that dark river,
While sinuously soft feet pass,
Begins to bleed and quiver.

The great dark voice breaks with a sob
Across the womb of night;
Above your grave the tom-toms throb,
And the hills are weird with light.

The great dark heart is like a well
Drained bitter by the sky,
And all the honeyed lies they tell
Come there to thirst and die.
No lie is strong enough to kill
The roots that work below;
From your rich dust and slaughtered will
A tree with tongues will grow.

A Brown Girl Dead

With two white roses on her breasts,
White candles at head and feet,
Dark Madonna of the grave she rests;
Lord Death has found her sweet.

Her mother pawned her wedding ring
To lay her out in white;
 he'd be so proud she'd dance and sing
To see herself tonight.

Lady, Lady

By ANNE SPENCER

Lady, Lady, I saw your face,
Dark as night withholding a star. . .
The chisel fell, or it might have been
You had borne so long the yoke of men.
Lady, Lady, I saw your hands,
Twisted, awry, like crumpled roots,
Bleached poor white in a sudsy tub,
Wrinkled and drawn from your rub-a-dub.
Lady, Lady I saw your heart,
And altared there in its darksome place
Were the tongues of flame the ancients knew,
Where the good God sits to spangle through.

The Black Finger

By ANGELINA GRIMKE

I have just seen a most beautiful thing
Slim and still,
Against a gold, gold sky,
A straight black cypress,
Sensitive,
Exquisite,
A black finger
Pointing upwards.
Why, beautiful still finger, are you black?
And why are you pointing upwards?

—From Opportunity

Poems

By CLAUDE McKAY

Like a Strong Tree

Like a strong tree that in the virgin earth
Sends far its roots through rock and loam and clay,
And proudly thrives in rain or time of dearth,
When the dry waves scare rainy sprites away;
Like a strong tree that reaches down, deep, deep,
For sunken water, fluid underground,
Where the great-ringed unsightly blind worms creep,
And queer things of the nether world abound:

So would I live in rich imperial growth,
Touching the surface and the depth of things,
Instinctively responsive unto both,
Tasting the sweets of being and the stings,
Sensing the subtle spell of changing forms,
Like a strong tree against a thousand storms.

Russian Cathedral

Bow down my soul in worship very low
And in the holy silences be lost.
Bow down before the marble man of woe,
Bow down before the singing angel host.
What jewelled glory fills my spirit's eye!
What golden grandeur moves the depths of me!
The soaring arches lift me up on high
Taking my breath with their rare symmetry.

Bow down my soul and let the wondrous light
Of Beauty bathe thee from her lofty throne
Bow down before the wonder of man's might.
Bow down in worship, humble and alone;
Bow lowly down before the sacred sight
Of man's divinity alive in stone.

White Houses

Your door is shut against my tightened face,
And I am sharp as steel with discontent;
But I possess the courage and the grace
To bear my anger proudly and unbent.
The pavement slabs burn loose beneath my feet,
A chafing savage, down the decent street,
And passion rends my vitals as I pass,
Where boldly shines your shuttered door of glass.
Oh I must search for wisdom every hour,
Deep in my wrathful bosom sore and raw,
And find in it the superhuman power
To hold me to the letter of your law!
Oh I must keep my heart inviolate
Against the potent poison of your hate.

Song of the Son

By JEAN TOOMER

Pour, O pour that parting soul in song,
O pour it in the saw-dust glow of night,
Into the velvet pine-smoke air tonight,
And let the valley carry it along,
And let the valley carry it along.
O land and soil, red soil and sweet-gum tree,
So scant of grass, so profligate of pines,
Now just before an epoch's sun declines
Thy son, I have in time returned to thee,
Thy son, I have in time returned to thee.
In time, although the sun is setting on
A song-lit race of slaves, it has not set;
Though late, O soil, it is not too late yet
To catch thy plaintive soul, leaving, soon gone,
Leaving, to catch thy plaintive soul soon gone.
O Negro slaves, dark purple ripened plums,
Squeezed, and bursting in the pine-wood air,
Passing, before they strip the old tree bare
One plum was saved for me, one seed becomes
An everlasting song, a singing tree,
Caroling softly souls of slavery,
What they were, and what they are to me,
Caroling softly souls of slavery.

—From "Cane", Boni and Liveright

Poems

By LANGSTON HUGHES

Poem

We have to-morrow
Bright before us
Like a flame

Yesterday, a night-gone thing
A sun-down name

And dawn to-day
Broad arch above the road we came,
We march.

—From The Crisis

Song

Lovely, dark, and lonely one
Bare your bosom to the sun
Do not be afraid of light
You who are a child of night.

Open wide your arms to life
Whirl in the wind of pain and strife
Face the wall with the dark closed gate
Beat with bare, brown fists
And wait.

Dream Variation

To fling my arms wide
In some place of the sun,
To whirl and to dance
Till the bright day is done.
Then rest at cool evening
Beneath a tall tree
While night comes gently
Dark like me.
That is my dream.
To fling my arms wide
In the face of the sun.
Dance! Whirl! Whirl!
Till the quick day is done.
Rest at pale evening,
A tall, slim tree,
Night coming tenderly
Black like me.

The Dream Keeper

Bring me all of your dreams
You dreamers.
Bring me all of your
Heart melodies.
That I may wrap them
In a blue cloud-cloth
Away from the too rough fingers
Of the world.

Poem

Being walkers with the dawn and morning
Walkers with the sun and morning,
We are not afraid of night,
Nor days of gloom,
Nor darkness,
Being walkers with the sun and morning.

Sea Charm

Sea charm
The sea's own children
Do not understand.
They know
But that the sea is strong
Like God's hand.
They know
But that sea wind is sweet
Like God's breath
And that the sea holds
A wide, deep death.

An Earth Song

It's an earth song,—
And I've been waiting long for an earth song.
It's a spring song,—
And I've been waiting long for a spring song.
    Strong as the shoots of a new plant
    Strong as the bursting of new buds
    Strong as the coming of the first child from its mother's
        womb.
It's an earth song,
A body-song,
A spring-song,
I have been waiting long for this spring song.

DAWN IN HARLEM

A phantasy by Winold Reiss

Jazz at Home

By J. A. ROGERS

JAZZ is a marvel of paradox: too fundamentally human, at least as modern humanity goes, to be typically racial, too international to be characteristically national, too much abroad in the world to have a special home. And yet jazz in spite of it all is one part American and three parts American Negro, and was originally the nobody's child of the levee and the city slum. Transplanted exotic—a rather hardy one, we admit—of the mundane world capitals, sport of the sophisticated, it is really at home in its humble native soil wherever the modern unsophisticated Negro feels happy and sings and dances to his mood. It follows that jazz is more at home in Harlem than in Paris, though from the look and sound of certain quarters of Paris one would hardly think so. It is just the epidemic contagiousness of jazz that makes it, like the measles, sweep the block. But somebody had to have it first: that was the Negro.

What after all is this taking new thing, that, condemned in certain quarters, enthusiastically welcomed in others, has nonchalantly gone on until it ranks with the movie and the dollar as the foremost exponent of modern Americanism? Jazz isn't music merely, it is a spirit that can express itself in almost anything. The true spirit of jazz is a joyous revolt from convention, custom, authority, boredom, even sorrow—from everything that would confine the soul of man and hinder its riding free on the air. The Negroes who invented it called their songs the "Blues," and they weren't capable of satire or deception. Jazz was their explosive attempt to cast off the blues and be happy, carefree happy even in the midst of sordidness and sorrow. And that is why it has been such a balm for modern ennui, and has become a safety valve for modern machine-ridden and convention-bound society. It is the revolt of the emotions against repression.

The story is told of the clever group of "jazz-specialists" who, originating dear knows in what scattered places, had found themselves and the frills of the art in New York and had been drawn to the gay Bohemias of Paris. In a little cabaret of Montmartre they had just "entertained" into the wee small hours fascinated society and royalty; and, of course, had been paid royally for it. Then, the entertainment over and the guests away, the "entertainers" entertained themselves with their very best, which is always impromptu, for the sheer joy of it. That is jazz.

In its elementals, jazz has always existed. It is in the Indian war-dance, the Highland fling, the Irish jig, the Cossack dance, the Spanish fandango, the Brazilian *maxixe,* the dance of the whirling dervish, the hula hula of the South Seas, the *danse du ventre* of the Orient, the *carmagnole* of the French Revolution, the strains of Gypsy music, and the ragtime of the Negro. Jazz proper, however, is something more than all these. It is a release of all the suppressed emotions at once, a blowing off of the lid, as it were. It is hilarity expressing itself through pandemonium; musical fireworks.

The direct predecessor of jazz is ragtime. That both are atavistically African there is little doubt, but to what extent it is difficult to determine. In its barbaric rhythm and exuberance there is something of the bamboula, a wild, abandoned dance of the West African and the Haytian Negro, so stirringly described by the anonymous author of Untrodden Fields of Anthropology, or of the *ganza* ceremony so brilliantly depicted in Maran's Batouala. But jazz time is faster and more complex than African music. With its cowbells, auto horns, calliopes, rattles, dinner gongs, kitchen utensils, cymbals, screams, crashes, clankings and monotonous rhythm it bears all the marks of a nerve-strung, strident, mechanized civilization. It is a thing of the jungles—modern man-made jungles.

The earliest jazz-makers were the itinerant piano players who would wander up and down the Mississippi from saloon to saloon, from dive to dive. Seated at the piano with a carefree air that a king might envy, their box-back coats flowing over the stool, their Stetsons pulled well over their eyes, and cigars at an angle of forty-five degrees, they would "whip the ivories" to marvellous chords and hidden racy, joyous meanings, evoking the intense delight of their hearers who would smother them at the close with huzzas and whiskey. Often wholly illiterate, these humble troubadours knowing nothing of written music or composition, but with minds like cameras, would listen to the rude improvisations of the dock laborers and the railroad gangs and reproduce them, reflecting perfectly the sentiments and the longings of these humble folk. The improvised bands at Negro dances in the South, or the little boys with their harmonicas and jews-harps each one putting his own individuality into the air, played also no inconsiderable part in its evolution. "Poverty," says J. A. Jackson of the Billboard, "compelled improvised instruments. Bones, tambourines, make-shift string instruments, tin can and hollow wood effects, all now utilized as musical novelties, were among early Negroes the product of necessity. When these were not available 'patting juba' prevailed. Present day 'Charleston' is but a variation of this. Its early expression was the 'patting' for the buck dance."

Jazzonia
By LANGSTON HUGHES

O, silver tree!
Oh, shining rivers of the soul!

In a Harlem cabaret
Six long-headed jazzers play.
A dancing girl whose eyes are bold
Lifts high a dress of silken gold.

Oh, singing tree!
Oh, shining rivers of the soul!

Were Eve's eyes
In the first garden
Just a bit too bold?
Was Cleopatra gorgeous
In a gown of gold?

Oh, shining tree!
Oh, silver rivers of the soul!

In a whirling cabaret
Six long-headed jazzers play.
—*From The Crisis*

The origin of the present jazz craze is interesting. More cities claim its birthplace than claimed Homer dead. New Orleans, San Francisco, Memphis, Chicago, all assert the honor is theirs. Jazz, as it is today, seems to have come into being this way, however: W. C. Handy, a Negro, having digested the airs of the itinerant musicians referred to, evolved the first classic, the Memphis Blues. Then came Jasbo Brown, a reckless musician of a Negro cabaret in Chicago, who played this and other blues, blowing his own extravagant moods and risqué interpretations into them, while hilarious with gin. To give further meanings to his veiled allusions he would make the trombone "talk" by putting a derby hat and later a tin can at its mouth. The delighted patrons would shout, "More, Jasbo. More, Jas, more." And so the name originated.

As to the jazz dance itself: at this time Shelton Brooks, a Negro comedian, invented a new "strut," called Walkin' the Dog. Jasbo's anarchic airs found in this strut a soul mate. Then as a result of their union came The Texas Tommy, the highest point of brilliant, acrobatic execution and nifty footwork so far evolved in jazz dancing. The latest of these dances is the Charleston, which has brought something really new to the dance step. The Charleston calls for activity of the whole body. One characteristic is a fantastic fling of the legs from the hip downwards. The dance ends in what is known as the "camel-walk"—in reality a gorilla-like shamble—and finishes with a peculiar hop like that of the Indian war dance. Imagine one suffering from a fit of rhythmic ague and you have the effect precisely.

Two Drawings by Winold Reiss

The cleverest Charleston dancers perhaps are urchins of five and six who may be seen any time on the streets of Harlem, keeping time with their hands, and surrounded by admiring crowds. But put it on a well-set stage, danced by a bobbed-hair chorus, and you have an effect that reminds you of the abandon of the Furies. And so Broadway studies Harlem. Not all of the visitors of the twenty or more well-attended cabarets of Harlem are idle pleasure seekers or underworld devotees. Many are serious artists, actors and producers seeking something new, some suggestion to be taken, too often in pallid imitation, to Broadway's lights and stars.

This makes it difficult to say whether jazz is more characteristic of the Negro or of contemporary America. As was shown, it is of Negro origin plus the influence of the American environment. It is Negro-American. Jazz proper however is in idiom—rhythmic, musical and pantomimic—thoroughly American Negro; it is his spiritual picture on that lighter comedy side, just as the spirituals are the picture on the tragedy side. The two are poles apart, but the former is by no means to be despised and it is just as characteristically the product of the peculiar and unique experience of the Negro in this country. The African Negro hasn't it, and the Caucasian never could have invented it. Once achieved, it is common property, and jazz has absorbed the national spirit, that tremendous spirit of go, the nervousness, lack of conventionality and boisterous good-nature characteristic of the American, white or black, as compared with the more rigid formal natures of the Englishman or German.

But there still remains something elusive about jazz that few, if any of the white artists, have been able to capture. The Negro is admittedly its best expositor. That elusive something, for lack of a better name, I'll call Negro rhythm. The average Negro, particularly of the lower classes, puts rhythm into whatever he does, whether it be shining shoes or carrying a basket on the head to market as the Jamaican women do. Some years ago while wandering in Cincinnati I happened upon a Negro revival meeting at its height. The majority present were women, a goodly few of whom were white. Under the influence of the "spirit" the sisters would come forward and strut—much of jazz enters where it would be least expected. The Negro women had the perfect jazz abandon, while the white ones moved lamely and woodenly. This same lack of spontaneity

Interpretations of Harlem Jazz

Jazz has come to stay because it is an expression of the times, of the breathless, energetic, superactive times in which we are living, it is useless to fight against it. Already its new vigor, its new vitality is beginning to manifest itself. . . . America's contribution to the music of the past will have the same revivifying effect as the injection of new, and in the larger sense, vulgar blood into dying aristocracy. Music will then be vulgarized in the best sense of the word, and enter more and more into the daily lives of people. . . . The Negro musicians of America are playing a great part in this change. They have an open mind, and unbiassed outlook. They are not hampered by conventions or traditions, and with their new ideas, their constant experiment, they are causing new blood to flow in the veins of music. The jazz players make their instruments do entirely new things, things finished musicians are taught to avoid. They are pathfinders into new realms.

And thus it has come about that serious modernistic music and musicians, most notably and avowedly in the work of the French modernists Auric, Satie and Darius Milhaud, have become the confessed debtors of American Negro jazz. With the same nonchalance and impudence with which it left the levee and the dive to stride like an upstart conqueror, almost overnight, into the grand salon, jazz now begins its conquest of musical Parnassus.

Whatever the ultimate result of the attempt to raise jazz from the mob-level upon which it originated, its true home is still its original cradle, the none too respectable cabaret. And here we have the seamy side to the story. Here we have some of the charm of Bohemia, but much more of the demoralization of vice. Its rash spirit is in Grey's popular song, *Runnin' Wild:*

Runnin' wild; lost control
Runnin' wild; mighty bold,
Feelin' gay and reckless too
Carefree all the time; never blue
Always goin' I don't know where
Always showin' that I don't care
Don' love nobody, it ain't worth while
All alone; runnin' wild.

is evident to a degree in the cultivated and inhibited Negro.

Musically jazz has a great future. It is rapidly being sublimated. In the more famous jazz orchestras like those of Will Marion Cook, Paul Whiteman, Sissle and Blake, Sam Stewart, Fletcher Henderson, Vincent Lopez and the Clef Club units, there are none of the vulgarities and crudities of the lowly origin or the only too prevalent cheap imitations. The pioneer work in the artistic development of jazz was done by Negro artists; it was the lead of the so-called "syncopated orchestras" of Tyers and Will Marion Cook, the former playing for the Castles of dancing fame, and the latter touring as a concertizing orchestra in the great American centers and abroad. Because of the difficulties of financial backing, these expert combinations have had to yield ground to white orchestras of the type of the Paul Whiteman and Vincent Lopez organizations that are now demonstrating the finer possibilities of jazz music. "Jazz," says Serge Koussevitzy, the new conductor of the Boston Symphony, "is an important contribution to modern musical literature. It has an epochal significance—it is not superficial, it is fundamental. Jazz comes from the soil, where all music has its beginning." And Stokowski says more extendedly of it:

Jazz reached the height of its vogue at a time when minds were reacting from the horrors and strain of war. Humanity welcomed it because in its fresh joyousness men found a temporary forgetfulness, infinitely less harmful than drugs or alcohol. It is partly for some such reasons that it dominates the amusement life of America today. No one can sensibly condone its excesses or minimize its social danger if uncontrolled; all culture is built upon inhibitions and control. But it is doubtful whether the "jazz-hounds" of high and low estate would use their time to better advantage. In all probability their tastes would find some equally morbid, mischievous vent. Jazz, it is needless to say, will remain a recreation for the industrious and a dissipator of energy for the frivolous, a tonic for the strong and a poison for the weak. (*Continued on page 712*)

Negro Art and America

By ALBERT C. BARNES

THAT there should have developed a distinctively Negro art in America was natural and inevitable. A primitive race, transported into an Anglo-Saxon environment and held in subjection to that fundamentally alien influence, was bound to undergo the soul-stirring experiences which always find their expression in great art. The contributions of the American Negro to art are representative because they come from the hearts of the masses of a people held together by like yearnings and stirred by the same causes. It is a sound art because it comes from a primitive nature upon which a white man's education has never been harnessed. It is a great art because it embodies the Negroes' individual traits and reflects their suffering, aspirations and joys during a long period of acute oppression and distress.

The most important element to be considered is the psychological complexion of the Negro as he inherited it from his primitive ancestors and which he maintains to this day. The outstanding characteristics are his tremendous emotional endowment, his luxuriant and free imagination and a truly great power of individual expression. He has in superlative measure that fire and light which, coming from within, bathes his whole world, colors his images and impels him to expression. The Negro is a poet by birth. In the masses, that poetry expresses itself in religion which acquires a distinction by extraordinary fervor, by simple and picturesque rituals and by a surrender to emotion so complete that ecstasy, amounting to automatisms, is the rule when he worships in groups. The outburst may be started by any unlettered person provided with the average Negro's normal endowment of eloquence and vivid imagery. It begins with a song or a wail which spreads like fire and soon becomes a spectacle of a harmony of rhythmic movement and rhythmic sound unequalled in the ceremonies of any other race. Poetry is religion brought down to earth and it is of the essence of the Negro soul. He carries it with him always and everywhere; he lives it in the field, the shop, the factory. His daily habits of thought, speech and movement are flavored with the picturesque, the rhythmic, the euphonious.

The white man in the mass cannot compete with the Negro in spiritual endowment. Many centuries of civilization have attenuated his original gifts and have made his mind dominate his spirit. He has wandered too far from the elementary human needs and their easy means of natural satisfaction. The deep and satisfying harmony which the soul requires no longer arises from the incidents of daily life. The requirements for practical efficiency in a world alien to his spirit have worn thin his religion and devitalized his art. His art and his life are no longer one and the same as they were in primitive man. Art has become exotic, a thing apart, an indulgence, a something to be possessed. When art is real and vital it effects the harmony between ourselves and nature which means happiness. Modern life has forced art into being a mere adherent upon the practical affairs of life which offer it no sustenance. The result has been that hopeless confusion of values which mistakes sentimentalism and irrational day-dreaming for art.

The Negro has kept nearer to the ideal of man's harmony with nature and that, his blessing, has made him a vagrant in our arid, practical American life. But his art is so deeply rooted in his nature that it has thrived in a foreign soil where the traditions and practices tend to stamp out and starve out both the plant and its flowers. It has lived because it was an achievement, not an indulgence. It has been his happiness through that mere self-expression which is its own immediate and rich reward. Its power converted adverse material conditions into nutriment for his soul and it made a new world in which his soul has been free. Adversity has always been his lot but he converted it into a thing of beauty in his songs. When he was the abject, down-trodden slave, he burst forth into songs which constitute America's only great music—the spirituals. These wild chants are the natural, naive, untutored, spontaneous utterance of the suffering, yearning, prayerful human soul. In their mighty roll there is a nobility truly superb. Idea and emotion are fused in an art which ranks with the Psalms and the songs of Zion in their compelling, universal appeal.

The emancipation of the Negro slave in America gave him only a nominal freedom. Like all other human beings he is a creature of habits which tie him to his past; equally set are his white brothers' habits toward him. The relationship of master and slave has changed but little in the sixty years of freedom. He is still a slave to the ignorance, the prejudice, the cruelty which were the fate of his forefathers. Today he has not yet found a place of equality in the social, educational or industrial world of the white man. But he has the same singing soul as the ancestors who created the single form of great art which America can claim as her own. Of the tremendous growth and prosperity achieved by America since emancipation day, the Negro has had scarcely a pittance. The changed times did, however, give him an opportunity to develop and strengthen the native, indomitable courage and the keen powers of mind which were not suspected during the days of slavery. The character of his song changed under the new civilization and his mental and moral stature now stands measurement with those of the white man of equal educational and civilizing opportunities. That growth he owes chiefly to his own efforts; the attendant strife has left unspoiled his native gift of song. We have in his poetry and music a true, infallible record of what the struggle has meant to his inner life. It is art of which America can well be proud.

The renascence of Negro art is one of the events of our age which no seeker for beauty can afford to overlook. It is as characteristically Negro as are the primitive African sculptures. As art forms, each bears comparison with the great art expressions of any race or civilization. In both ancient and modern Negro art we find a faithful expression of a people and of an epoch in the world's evolution.

The Negro renascence dates from about 1895 when two men, Paul Laurence Dunbar and Booker T. Washington, began to attract the world's attention. Dunbar was a poet, Washington an educator in the practical business of life. They lived in widely-distant parts of America, each working independently of the other. The leavening power of each upon the Negro spirit was tremendous; each fitted into and reinforced the other; their combined influences brought to birth a new epoch for the American Negro. Washington showed that by a new kind of education the Negro could attain to an economic condition that enables him to preserve his identity, free his soul and make himself an important factor in American life. Dunbar revealed the virgin field which the Negro's own talents and conditions of life offered for creating new forms of beauty. The race became self-conscious and pride of race supplanted the bitter wail of unjust persecution. The Negro saw and followed the path that was to lead him out of the wilderness and back to his own heritage through the means of his own endowments. Many new poets were discovered, while education had a tremendous quickening. The yield to art was a new expression of Negro genius in a form of poetry which connoisseurs place in the class reserved for the disciplined art of all races. Intellect and culture of a high order became the goals for which they fought, and with a marked degree of success.

Only through bitter and long travail has Negro poetry attained to its present high level as an art form and the struggle has produced much writing which, while less perfect in form, is no less important as poetry. We find nursery rhymes, dances, love-songs, paeans of joy, lamentations, all revealing unerringly the spirit of the race in its varied contacts with life. There has grown a fine tradition which is fundamentally Negro in character. Every phase of that growth in alien surroundings is marked with reflections of the multitudinous vicissitudes that cumbered the path from slavery to culture. Each record is loaded with feeling, powerfully expressed in uniquely Negro forms. The old chants, known as spirituals, were pure soul, their sadness untouched by vindictiveness. After the release from slavery, bitterness crept into their songs. Later, as times changed, we find self-assertion, lofty aspirations and only a scattered cry for vengeance. As he grew in culture, there came expressions of the deep consolation of resignation which is born of the wisdom that the Negro race is its own, all-sufficient justification. Naturally, sadness is the note most often struck; but the frequently-expressed joy, blithesome, carefree, overflowing joy, reveals what an enviable creature the Negro is in his happy moods. No less evident is that native understanding and wisdom which—from the homely and crude expressions of their slaves, to the scholarly and cultured contributions of today—we know go with the Negro's endowment. The black scholar, seer, sage, prophet sings his message; that explains why the Negro tradition is so rich and is so firmly implanted in the soul of the race.

The Negro tradition has been slow in forming but it rests upon the firmest of foundations. Their great men and women of the past—Wheatley, Sojourner Truth, Douglass, Dunbar, Washington—have each laid a personal and imperishable stone in that foundation. A host of living Negroes, better educated and unalterably faithful to their race, are still building, and each with some human value which is an added guarantee that the tradition will be strengthened and made serviceable for the new era that is sure to come when more of the principles of humanity and rationality become the white man's guides. Many living Negroes—Du Bois, Cotter, Grimke, Braithwaite, Burleigh, the Johnsons, Mackay, Dett, Locke, Hayes, and many others—know the Negro soul and lead it to richer fields by their own ideals of culture, art and citizenship. It is a healthy development, free from that pseudo-culture which stifles the soul and misses rational happiness as the goal of human life. Through the compelling powers of his poetry and music the American Negro is revealing to the rest of the world the essential oneness of all human beings.

The cultured white race owes to the soul-expressions of its black brother too many moments of happiness not to acknowledge ungrudgingly the significant fact that what the Negro has achieved is of tremendous civilizing value. We see that in certain qualities of soul essential to happiness our own endowment is comparatively deficient. We have to acknowledge not only that our civilization has done practically nothing to help the Negro create his art but that our unjust oppression has been powerless to prevent the black man from realizing in a rich measure the expressions of his own rare gifts. We have begun to imagine that a better education and a greater social and economic equality for the Negro might produce something of true importance for a richer and fuller American life. The unlettered black singers have taught us to live music that rakes our souls and gives us moments of exquisite joy. The later Negro has made us feel the majesty of Nature, the ineffable peace of the woods and the great open spaces. He has shown us that the events of our every-day American life contain for him a poetry, rhythm and charm which we ourselves had never discovered. Through him we have seen the pathos, comedy, affection, joy of his own daily life, unified into humorous dialect verse or perfected sonnet that is a work of exquisite art. He has taught us to respect the sheer manly greatness of the fibre which has kept his inward light burning with an effulgence that shines through the darkness in which we have tried to keep him. All these visions, and more, he has revealed to us. His insight into realities has been given to us in vivid images loaded with poignancy and passion. His message has been lyrical, rhythmic, colorful. In short, the elements of beauty he has controlled to the ends of art.

THIS mystic whom we have treated as a vagrant has proved his possession of a power to create out of his own soul and our own America, moving beauty of an individual character whose existence we never knew. We are beginning to recognize that what the Negro singers and sages have said is only what the ordinary Negro feels and thinks, in his own measure, every day of his life. We have paid more attention to that every-day Negro and have been surprised to learn that nearly all of his activities are shot through and through with music and poetry. When we take to heart the obvious fact that what our prosaic civilization needs most is precisely the poetry which the average Negro actually lives, it is incredible that we should not offer the consideration which we have consistently denied to him. If at that time, he is the simple, ingenuous, forgiving, good-natured, wise and obliging person that he has been in the past, he may consent to form a working alliance with us for the development of a richer American civilization to which he will contribute his full share.

The Negro Digs Up His Past

By ARTHUR A. SCHOMBURG

THE American Negro must remake his past in order to make his future. Though it is orthodox to think of America as the one country where it is unnecessary to have a past, what is a luxury for the nation as a whole becomes a prime social necessity for the Negro. For him, a group tradition must supply compensation for persecution, and pride of race the antidote for prejudice. History must restore what slavery took away, for it is the social damage of slavery that the present generations must repair and offset. So among the rising democratic millions we find the Negro thinking more collectively, more retrospectively than the rest, and apt out of the very pressure of the present to become the most enthusiastic antiquarian of them all.

Vindicating evidences of individual achievement have as a matter of fact been gathered and treasured for over a century: Abbé Gregoire's liberal-minded book on Negro notables in 1808 was the pioneer effort; it has been followed at intervals by less-known and often less discriminating compendiums of exceptional men and women of African stock, But this sort of thing was on the whole pathetically overcorrective, ridiculously over-laudatory; it was apologetics turned into biography. A true historical sense develops slowly and with difficulty under such circumstances. But today, even if for the ultimate purpose of group justification, history has become less a matter of argument and more a matter of record. There is the definite desire and determination to have a history, well documented, widely known at least within race circles, and administered as a stimulating and inspiring tradition for the coming generations.

Gradually as the study of the Negro's past has come out of the vagaries of rhetoric and propaganda and become systematic and scientific, three outstanding conclusions have been established:

First, that the Negro has been throughout the centuries of controversy an active collaborator, and often a pioneer, in the struggle for his own freedom and advancement. This is true to a degree which makes it the more surprising that it has not been recognized earlier.

Second, that by virtue of their being regarded as something "exceptional," even by friends and well-wishers, Negroes of attainment and genius have been unfairly disassociated from the group, and group credit lost accordingly.

Third, that the remote racial origins of the Negro, far from being what the race and the world have been given to understand, offer a record of creditable group achievement when scientifically viewed, and more important still, that they are of vital general interest because of their bearing upon the beginnings and early development of culture.

With such crucial truths to document and establish, an ounce of fact is worth a pound of controversy. So the Negro historian today digs under the spot where his predecessor stood and argued. Not long ago, the Public Library of Harlem housed a special exhibition of books, pamphlets, prints and old engravings, that simply said, to sceptic and believer alike, to scholar and school-child, to proud black and astonished white, "Here is the evidence." Assembled from the rapidly growing collections of the leading Negro book-collectors and research societies, there were in these cases, materials not only for the first true writing of Negro history, but for the rewriting of many important paragraphs of our common Amer-

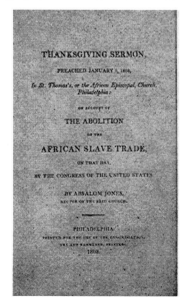

From the Schomburg Collection, some of the documentary evidences of early scholarship, progressive group organization, and pioneer social reform

ican history. Slow though it be, historical truth is no exception to the proverb.

Here among the rarities of early Negro Americana was Jupiter Hammon's Address to the Negroes of the State of New York, edition of 1787, with the first American Negro poet's famous "If we should ever get to Heaven, we shall find nobody to reproach us for being black, or for being slaves." Here was Phillis Wheatley's Mss. poem of 1767 addressed to the students of Harvard, her spirited encomiums upon George Washington and the Revolutionary Cause, and John Marrant's St. John's Day eulogy to the 'Brothers of African Lodge No. 459' delivered at Boston in 1784. Here too were Lemuel Haynes' Vermont commentaries on the American Revolution and his learned sermons to his white congregation in Rutland, Vermont, and the sermons of the year 1808 by the Rev. Absalom Jones of St. Thomas Church, Philadelphia, and Peter Williams of St. Philip's, New York, pioneer Episcopal rectors who spoke out in daring and influential ways on the Abolition of the Slave Trade. Such things and many others are more than mere items of curiosity: they educate any receptive mind.

Reinforcing these were still rarer items of Africana and foreign Negro interest, the volumes of Juan Latino, the best Latinist of Spain in the reign of Philip V, incumbent of the chair of Poetry at the University of Granada, and author of Poems printed Granatae 1573 and a book on the Escurial published 1576; the Latin and Dutch treatises of Jacobus Eliza Capitein, a native of West Coast Africa and graduate of the University of Leyden, Gustavus Vassa's celebrated autobiography that supplied so much of the evidence in 1796 for Granville Sharpe's attack on slavery in the British colonies, Julien Raymond's Paris exposé of the disabilities of the free people of color in the then (1791) French colony of Hayti, and Baron de Vastey's Cry of the Fatherland, the famous polemic by the secretary of Christophe that precipitated the Haytian struggle for independence. The cumulative effect of such evidences of scholarship and moral prowess is too weighty to be dismissed as exceptional.

But weightier surely than any evidence of individual talent and scholarship could ever be, is the evidence of important collaboration and significant pioneer initiative in social service and reform, in the efforts toward race emancipation, colonization and race betterment. From neglected and rust-spotted pages comes testimony to the black men and women who stood shoulder to shoulder in courage and zeal, and often on a parity of intelligence and public talent, with their notable white benefactors. There was the already cited work of Vassa that aided so materially the efforts of Granville Sharpe, the record of Paul Cuffee, the Negro colonization pioneer, associated so importantly with the establishment of Sierra Leone as a British colony for the occupancy of free people of color in West Africa; the dramatic and history-making exposé of John Baptist Phillips, African graduate of Edinburgh, who compelled through Lord Bathurst in 1824 the enforcement of the articles of capitulation guaranteeing freedom to the blacks of Trinidad. There is the record of the pioneer colonization project of Rev. Daniel Coker in conducting a voyage of ninety expatriates to West Africa in 1820, of the missionary efforts of Samuel Crowther in Sierra Leone, first Anglican bishop of his diocese, and that of the work of John Russwurm, a leader in the work and foundation of the American Colonization Society.

When we consider the facts, certain chapters of American history will have to be reopened. Just as black men were influential factors in the campaign against the slave trade, so they were among the earliest instigators of the abolition movement. Indeed there was a dangerous calm between the agitation for the suppression of the slave trade and the beginning of the campaign for emancipation. During that interval colored men were very influential in arousing the attention of public men who in turn aroused the conscience of the country. Continuously between 1808 and 1845, men like Prince Saunders, Peter Williams, Absalom Jones, Nathaniel Paul, and Bishops Varick and Richard Allen, the founders of the two wings of African Methodism, spoke out with force and initiative, and men like Denmark Vesey (1822), David Walker (1828) and Nat Turner (1831) advocated and organized schemes for direct action. This culminated in the gener-

Marrant's Sermon to the first Lodge of Negro Masons in 1787

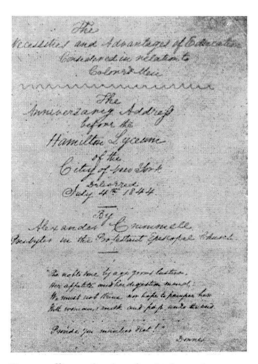

Crummell's early plea for higher education: "Provide you manlier diet"

The ex-slave turned emancipator: a not unusual rôle

ally ignored but important conventions of Free People of Color in New York, Philadelphia and other centers, whose platforms and efforts are to the Negro of as great significance as the nationally cherished memories of Faneuil and Independence Halls. Then with Abolition comes the better documented and more recognized collaboration of Samuel R. Ward, William Wells Brown, Henry Highland Garnett, Martin Delaney, Harriet Tubman, Sojourner Truth, and Frederick Douglass with their great colleagues, Tappan, Phillips, Sumner, Mott, Stowe and Garrison.

But even this latter group who came within the limelight of national and international notice, and thus into open comparison with the best minds of their generation, the public too often regards as a group of inspired illiterates, eloquent echoes of their Abolitionist sponsors. For a true estimate of their ability and scholarship, however, one must go with the antiquarian to the files of the Anglo-African Magazine, where page by page comparisons may be made. Their writings show Douglass, McCune Smith, Wells Brown, Delaney, Wilmot Blyden and Alexander Crummell to have been as scholarly and versatile as any of the noted publicists with whom they were associated. All of them labored internationally in the cause of their fellows; to Scotland, England, France, Germany and Africa, they carried their brilliant offensive of debate and propaganda, and with this came instance upon instance of signal foreign recognition, from academic, scientific, public and official sources. Delaney's Principia of Ethnology won public reception from learned societies, Penington's discourses an honorary doctorate from Heidelberg, Wells Brown's three years mission the entree of the salons of London and Paris, and Douglass' tours receptions second only to Henry Ward Beecher's.

After this great era of public interest and discussion, it was Alexander Crummell, who, with the reaction already setting in, first organized Negro brains defensively through the founding of the American Negro Academy in 1874 at Washington. A New York boy whose zeal for education had suffered a rude shock when refused admission to the Episcopal Seminary by Bishop Onderdonk, he had been befriended by John Jay and sent to Cambridge University, England, for his education and ordination. On his return, he was beset with the idea of promoting race scholarship, and the Academy was the final result. It has continued ever since to be one of the bulwarks of our intellectual life, though unfortunately its members have had to spend too much of their energy and effort answering detractors and disproving popular fallacies. Only gradually have the men of this group been able to work toward pure scholarship. Taking a slightly different start, The Negro Society for Historical Research was later organized in New York, and has succeeded in stimulating the collection from all parts of the world of books and documents dealing with the Negro. It has also brought together for the first time cooperatively in a single society African, West Indian and Afro-American scholars. Direct offshoots of this same effort are the extensive private collections of Henry P. Slaughter of Washington, the Rev. Charles D. Martin of Harlem, of Arthur Schomburg of Brooklyn, and of the late John E. Bruce, who was the enthusiastic and far-seeing pioneer of this movement. Finally and more recently, the Association for the Study of Negro Life and History has extended these efforts into a scientific research project of great achievement and promise. Under the direction of Dr. Carter G. Woodson, it has con-

tinuously maintained for nine years the publication of the learned quarterly, The Journal of Negro History, and with the assistance and recognition of two large educational foundations has maintained research and published valuable monographs in Negro history. Almost keeping pace with the work of scholarship has been the effort to popularize the results, and to place before Negro youth in the schools the true story of race vicissitude, struggle and accomplishment. So that quite largely now the ambition of Negro youth can be nourished on its own milk.

Such work is a far cry from the puerile controversy and petty braggadocio with which the effort for race history first started. But a general as well as a racial lesson has been learned. We seem lately to have come at last to realize what the truly scientific attitude requires, and to see that the race issue has been a plague on both our historical houses, and that history cannot be properly written with either bias or counter-bias. The blatant Caucasian racialist with his theories and assumptions of race superiority and dominance has in turn bred his Ethiopian counterpart—the rash and rabid amateur who has glibly tried to prove half of the world's geniuses to have been Negroes and to trace the pedigree of nineteenth century Americans from the Queen of Sheba. But fortunately today there is on both sides of a really common cause less of the sand of controversy and more of the dust of digging.

Of course, a racial motive remains—legitimately compatible with scientific method and aim. The work our race students now regard as important, they undertake very naturally to overcome in part certain handicaps of disparagement and omission too well-known to particularize. But they do so not merely that we may not wrongfully be deprived of the spiritual nourishment of our cultural past, but also that the full story of human collaboration and interdependence may be told and realized. Especially is this likely to be the effect of the latest and most fascinating of all of the attempts to open up the closed Negro past, namely the important study of African cultural origins and sources. The bigotry of civilization which is the taproot of intellectual prejudice begins far back and must be corrected at its source. Fundamentally it has come about from that depreciation of Africa which has sprung up from ignorance of her true role and position in human history and the early development of culture. The Negro has been a man without a history because he has been considered a man without a worthy culture. But a new notion of the cultural attainment and potentialities of the African stocks has recently come about, partly through the corrective influence of the more scientific study of African institutions and early cultural history, partly through growing appreciation of the skill and beauty and in many cases the historical priority of the African native crafts, and finally through the signal recognition which first in France and Germany, but now very generally the astonishing art of the African sculptures has received. Into these fascinating new vistas, with limited horizons lifting in all directions, the mind of the Negro has leapt forward faster than the slow clearings of scholarship will yet safely permit. But there is no doubt that here is a field full of the most intriguing and inspiring possibilities. Already the Negro sees himself against a reclaimed background, in a perspective that will give pride and self-respect ample scope, and make history yield for him the same values that the treasured past of any people affords.

The Art of the Ancestors

FROM one of the best extant collections of African art, that of the Barnes Foundation of Merion, Pennsylvania, come these exemplars of the art of the ancestors. Primitive African wood and bronze sculpture is now universally recognized as "a notable instance of plastic representation." Long after it was known as ethnological material, it was artistically "discovered" and has exerted an important influence upon modernist art, both in France and Germany. Attested influences are to be found in the work of Matisse, Picasso, Modigliani, Archipenko, Lipschitz, Lembruch and others, and in Paris centering around Paul Guillaume, one of its pioneer exponents, a coterie profoundly influenced by the aesthetic of this art has developed.

Masterful over its material, in a powerful simplicity of conception, design and effect, it is evidence of an aesthetic endowment of the highest order. The Negro in his American environment has turned predominantly to the arts of music, the dance, and poetry, an emphasis quite different from that of African culture. But beyond this as evidence of a fundamental artistic bent and versatility, there comes from the consideration of this ancient plastic art another modern and practical possibility and hope, that it may exert upon the artistic development of the American Negro the influence that it has already had upon modern European artists. It may very well be taken as the basis for a characteristic school of expression in the plastic and pictorial arts, and give to us again a renewed mastery of them, a mine of fresh motifs, and a lesson in simplicity and originality of expression. Surely this art, once known and appreciated, can scarcely have less influence upon the blood descendants than upon those who inherit by tradition only. And at the very least, even for those not especially interested in art, it should definitely establish the enlightening fact that the Negro is not a cultural foundling without an inheritance.   A. L.

Dahomey (Bronze)

Soudan-Niger

Baoule

Yabouba

Heritage

By COUNTÉE CULLEN

Sculpture reproduced by courtesy of the Barnes Foundation

WHAT is Africa to me:
Copper sun, a scarlet sea,
Jungle star and jungle track,
Strong bronzed men and regal black
Women from whose loins I sprang
When the birds of Eden sang?
One three centuries removed
From the scenes his fathers loved
Spicy grove and banyan tree,
What is Africa to me?

Africa? A book one thumbs
Listlessly till slumber comes.
Unremembered are her bats
Circling through the night, her cats
Crouching in the river reeds
Stalking gentle food that feeds
By the river brink; no more
Does the bugle-throated roar
Cry that monarch claws have leapt
From the scabbards where they slept.
Silver snakes that once a year
Doff the lovely coats you wear
Seek no covert in your fear
Lest a mortal eye should see:
What's your nakedness to me?

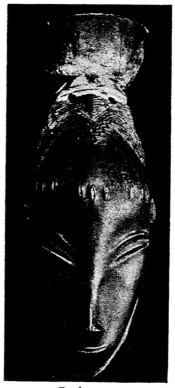

Bushongo

African sculpture

All day long and all night through
One thing only I must do
Quench my pride and cool my blood,
Lest I perish in their flood,
Lest a hidden ember set
Timber that I thought was wet
Burning like the dryest flax,
Melting like the merest wax,
Lest the grave restore its dead.
Stubborn heart and rebel head.
Have you not yet realized
You and I are civilized?

So I lie and all day long
Want no sound except the song
Sung by wild barbaric birds
Goading massive jungle herds,
Juggernauts of flesh that pass
Trampling tall defiant grass
Where young forest lovers lie
Plighting troth beneath the sky.

Ivory Coast—ceremonial mask

So I lie, who always hear
Though I cram against my ear
Both my thumbs, and keep them there,
Great drums beating through the air.
So I lie, whose fount of pride,
Dear distress, and joy allied,
Is my sombre flesh and skin
With the dark blood dammed within.
Thus I lie, and find no peace
Night or day, no slight release
From the unremittant beat
Made by cruel padded feet,
Walking through my body's street.
Up and down they go, and back
Treading out a jungle track.
So I lie, who never quite
Safely sleep from rain at night
While its primal measures drip
Through my body, crying, "Strip!
Doff this new exuberance,
Come and dance the Lover's Dance."
In an old remembered way
Rain works on me night and day.
Though three centuries removed
From the scenes my fathers loved.

My conversion came high-priced.
I belong to Jesus Christ,
Preacher of humility:
Heathen gods are naught to me—
Quaint, outlandish heathen gods
Black men fashion out of rods,
Clay and brittle bits of stone,
In a likeness like their own.

"Father, Son and Holy Ghost"
Do I make an idle boast,
Jesus of the twice turned cheek,
Lamb of God, although I speak
With my mouth, thus, in my heart
Do I not play a double part?
Ever at thy glowing altar
Must my heart grow sick and falter
Wishing He I served were black.
Thinking then it would not lack
Precedent of pain to guide it
Let who would or might deride it;
Surely then this flesh would know
Yours had borne a kindred woe.
Lord, I fashion dark gods, too,
Daring even to give to You
Dark, despairing features where
Crowned with dark rebellious hair,
Patience wavers just so much as
Mortal grief compels, while touches
Faint and slow, of anger, rise
To smitten cheek and weary eyes.

Lord, forgive me if my need
Sometimes shapes a human creed.

Zouenouia

The Dilemma of Social Pattern

By MELVILLE J. HERSKOVITS

GLIMPSES of the whirring cycle of life in Harlem leave the visitor bewildered at its complexity. There is constantly before one the tempting invitation to compare and contrast the life there with that of other communities one has had the opportunity of observing. Should I not find there, if anywhere, the distinctiveness of the Negro, of which I had heard so much? Should I not be able to discover there his ability, of which we are so often told, to produce unique cultural traits, which might be added to the prevailing white culture, and, as well, to note his equally well-advertised inability to grasp the complex civilization of which he constitutes a part?

And so I went, and what I found was churches and schools, club-houses and lodge meeting-places, the library and the newspaper offices and the Y. M. C. A. and busy 135th Street and the hospitals and the social service agencies. I met persons who were lawyers and doctors and editors and writers, who were chauffeurs and peddlers and longshoremen and real estate brokers and capitalists, teachers and nurses and students and waiters and cooks. And all Negroes. Cabarets and theaters, drug-stores and restaurants just like those everywhere else. And finally, after a time, it occurred to me that what I was seeing was a community just like any other American community. The same pattern, only a different shade!

Where, then, is the "peculiar" community of which I had heard so much? Is the cultural genius of the Negro, which is supposed to have produced jazz and the spiritual, the West African wood-carving and Bantu legalism, non-existent in this country, after all? To what extent, if any, has this genius developed a culture peculiar to it in America? I did not find it in the great teeming center of Negro life in Harlem, where, if anywhere, it should be found. May it not then be true that the Negro has become acculturated to the prevailing white culture and has developed the patterns of culture typical of American life?

Let us first view the matter historically. In the days after the liberation of the Negroes from slavery, what was more natural than that they should strive to maintain, as nearly as possible, the standards set up by those whom they had been taught to look up to as arbiters—the white group? And we see, on their part, a strong conscious effort to do just this. They went into business and tried to make

Looked at in its externals, Negro life, as reflected in Harlem registers a ready—almost a feverishly rapid—assimilation of American patterns, what Mr. Herskovits calls "complete acculturation." It speaks well both for the Negro and for American standards of living that this is so. Internally, perhaps it is another matter. Does democracy require uniformity? If so, it threatens to be safe, but dull. Social standards must be more or less uniform, but social expressions may be different. Old folkways may not persist, but they may leave a mental trace, subtly recorded in emotional temper and coloring social reactions. In the article which follows this Mr. Bercovici tells of finding, by intuition rather than research, something "unique" in Harlem—back of the external conformity, a race-soul striving for social utterance

money as their white fellows did. They already had adopted the white forms of religious faith and practise, and now they began to borrow lodges and other types of organization. Schools sprang up in which they might learn, not the language and technique of their African ancestors, but that of this country, where they lived. The "respected" members of the community were those who lived upright lives such as the "respected" whites lived—they paid their debts, they walked in the paths of sexual morality according to the general pattern of the prevailing Puritanical culture, and they went to church as was right and proper in every American town. The matter went so far that they attempted to alter their hair to conform to the general style, and the fortunes made by those who sold hair-straightening devices and medicines are a matter of record.

In Harlem we have today, essentially, a typical American community. You may look at the Negroes on the street. As to dress and deportment, do you find any vast difference between them and the whites among whom they carry on their lives? Notice them as they go about their work—they do almost all of the things the whites do, and in much the same way. The popular newspapers in Harlem are not the Negro papers—there is even no Negro daily—but the city newspapers which everyone reads. And there is the same gossipy reason why the Harlemites read their own weeklies as that which causes the inhabitants of Chelsea, of the Bronx, of Putnam, Connecticut, or of West Liberty, Ohio, to read theirs. When we come to the student groups in Harlem, we find that the same process occurs—the general culture-pattern has taken them horse, foot and artillery. Do the whites organize Greek-letter fraternities and sororities in colleges, with pearl-studded pins and "houses"? You will find a number of Negro fraternities and sororities with just the same kind of insignia and "houses." Negro community centers are attached to the more prosperous churches just as the same sort of institutions are connected with white churches. And they do the same sort of things there; you can see swimming and gymnasium classes and sewing classes and nutrition talks and open forums and all the rest of it that we all know so well.

When I visit the Business Men's Association, the difference between this gathering and that of my Rotary Club is imperceptible. And on the other end of the economic scale that equally applies to Negro and white, and which prevails all over the country, we find the Socialist and labor groups. True, once in a while an element peculiarly Negro does manifest itself; thus I remember vividly the bitter complaints of one group of motion picture operators at the prejudices which prevent them from enjoying the benefits of the white union. And, of course, you will meet with this sort of thing whenever the stream of Negro life conflicts with the more general pattern of the "color line." But even here I noticed that the *form* of the organization of these men was that assumed by their white fellow-workers, and similarly when I attended a Socialist street-meeting in Harlem, I found that the general economic motif comes in for much more attention than the problems which are of interest to the Negro per se.

Perhaps the most striking example of complete acceptance of the general pattern is in the field of sex relations. I shall never forget the storm of indignation which I aroused among a group of Negro men and women with whom I chanced to be talking on one occasion, when, *a propos* of the question of the treatment of the Negro woman in literature, I inadvertently remarked that even if the sexual looseness generally attributed to her were true, it was nothing of which to be essentially ashamed, since such a refusal to accept the Puritanical modes of procedure generally considered right and proper might contribute a welcome leaven to the conventionality of current sex *mores*. The reaction, prompt and violent, was such as to show with tremendous clarity the complete acculturation of these men and women to the accepted standards of sex behavior. There was not even a shade of doubt but that sexual rigidity is the ultimate ideal of relations between men and women, and certainly there was no more indication of a leaning toward the customs to be found in ancestral Africa than would be found among a group of whites.

Or, let us consider the position of the Negro intellectuals, the writers and artists. The proudest boast of the modern young Negro writer is that he writes of humans, not of Negroes. His literary ideals are not the African folk-tale and conundrum, but the vivid expressionistic style of the day—he seeks to be a writer, not a Negro writer. It was this point, indeed, which was especially stressed at a dinner recently given in New York City for a group of young Negro writers on the occasion of the publication of a novel by one of their number. Member after member of the group stated this position as his own—not Negro as such, but human—another striking example of the process of acculturation.

The problem then may be presented with greater clarity. Does not the Negro have a mode of life that is essentially similar to that of the general community of which he is a part? Or can it be maintained that he possesses a distinctive, inborn cultural genius which manifests itself even in America? To answer this, we must answer an even more basic question: what is cultural genius? For the Negro came to America endowed, as all people are endowed, with a culture, which had been developed by him through long ages in Africa. Was it innate? Or has it been sloughed off, forgotten, in the generations since he was brought into our culture?

To understand the problem with which we are presented, it may be well to consider what this thing, culture, is, and the extent to which we can say that it falls into patterns. By the word culture, I do not mean the refinements of our particular civilization which the word has come to connote, but simply those elements of the environment which are the handiwork of man himself. Thus, among ourselves, we might consider a spinning machine, or the democratic theory of society, or a fork, or the alphabet as much a cultural fact as a symphonic tone-poem, a novel, or an oil painting.

We may best come to an understanding of culture through a consideration of some of the phases of primitive life, where the forces at work are not overshadowed by the great imponderable fact of dense masses of population. As we look over the world, we see that there is no group of men, however simply they may live their lives, without the thing we call culture. And, what is more important, the culture they possess as the result of their own historical background— is an adult affair, developed through long centuries of trial and error, and something constantly changing. Man, it has been said, is a culture-building animal. And he is nowhere without the particular culture which his group have built. It is true that the kinds of culture which he builds are bewilderingly different—to compare the civilization of the Eskimo, the Australian, the Chinese, the African, and of ourselves leaves the student with a keener sense of their differences, both as to form and complexity, rather than with any feeling of resemblances among them. But one thing they do have in common: the cultures, when viewed from the outside, are stable. In their main elements they go along much as they always have gone, unless some great historical accident (like the discovery of the steam engine in our culture or the intrusion of the Western culture on that of the Japanese or the transplanting of Negro slaves from Africa to America) occurs to upset the trend and to direct the development of the culture along new paths. To the persons within the cultures, however, they seem even more than just stable. They seem fixed, rigid, all-enduring—indeed, they are so taken for granted that, until comparatively recent times, they were never studied at all.

But what is it that makes cultures different? There are those, of course, who will maintain that it is the racial factor. They will say that the bewildering differences between the cultures of the Englishman, the Chinaman, the Bantu and the Maya, for example, are the result of differences in innate racial endowment, and that every race has evolved a culture peculiarly fitted to it. All this sounds very convincing until one tries to define the term "race." Certain anthropologists are trying, even now, to discover criteria which will scientifically define the term "Negro." One of the most distinguished of these, Professor T. Wingate Todd, has been working steadily for some years in the attempt and the net results are certain hypotheses which he himself calls tentative. The efforts of numerous psychological testers to establish racial norms for intelligence are vitiated by the two facts that first, as many of them will admit, it is doubtful just what it is they are testing, and, in the second place, that races are mixed. This is particularly true in the case of the Negroes; in New York City, less than 2 per cent of the group from whom I obtained genealogical material claimed pure Negro ancestry, and while this percentage is undoubtedly low, the fact remains that the vast majority of Negroes in America are of mixed ancestry.

If ability to successfully live in one culture were restricted to persons of one race, how could we account for the fact that we see persons of the most diverse races living together, for example, in this country, quite as though they were naturally endowed with the ability to meet the problems of living here, while again we witness an entire alien people adopting our civilization, to use the Japanese again for illustration?

OUR civilization is what it is because of certain historic events which occurred in the course of its development. So we can also say for the civilization of the African, of the Eskimo, of the Australian. And the people who lived in these civilizations like ourselves, view the things they do—as a result of living in them—not as inbred, but as inborn. To the Negro in Africa, it would be incomprehensible for a man to work at a machine all day for a few bits of paper to be given him at the end of his work-day, and in the same way, the white traveler stigmatizes the African as lazy because he will not see the necessity for entering on a gruelling forced march so as to reach a certain point in a given time. And when we turn to our civilization, we find that it has many culture-patterns, as we may term these methods of behavior. They are ingrained in us through long habituation, and their violation evokes a strong emotional response in us, no matter what our racial background. Thus for a person to eat with a knife in place of a fork, or to go about the streets hatless, or for a woman to wear short dresses when long ones are in fashion, are all violations of the patterns we have been brought up to feel right and proper, and we react violently to them. More serious, for a young man not to "settle down" and make as much money as he can is regarded as bordering on the immoral, while, in the régime of sex, the rigid patterns have been remarked upon, as has been the unmitigated condemnation which the breaking of these taboos calls forth. The examples which I have given above of the reaction of the Negro to the general cultural patterns of this country might be multiplied to include almost as many social facts as are observable, and yet, wherever we might go, we would find the Negro reacting to the same situations in much the same fashion as his white brother.

What, then, is the particular Negro genius for culture? Is there such a thing? Can he contribute something of his vivid, and yet at the same time softly gracious personality to the general culture in which he lives? What there is today in Harlem distinct from the white culture which surrounds it, is, as far as I am able to see, merely a remnant from the peasant days in the South. Of the African culture, not a trace. Even the spirituals are an expression of the emotion of the Negro playing through the typical religious pattern of white America. But from that emotional quality in the Negro, which is to be sensed rather than measured, comes the feeling that, though strongly acculturated to the prevalent pattern of behavior, the Negroes may, at the same time, influence it somewhat eventually through the appeal of that quality.

THAT they have absorbed the culture of America is too obvious, almost, to be mentioned. They have absorbed it as all great racial and social groups in this country have absorbed it. And they face much the same problems as these groups face. The social ostracism to which they are subjected is only different in extent from that to which the Jew is subjected. The fierce reaction of race-pride is quite the same in both groups. But, whether in Negro or in Jew, the protest avails nothing, apparently. All racial and social elements in our population who live here long enough become acculturated, Americanized in the truest sense of the word, eventually. They learn our culture and react according to its patterns, against which all the protestations of the possession of, or of hot desire for, a peculiar culture mean nothing.

As we turn to Harlem we see its social and economic and political makeup a part of the larger whole of the city—separate from it, it is true, but still essentially not different from any other American community in which the modes of life and of action are determined by the great dicta of "what is done." In other words, it represents, as do all American communities which it resembles, a case of complete acculturation. And so, I return again to my reaction on first seeing this center of Negro activity, as the complete description of it: "Why, it's the same pattern, only a different shade!"

Our Land

By LANGSTON HUGHES

Drawings by Winold Reiss

We should have a land of sun,
Of gorgeous sun,
And a land of fragrant water
Where the twilight is a soft bandanna handkerchief
Of rose and gold,
And not this land
Where life is cold.

We should have a land of trees,
Of tall thick trees,
Bowed down with chattering parrots
Brilliant as the day,
And not this land where birds are gray.

Ah, we should have a land of joy,
Of love and joy and wine and song,
And not this land where joy is wrong.

—From Opportunity

The Rhythm of Harlem

By KONRAD BERCOVICI

WHEN, in the course of my study of New York City, I visited Harlem, a white and a colored man put the very same question to me, in exactly the same words. They have branded themselves in my memory:

"Why do you go to Harlem? For material?"

And what they meant was: "Would you have developed such an enthusiasm if you did not have to write—or want to write—about Negroes?"

That Harlem was a revelation to me; that I enjoyed its colorfulness and vividness of life as much as I have enjoyed anything in this country, would not have been enough of an answer for either of my interrogators. The colored people did not believe my friendship. The white ones suspected it. The question put to me was the quintessence of the colored man's attitude toward the white man and the white man's attitude toward another white man who shows an interest in the life of the colored people.

I am now, perhaps, better fitted to understand a good many things that happened to me in Harlem. I have been through Louisiana and Tennessee. . . . I understand better the gaze in the eyes of my Negro friends, and the drooping corners of the mouths of the white ones, one sniffing and the other sneering at my interest. It is this suspicion which lives in Harlem, fostered by the years of slavery. It has raised a second wall to surmount; thicker even than the wall the white man has raised between himself and the colored population. Culture, friendship may after all be unable to tear either of these walls down.

The white man does not believe that the Christian Negro, praying in a Christian church, to the Christian God, is entitled to do so. Does he believe that his God is listening to the Negroes' prayers? The colored man thinks that praying in a Christian church to a Christian God in a Christian language entitles him to the white God's mercy and to equality. I wondered and still wonder why the colored people have not evolved a religion of their own, a church of their own and a God of their own.

AN awakened consciousness of race stirs Harlem. Backs are straightened out and heads are raised. Eyes look to their own level when they seek those of other people. The feeling is still one of being better than thou, but underneath that, it seemed to me, there was a striving for another culture that was not an imitative one. Surely greater difficulties beset this undercurrent than one would casually think. The greatest of them all is the one of language. For in the same word-figures one limits himself to the same thought as the others using similar word-figures. At bottom, the white man's feeling of superiority is based on the fact that the Negroes have no language of their own. Had they preserved their African tongue it would have been different.

"We are as good and as bad as the white man, neither better nor worse" is the feeling of Harlem. It is not the winning attitude for a people so different! Different from the whites would be the right starting point for a new culture. For the few hundred thousand Negroes in Harlem will ultimately be to the colored race living in the United States the intellectual center from which its culture will emanate. To pile up wealth as the white man has done will not further them. To pile up industrial organizations, institutions, universities, charities and armies will not do it.

A different culture, a different music, a different art, of which the Negroes are capable and which should be like a gift to the races they live with, will do it.

They are not inferiors. They do not have to strive for equality. They are different. Emphasizing that difference in their lives, in their culture, is what will give them and what should give them their value. They should take a leaf out of the race life of the Jews. The Jews have maintained their racial entity by being different. Where and when they have ceased to do so, they have ceased to exist as such without in any way changing the attitude of their neighbors. Quite the opposite. The non-Jew is less friendly to the unorthodox than to the orthodox Jew.

I LISTENED to the preachers in the churches of Harlem. I understood the language. But was there not something unsaid in the preachment? Was the preacher, the minister, not fashioning another God for himself and for his congregation while he spoke? It seemed impossible that they should all be serving the same one.

I went to the theater. Colored actors were playing a play of colored people. And there, too, the whole thing seemed to me a translation from an unspoken language lying dormant in the souls of the people, which they had forgotten and yet translated from. The color of the voice, the tone, the rhythm, the music of the phrase was something peculiarly their own. Beautiful? Yes. But different. The words never meant anything to me. There was another medium of communication. Words of another language should have gone with that music, with that rhythm, with that cadence. The thought process that animated them was so different it required another medium than the one used.

I have heard their music and I have seen their dances. Beautiful? Yes. But how totally unlike the music of the rest of the people, and the dance of the rest of the people. I was a stranger to it. It was a stranger to me. We remained strangers.

I have heard Harlem men planning business, planning politics, speaking of life and death. And in all of this, though the surface was clear and understandable, there was another element under the surface, hardly hinted at in the words spoken.

Long after the white people have ceased, if they ever do cease, to have any feeling of superiority toward the colored race, there will still remain that feeling of essential difference. It is up to the colored people to direct their creative thought into such channels as will give them a distinctive superiority. Only then will one's friendship be neither suspected nor reproached.

Color Lines

By WALTER F. WHITE

THE hushed tenseness within the theatre was broken only by the excited chattering between the scenes which served as oases of relief. One reassured himself by touching his neighbor or gripping the edge of the bench as a magnificently proportioned Negro on the tiny Provincetown Theatre stage, with a voice of marvelous power and with a finished artistry enacted Eugene O'Neill's epic of human terror, The Emperor Jones. For years I had nourished the conceit that nothing in or of the theatre could thrill me—I was sure my years of theatre-going had made me immune to the tricks and the trappings which managers and actors use to get their tears and smiles and laughs. A few seasons ago my shell of conceit was cracked a little—in that third act of Karel Capek's R. U. R. when Rossum's automatons swarmed over the parapet to wipe out the last human being. But the chills that chased each other up and down my spine then were only pleasurable tingles compared to the sympathetic terror evoked by Paul Robeson as he fled blindly through the impenetrable forest of the "West Indian island not yet self-determined by white marines."

Nor was I alone. When, after remaining in darkness from the second through the eighth and final scene, the house was flooded with light, a concerted sigh of relief welled up from all over the theatre. With real joy we heard the reassuring roar of taxicabs and muffled street noises of Greenwich Village and knew we were safe in New York. Wave after wave of applause, almost hysterical with relief, brought Paul Robeson time and time again before the curtain to receive the acclaim his art had merited. Almost shyly he bowed again and again as the storm of handclapping and bravos surged and broke upon the tiny stage. His color—his race—all, all were forgotten by those he had stirred so deeply with his art.

Outside in narrow, noisy Macdougal Street the four of us stood. Mrs. Robeson, alert, intelligent, merry, an expert chemist for years in one of New York's leading hospitals; Paul Robeson, clad now in conventional tweeds in place of the ornate, gold-laced trappings of the Emperor Jones; my wife and I. We wanted supper and a place to talk. All about us blinked invitingly the lights of restaurants and inns of New York's Bohemia. Place after place was suggested and discarded. Here a colored man and his companion had been made to wait interminably until, disgusted, they had left. There a party of four colored people,

The color line, we say—but there are many color lines. One bars the man but not the artist; another the man who looks black but not the man who looks white, regardless of race; another divides the black from the mulatto. Some cross the lines, and some refuse to do so. Mr. White explores these tangled inhibitions and their bearing on the human spirit— the personal aspects of race and color prejudice. In the succeeding article Dean Miller studies the mass effects of prejudice, viewing it dispassionately as a factor in social development

all university graduates, had been told flatly by the proprietress, late of North Carolina, she did not serve "niggers." At another, other colored people had been stared at so rudely they had bolted their food and left in confusion. The Civil Rights Act of New York would have protected us—but we were too much under the spell of the theatre we had just quitted to want to insist on the rights the law gave us. So we mounted a bus and rode seven miles or more to colored Harlem where we could be served with food without fear of insult or contumely. The man whose art had brought homage to his feet from sophisticated New York could not enter even the cheapest of the eating places of lower New York with the assurance that some unpleasantness might not come to him before he left.

What does race prejudice do to the inner man of him who is the victim of that prejudice? What is the feeling within the breast of the Paul Robesons, the Roland Hayes's, the Harry Burleighs, as they listen to the applause of those whose kind receive them as artists but refuse to accept them as men? It is of this inner conflict of the black man in America—or, more specifically in New York City, I shall try to speak.

I approach my task with reluctance—it is no easy matter to picture that effect which race or color prejudice has on the Negro of fineness of soul who is its victim. Of wounds to the flesh it is easy to speak. It is not difficult to tell of lynchings and injustices and race proscription. Of wounds to the spirit which are a thousand times more deadly and cruel it is impossible to tell in entirety. On the one hand lies the Scylla of bathos and on the other the Charybdis of insensivity to subtler shadings of the spirit. If I can evoke in your mind a picture of what results proscription has brought, I am content.

With its population made up of peoples from every corner of the earth, New York City is, without doubt, more free from ordinary manifestations of prejudice than any other city in the United States. Its Jewish, Italian, German, French, Greek, Czechoslovakian, Irish, Hungarian quarters with their teeming thousands and hundreds of thousands form so great a percentage that "white, Gentile, Protestant" Nordics have but little opportunity to develop their prejudices as they do, for example, in Mississippi or the District of Columbia. It was no idle joke when some forgotten wit remarked, "The Jews own New York, the Irish run it and the Negroes enjoy it."

New York's polyglot population which causes such distress

to the Lothrop Stoddards and the Madison Grants, by a curious anomaly, has created more nearly than any other section that democracy which is the proud boast but rarely practiced accomplishment of these United States. The Ku Klux Klan has made but little headway in New York City for the very simple reason that the proscribed outnumber the proscribers. Thus race prejudice cannot work its will upon Jew or Catholic—or Negro, as in other more genuinely American centers. This combined with the fact that most people in New York are so busy they haven't time to spend in hating other people, makes New York as nearly ideal a place for colored people as exists in America.

Despite these alleviating causes, however, New York is in the United States where prejudice appears to be indigenous. Its population includes many Southern whites who have brought North with them their hatreds. There are here many whites who are not Southern but whose minds have indelibly fixed upon them the stereotype of a Negro who is either a buffoon or a degenerate beast or a subservient lackey. From these the Negro knows he is ever in danger of insult or injury. This situation creates various attitudes of mind among those who are its victims. Upon most the acquisition of education and culture, of wealth and sensitiveness causes a figurative and literal withdrawal, as far as is humanly possible or as necessity permits, from all contacts with the outside world where unpleasant situations may arise. This naturally means the development of an intensive Negro culture and a definitely bounded city within a city. Doubtless there are some advantages, but it is certain that such voluntary segregation works a greater loss upon those within and those without the circle.

Upon those within, it cuts off to a large extent the world of music, of the theatre, of most of those contacts which mean growth and development and which denied, mean stagnation and spiritual atrophy. It develops as well a tendency towards self-pity, towards a fatal conviction that they of all peoples are most oppressed. The harmful effects of such reactions are too obvious to need elaboration.

Upon those without, the results are equally mischievous. First there is the loss of that deep spirituality, that gift of song and art, that indefinable thing which perhaps can best be termed the over-soul of the Negro, which has given America the only genuinely artistic things which the world recognizes as distinctive American contributions to the arts.

More conventional notions as Thomas Dixon and Octavus Roy Cohen and Irvin Cobb have falsely painted them, of what the Negro is and does and thinks continue to persist, while those who represent more truly the real Negro avoid all contact with other races.

There are, however, many other ways of avoidance of proscription and prejudice. Of these one of no small importance is that popularly known as "passing," that

is, those whose skin is of such color that they can pass as white may do so. This is not difficult; there are so many swarthy races represented in New York's population that even colored people who could easily be distinguished by their own race as Negroes, pass as French or Spanish or Cuban with ease. Of these there are two classes. First are those who for various reasons disappear entirely and go over the line to become white in business, social and all other relationships. The number of these is very large—much larger that is commonly suspected. To my personal knowledge one of the prominent surgeons of New York City who has an elaborately furnished suite of offices in an exclusive neighborhood, whose fees run often into four figures, who moves with his family in society of such standing that the names of its members appear frequently in the society columns of the metropolitan press, is a colored man from a Southern city. There he grew tired of the proscribed life he was forced to lead, decided to move North and forget he was a colored man. He met with success, married well and he and his wife and their children form as happy a family circle as one could hope to see. O'Neill's All God's Chillun Got Wings to the contrary, his wife loves him but the more for his courage in telling her of his race when first they met and loved.

This doctor's case is not an exception. Colored people know many of their own who have done likewise. In New York there is at least one man high in the field of journalism, a certain famous singer, several prominent figures of the stage, in fact, in almost any field that could be mentioned there are those who are colored but who have left their race for wider opportunity and for freedom from race prejudice. Just a few days before this article is being written I received a note from a woman whose name is far from being obscure in the world of the arts. The night before, she wrote me, there had been a party at her studio. Among the guests were three Southern whites who, in a confidential mood, had told her of a plan the Ku Klux Klan was devising for capitalizing in New York prejudice against the Negro. When I asked her why she had given me the information she told me her father, resident at the time of her birth in a Southern state, was a Negro.

The other group is made up of the many others who "pass" only occasionally. Some of these do so for business reasons, others when they go out to dine or to the theatre.

If a personal reference may be forgiven, I have had the unique experience within the past seven years of investigating some thirty-seven lynchings and eight race riots by the simple method of *not* telling those whom I was investigating of the Negro blood within my veins.

Large as is the number of those who have crossed the line, they form but a small percentage of those who might follow such an example but who do not. The

Baptism
By CLAUDE McKAY

Into the furnace let me go alone;
Stay you without in terror of the heat.

I will go naked in—for thus 'tis sweet—
Into the wierd depths of the hottest zone.
I will not quiver in the frailest bone,
You will not note a flicker of defeat;
My heart shall tremble not its fate to meet,
Nor mouth give utterance to any moan.
The yawning oven spits forth fiery spears;
Red aspish tongues shout wordlessly my name.
Desire destroys, consumes my mortal fears,
Transforming me into a shape of flame.

I will come out, back to your world of tears,
A stronger soul within a finer frame.
            —*From Harlem Shadows, Harcourt, Brace & Co.*

constant hammering of three hundred years of oppression has resulted in a race consciousness among the Negroes of the United States which is amazing to those who know how powerful it is. In America, as is well known, all persons with any discernible percentage of Negro blood are classed as Negroes, subject therefore to all of the manifestations of prejudice. They are never allowed to forget their race. By prejudice ranging from the more violent forms like lynching and other forms of physical violence down to more subtle but none the less effective methods, Negroes of the United States have been welded into a homogeneity of thought and a commonness of purpose in combatting a common foe. These external and internal forces have gradually created a state of mind among Negroes which is rapidly becoming more pronounced where they realize that just so long as one Negro can be made the victim of prejudice because he *is* a Negro, no other Negro is safe from that same oppression. This applies geographically, as is seen in the support given by colored people in cities like Boston, New York and Chicago to those who oppose lynching of Negroes in the South, and it applies to that large element of colored people whose skins are lighter who realize that their cause is common with that of all Negroes regardless of color.

Unfortunately, however, color prejudice creates certain attitudes of mind on the part of some colored people which form color lines within the color line. Living in an atmosphere where swarthiness of skin brings, almost automatically, denial of opportunity, it is as inevitable as it is regrettable that there should grow up among Negroes themselves distinctions based on skin color and hair texture. There are many places where this pernicious custom is more powerful than in New York—for example, there are cities where only mulattoes attend certain churches while those whose skins are dark brown or black attend others. Marriages between colored men and women whose skins differ markedly in color, and indeed, less intimate relations are frowned upon. Since those of lighter color could more often secure the better jobs an even wider chasm has come between them, as those with economic and cultural opportunity have progressed more rapidly than those whose skin denied them opportunity.

Thus, even among intelligent Negroes there has come into being the fallacious belief that black Negroes are less able to achieve success. Naturally such a condition had led to jealousy and suspicion on the part of darker Negroes, chafing at their bonds and resentful of the patronizing attitude of those of lighter color.

In New York City this feeling between black and mulatto has been accentuated by the presence of some 40,000 Negroes from the West Indies, and particularly by the propaganda of Marcus Garvey and his Universal Negro Improvement Association. In contrast to the division between white and colored peoples in the United States, there is in the West Indies, as has been pointed out by Josiah Royce and others, a tri-partite problem of race relations with whites, blacks and mulattoes. The latter mingle freely with whites in business and other relations and even socially. But neither white nor mulatto has any extensive contact on an equal plane with the blacks. It is this system which has enabled the English whites in the islands to rule and exploit though they as rulers are vastly inferior numerically to blacks and mulattoes.

The psychology thus created is visible among many of the West Indian Negroes in New York. It was the same background of the English brand of race prejudice which actuated Garvey in preaching that only those who were of unmixed Negro blood were Negroes. It is true beyond doubt that such a doctrine created for a time greater antagonisms among colored people, but an inevitable reaction has set in which, in time, will probably bring about a greater unity than before among Negroes in the United States.

We have therefore in Harlem this strange mixture of reaction not only to prejudice from without but to equally potent prejudices from within. Many are the comedies and many are the tragedies which these artificial lines of demarcation have created. Yet with all these forces and counter forces at work, there can be seen emerging some definite and hopeful signs of racial unity. Though it hearkens back to the middle ages, this is essential in the creation of a united front against that race and color prejudice with which the Negro, educated or illiterate, rich or poor, native or foreign-born, mulatto, octaroon, quadroon, or black, must strive continuously.

The Harvest of Race Prejudice

By KELLY MILLER

PREJUDICE is a state of mind. Some affect to believe that it is an innate passion parallel with instinct, and is therefore unalterable. Others maintain that it is a stimulated animosity modifiable by time, place and condition, and is on the same footing with other shallow obliterative feelings. But whatever the basis of race prejudice, whether natural or acquired, we do know certainly that it is a pressing, persistent fact, easily stimulated and appeased with difficulty. It forms a barrier between the races which is as real as the seas and as apparent as the mountains.

Like a two-edged sword, race prejudice cuts both ways. It weakens the energies and paralyzes the moral muscle of the white race; it stultifies the conscience and frustrates the normal workings of democracy and Christianity. It fosters a double standard of ethics, and leads to lawlessness, lynching, and all manner of national disgrace. The elements of the white race that are most thoroughly obsessed by this passion show the lowest average of intellectual, moral and spiritual achievement. The Ku Klux Klan spreads its virus through our democracy; Nordicism carries it to the ends of the earth. Its effects are nationally and internationally threatening, and the American people and the Nordic civilization of which they are a part must stop to consider whether in this evil fruit they are not nurturing the fatal seeds of world dissension and catastrophe.

But our present concern is mainly to describe prejudice as

i; affects the Negro. Here the harvest of prejudice is ripe for the sociologist's gleaning. The outstanding and all-inclusive effect of race prejudice on the Negro can be summed up in one word, *segregation*. This is but the outer embodiment of the inner feeling of the white race. Whatever the nature and origin of this attitude, it is well nigh universal in the scope of its operation. The watch word is "miscegenation"; the rallying cry is "social equality." The cunning propagandist knows how to play upon these alarms and to adjust their appeal to the varying moods of popular passion and prejudice as a skilled musician plays upon his favorite instrument. Until recently the Negro has been the victim, with little capacity to resist.

This attitude of the white race has decreed residential segregation. Several municipalities have sought to embody this feeling in restrictive ordinances. In their too hasty zeal they over-rode the reaches of the constitution and the law; Negroes, through the National Association for the Advancement of Colored People, contested the constitutionality of these ordinances and won a unanimous decision from the Supreme Court. Yet the legal victory merely modified the details of procedure; it had little effect upon the actual fact of segregation, which operates as effectively without the law as within it, except as to the finality of its boundaries.

The most gigantic instance of racial segregation in the United States is seen in Harlem. There is no local law prescribing it. There does not have to be. And yet, under the normal operation of race prejudice, we find 200,000 Negroes shut in segregated areas as sharply marked as the aisles of a church. This is but an example of what it taking place in every city and center where the Negro resorts in great numbers. The recent tide of Northern migration has greatly emphasized this tendency. In Boston, New York, Philadelphia, Baltimore, Washington, Pittsburgh, Detroit, Indianapolis and Chicago, the Negro contingent lives in wards and sections of wards which the politician and the real estate dealer know as well as the mariners know the depths and shallows of the seas.

We may then take Harlem as a fair specimen of the harvest of race prejudice throughout the United States. Here we have the largest Negro community in the world. It is a city within a city, a part of, and yet apart from the general life of greater New York. We need not stop here to dilate upon the inhumanity, the cruelty or the hardships of race prejudice. The outstanding fact and the consequences immediately flowing from it suffice for the present purpose.

These Negro communities are everywhere extending their boundaries without tending to any fixed limits we can now set. In Chicago the rapidly expanding boundary of the black belt precipitated the lamentable race riot. The issue is still the cause of race agitation in milder form in all parts

of the country. The whites are trying to keep back the rising tide of black invasion into residential areas previously regarded as exclusively theirs. The Negroes are pushing over the boundaries of racial restriction in quest of more room and better facilities. We may expect this minor border warfare to continue until the matter settles itself by custom, understanding and acceptance. Thus it is that the sharp accentuation of race consciousness on the part of the white race is developing a counter-tendency on the part of the Negro. This is the first fruit of segregation.

If Negroes were indiscriminately interspersed among the white population of New York, race consciousness would weaken to the point of disappearance. Three hundred thousand Negroes intermingled among six million whites would be unnoticeable. But when segregated in two or three centers the African contingent becomes not only apparent, but impressive. Whenever p e o p l e are thrown together they begin to think of their common interests. A common consciousness emerges which shortly expresses itself in organized endeavor. The Negro race as a whole has hitherto had a somewhat vague and indefinite collective consciousness stimulated in large part by stress of outside compulsion. But the race is too numerous, too widespread in territory and too diverse in interests to give this conscious edge. Harlem furnishes the needed pressure. The Garvey movement furnishes the most extreme focussing of this feeling. Marcus Garvey found in Harlem not only a mass of Negroes surrounded and overshadowed by whites, but also a considerable group of West Indians, who, in many ways, felt themselves isolated and circumscribed by the native Afro-Americans. Shrewdly enough he seized upon this group as the basis of his focal operation. He preached the impossibility of racial entente on the same soil and under the same political and social régime, and urged a racial hegira. His philosophy does not in this connection interest us. But he has shown to the world the possibility of focussing the racial mind, and of mobilizing racial resources about a formulated ideal.

Another fruit of prejudice is the direction which race effort and organization has been impelled to take; until recently the Negro has been thrown quite too much on the defensive. The National Association for the Advancement of Colored People arose to cope with this situation on the basis of fight and protest. Their fundamental philosophy is based upon the belief that race prejudice is medicable by legal and judicial process. Their method is militant; their mood is optimistic. Equality is their goal; the elimination of prejudice their objective. The Urban League, on the other hand, represents the ameliorative method which hopes that in the long run smooth working relations will be effected on the basis of mutual forbearance and good will. Its main attack is local, urban (*Continued on page* 711)

I, TOO

By LANGSTON HUGHES

I, too, sing America.

I am the darker brother.
They send me to eat in the kitchen
When company comes.
But I laugh,
And eat well,
And grow strong.

Tomorrow
I'll sit at the table
When company comes
Nobody 'll dare
Say to me,
"Eat in the kitchen"
Then.

Besides, they'll see how beautiful I am
And be ashamed,—

I, too, am America.

Breaking Through

By EUNICE ROBERTA HUNTON

HARLEM is a modern ghetto. True, that is a contradiction in terms, but prejudice has ringed this group around with invisible lines and bars. Within the bars you will find a small city, self-sufficient, complete in itself— a riot of color and personality, a medley of song and tears, a canvas of browns and golds and flaming reds. And yet bound.

In it are some who year in and year out never leave the narrow confines of Harlem. There are those who make rare excursions into the larger shopping districts and rarer still to the theatrical center. There are those whose work takes them down to New York's factories, office buildings, hotels, restaurants and places of amusement, but they know these places only in working hours; their life is the life of Harlem. There are those who, still ghetto-bound mentally, have been pressed through the bars of the cage, but they have been caught up and placed in tiny ghettos of their own in other sections of Manhattan, Brooklyn, the Bronx and on Long Island. Their lives too are race-bound. But there is another group, which is not Harlem bound, whose contacts are many, whose sphere of activity is wide and ever widening. Theirs is New York in its entirety; theirs is the opportunity of giving Harlem to New York and New York to Harlem.

Education is the way out of the ghetto. Age submits, but youth—even though the door be barred—revolts. In many instances age contributes to the burden by pressing youth into the beaten paths of experience, by insisting upon teaching, preaching and medicine as the appropriate professional goals. Now youth is revolting and getting away from the compromise so often expressed in words like these: "Well, I'll take it up any way, even if I cannot practice it, perhaps I can teach it." Youth is escaping into business, art and the technical professions. A few even are escaping into the broad freedom of the leisure class.

In sharp contrast with these rebels of success who are seeking to work out their own destiny, these individualists who often appear in the first instance to be deserting the race, are the conscious pathbreakers—those who protest at proscription. We find them of varied ardors and enthusiasms, often misguided, from those who won't go to a colored church or who will break into a white block to those who organize some definite assault on occupational proscription. Whereas many who break the bonds are actuated solely by the desire to get the best for themselves in spite of proscription, a few realize that they are blazing a trail that others of the race may follow. This kind of thing is instanced by the young man who about seven years ago succeeded in becoming the first interne known to be of Negro extraction in a New York city hospital, or by the older surgeon who a little while ago became the first of his race to be permitted to conduct operations in one of the city's large hospitals. This being "first" means a great deal in the life of the racial group. There is a constant struggle among young men and women to be the "first" to do a certain thing, for the pioneer in any thing significant occupies, if only for a little while, an exalted position while a large portion of the race indulges in a mild form of hero worship. These achievements are the pride of the race; this business of reaching new heights is taken very seriously by the ghetto bound, for each is a milestone on the road of progress which leads to the goal of unrestricted opportunity.

These achievements have not always been regarded as breaking paths for others to follow. There was a time, in fact, when they were truly exceptional, when there was a first and never a second, when the proud possessor of such a record was even jealous and fearful lest some one rob him of his uniqueness. Now among leaders and youth there is prevalent the relay spirit which seeks to "keep openings open."

THERE is also some tugging from without at the ropes that bind the ghetto. It is the result of the efforts of the whites because of curiosity, self-interest, a spasm of self-righteousness or—very rarely—genuine interest, to establish a contact with those within the ghetto. It takes the form of the establishment of various organizations within the ghetto and organizations outside the ghetto to "help" those inside. We see it in the Christian societies, in the numerous clinics, health organizations and social service bureaus which are operating in Harlem, in the rapidly increasing group of whites who are attending civic and social affairs there and for varied reasons attempting to establish understanding and friendship with those within.

In many cases this is no conscious attempt to break the ghetto bonds; indeed it may be a deliberate attempt to go in and satisfy the needs of the inhabitants to prevent their leaving the ghetto. Sometimes the ruse is successful but more often, in the long run, it defeats its own end, for it sets an example of broadness that the ghetto-bound spirit eagerly seizes upon. Having secured a taste of the world outside, the ghetto youth is eager to get more of it and the determination to grow strong and break through increases.

There is another side of the picture; it is a tale of long dark years of dismal failure, of brave struggles to rise above mediocrity, of bitter fights for existence, a tale twisted with heartaches and heartbreaks, a tale drenched in sweat and blood, but still shot through with flashes of sunlight upon pure gold. It takes rare courage to fight a fight that more often than not ends in death, poverty or prostitution of genius. But it is to these who make this fight despite the tremendous odds, despite the deterring pessimism of those who see in the tangle of prejudice that surround the ghetto a hopeless barrier, that we must look for the breaking of the bonds now linked together by ignorance and misunderstanding.

Four Portraits of Negro Women

Drawn by Winold Reiss

A Woman from the Virgin Islands

The Librarian

Two Public School Teachers

ELISE JOHNSON McDOUGALD

The Double Task

The Struggle of Negro Women for Sex and Race Emancipation

By ELISE JOHNSON McDOUGALD

THROUGHOUT the long years of history, woman has been the weather-vane, the indicator, showing in which direction the wind of destiny blows. Her status and development have augured now calm and stability, now swift currents of progress. What then is to be said of the Negro woman today?

In Harlem, more than anywhere else, the Negro woman is free from the cruder handicaps of primitive household hardships and the grosser forms of sex and race subjugation. Here she has considerable opportunity to measure her powers in the intellectual and industrial fields of the great city. Here the questions naturally arise: "What are her problems?" and "How is she solving them?"

To answer these questions, one must have in mind not any one Negro woman, but rather a colorful pageant of individuals, each differently endowed. Like the red and yellow of the tiger-lily, the skin of one is brilliant against the star-lit darkness of a racial sister. From grace to strength, they vary in infinite degree, with traces of the race's history left in physical and mental outline on each. With a discerning mind, one catches the multiform charm, beauty and character of Negro women; and grasps the fact that their problem cannot be thought of in mass.

Because only a few have caught this vision, the attitude of mind of most New Yorkers causes the Negro woman serious difficulty. She is conscious that what is left of chivalry is not directed toward her. She realizes that the ideals of beauty, built up in the fine arts, exclude her almost entirely. Instead, the grotesque Aunt Jemimas of the street-car advertisements proclaim only an ability to serve, without grace or loveliness. Nor does the drama catch her finest spirit. She is most often used to provoke the mirthless laugh of ridicule; or to portray feminine viciousness or vulgarity not peculiar to Negroes. This is the shadow over her. To a race naturally sunny comes the twilight of self-doubt and a sense of personal inferiority. It cannot be denied that these are potent and detrimental influences, though not generally recognized because they are in the realm of the mental and spiritual. More apparent are the economic handicaps which follow her recent entrance into industry. It is conceded that she has special difficulties because of the poor working conditions and low wages of her men. It is not surprising that only the determined women forge ahead to results other than mere survival. The few who do prove their mettle stimulate one to a closer study of how this achievement is won in Harlem.

Better to visualize the Negro woman at her job, our vision of a host of individuals must once more resolve itself into groups on the basis of activity. First, comes a very small leisure group—the wives and daughters of men who are in business, in the professions and in a few well-paid personal service occupations. Second, a most active and progressive group, the women in business and the professions. Third, the many women in the trades and industry. Fourth, a group weighty in numbers struggling on in domestic service, with an even less fortunate fringe of casual workers, fluctuating with the economic temper of the times.

The first is a pleasing group to see. It is picked for outward beauty by Negro men with much the same feeling as other Americans of the same economic class. Keeping their women free to preside over the family, these women are affected by the problems of every wife and mother, but touched only faintly by their race's hardships. They do share acutely in the prevailing difficulty of finding competent household help. Negro wives find Negro maids unwilling generally to work in their own neighborhoods, for various reasons. They do not wish to work where there is a possibility of acquaintances coming into contact with them while they serve and they still harbor the misconception that Negroes of any station are unable to pay as much as persons of the other race. It is in these homes of comparative ease that we find the polite activities of social exclusiveness. The luxuries of well-appointed homes, modest motors, tennis, golf and country clubs, trips to Europe and California, make for social standing. The problem confronting the refined Negro family is to know others of the same achievement. The search for kindred spirits gradually grows less difficult; in the past it led to the custom of visiting all the large cities in order to know similar groups of cultured Negro people.

A spirit of stress and struggle characterizes the second two groups. These women of business, profession and trade are the hub of the wheel of progress. Their burden is two-fold. Many are wives and mothers whose husbands are insufficiently paid, or who have succumbed to social maladjustment and have abandoned their families. An appalling number are widows. They face the great problem of leaving home each day and at the same time trying to rear children in their spare time—this too in neighborhoods where rents are large, standards of dress and recreation high and costly, and social danger on the increase.

The great commercial life of New York City is only slightly touched by the Negro woman of our second group. Negro business men offer her most of their work, but their number is limited. Outside of this field, custom is once more against her and competition is keen for all. However, Negro girls are training and some are holding exceptional jobs. One of the professors in a New York college has had a young colored woman as secretary for the past three years. Another holds the head clerical position in an organization where reliable handling of detail and a sense of business ethics are essential. For four years she has steadily advanced. Quietly these women prove their worth, so that when a vacancy exists and there is a call, it is difficult to find even one competent colored secretary who is not employed. As a result of opportunity in clerical work in the educational system of New York City a number have qualified for such positions, one being appointed within the year to the office work of a high school. In other departments the civil service in New York City is no longer free from discrimination. The casual personal interview, that tenacious and retrogressive practice introduced in the Federal administration during the World War has spread and often nullifies the Negro woman's success in written tests. The successful young woman just cited above was three times "turned down" as undesirable on the basis of the personal interview. In the great mercantile houses, the many young Negro girls who might be well suited to salesmanship are barred from all but the menial positions. Even so, one Negro woman, beginning as a uniformed maid, has pulled herself up to the position of "head of stock."

Again, the telephone and insurance companies which receive considerable patronage from Negroes deny them proportionate employment. Fortunately, this is an era of changing customs. There is hope that a less selfish racial attitude will prevail. It is a heartening fact that there is an increasing number of Americans who will lend a hand in the game fight of the worthy.

In the less crowded professional vocations, the outlook is more cheerful. In these fields, the Negro woman is dependent largely upon herself and her own race for work. In the legal, dental, medical and nursing professions, successful women practitioners have usually worked their way through college and are "managing" on the small fees that can be received from an underpaid public. Social conditions in America are hardest upon the Negro because he is lowest in the economic scale. This gives rise to a demand for trained college women in the profession of social work. It has met with a response from young college women, anxious to devote their education and lives to the needs of the submerged classes. In New York City, some fifty-odd women are engaged in social work, other than nursing. In the latter profession there are over two hundred and fifty. Much of the social work has been pioneer in nature: the pay has been small with little possibility of advancement. For even in work among Negroes, the better paying positions are reserved for whites. The Negro college woman is doing her bit in this field at a sacrifice, along such lines as these: in the correctional departments of the city, as probation officers, investigators, and police women; as Big Sisters attached to the Childrens' Court; as field workers and visitors for relief organizations and missions; as secretaries for travelers-aid and mission societies; as visiting teachers and vocational guides for the schools of the city; and, in the many branches of public health nursing, in schools, organizations devoted to preventive and educational medicine, in hospitals and in private nursing.

In New York City, nearly three hundred Negro women share the good conditions in the teaching profession. They measure up to the high pedagogical requirements of the city and state law and are increasingly, leaders in the community. Here too the Negro woman finds evidence of the white workers' fear of competition. The need for teachers is still so strong that little friction exists. When it does seem to be imminent, it is smoothed away, as it recently

was at a meeting of school principals. From the floor, a discussion began with: "What are we going to do about this problem of the increasing number of Negro teachers coming into our schools?" It ended promptly through the suggestion of another principal: "Send all you get and don't want over to my school. I have two now and I'll match their work to any two of your best whom you name." One might go on to such interesting and more unusual professions as journalism, chiropody, bacteriology, pharmacy, etc., and find that, though the number in any one may be small, the Negro woman is creditably represented in practically every one. According to individual ability she is meeting with success.

Closing the door on the home anxieties, the woman engaged in trades and in industry faces equally serious difficulty in competition in the open working field. Custom is against her in all but a few trade and industrial occupations. She has, however been established long in the dressmaking trade among the helpers and finishers, and more recently among the drapers and fitters in some of the best establishments. Several Negro women are themselves proprietors of shops in the country's greatest fashion district. Each of them has, against great odds, convinced skeptical employers of her business value; and, at the same time, has educated fellow workers of other races, doing much to show the oneness of interest of all workers. In millinery, power sewing-machine operating on cloth, straw and leather, there are few Negro women. The laissez-faire attitude of practically all trade unions makes the Negro woman an unwilling menace to the cause of labor.

In trade cookery, the Negro woman's talent and past experience is recognized. Her problem here is to find employers who will let her work her way to managerial positions, in tea-rooms, candy shops and institutions. One such employer became convinced that the managing cook, a young colored graduate of Pratt Institute, would continue to build up a business that had been failing. She offered her a partnership. As in the cases of a number of such women, her barrier was lack of capital. No matter how highly trained, nor how much speed and business acumen has been acquired, the Negro's credit is held in doubt. An exception in this matter of capital will serve to prove the rule. Thirty years ago, a young Negro girl began learning all branches of the fur trade. She is now in business for herself, employing three women of her race and one Jewish man. She has made fur experts of still another half-dozen colored girls. Such instances as these justify the prediction that the foothold gained in the trade world will, year by year, become more secure.

Because of the limited fields for workers in this group, many of the unsuccessful drift into the fourth social grade, the domestic and casual workers. These drifters increase the difficulties of the Negro woman suited to housework. New standards of household management are forming and the problem of the Negro woman is to meet these new business-like ideals. The constant influx of workers unfamiliar with household conditions in New York keeps the situation one of turmoil. The Negro woman, moreover, is revolting against residential domestic service. It is a last stand in her fight to maintain a semblance of family life. For this reason, principally, the number of day or casual workers is on the increase. Happiness is almost impossible under the strain of these conditions. Health and morale suffer, but how else can her children, loose all afternoon, be gathered together at night-fall? Through it all she manages to give satisfactory service and the Negro woman is sought after for this unpopular work largely because her honesty, loyalty and cleanliness have stood the test of time. Through her drudgery, the women of other groups find leisure time for progress. This is one of her contributions to America.

IT is apparent from what has been said, that even in New York City, Negro women are of a race which is free neither economically, socially nor spiritually. Like women in general, but more particularly like those of other oppressed minorities, the Negro woman has been forced to submit to over-powering conditions. Pressure has been exerted upon her, both from without and within her group. Her emotional and sex life is a reflex of her economic station. The women of the working class will react, emotionally and sexually, similarly to the working-class women of other races. The Negro woman does not maintain any moral standard which may be assigned chiefly to qualities of race, any more than a white woman does. Yet she has been singled out and advertised as having lower sex standards. Superficial critics who have had contact only with the lower grades of Negro women, claim that they are more immoral than other groups of women. This I deny. This is the sort of criticism which predicates of one race, to its detriment, that which is common to all races. Sex irregularities are not a matter of race, but of socio-economic conditions. Research shows that most of the African tribes from which the Negro sprang have strict codes for sex relations. There is no proof of inherent weakness in the ethnic group.

Gradually overcoming the habitual limits imposed upon her by slave masters, she increasingly seeks legal sanction for the consummation and dissolution of sex contracts. Contrary to popular belief, illegitimacy among Negroes is cause for shame and grief. When economic, social and biological forces combined bring about unwed motherhood, the reaction is much the same as in families of other racial groups. Secrecy is maintained if possible. Generally the married aunt, or even the mother, claims that the illegitimate child is her own. The foundling asylum is seldom sought. Schooled in this kind of suffering in the days of slavery, Negro women often temper scorn with sympathy for weakness. Stigma does fall upon the unmarried mother, but perhaps in this matter the Negroes' attitude is nearer the modern enlightened ideal for the social treatment of the unfortunate. May this not be considered another contribution to America?

With all these forces at work, true sex equality has not been approximated. The ratio of opportunity in the sex, social, economic and political spheres is about that which exists between white men and women. In the large, I would say that the Negro woman is the cultural equal of her man because she is generally kept in school longer. Negro boys, like white boys, are usually put to work to subsidize the family income. The growing economic independence of Negro working women is causing her to rebel against the domineering family attitude of the cruder working-class Negro man. The masses of Negro men are engaged in menial occupations throughout the working day. Their baffled and suppressed desires to determine their economic life are manifested in over-bearing domination at home. Working mothers are unable to instill different ideals in their sons. Conditions change slowly. Nevertheless, education and opportunity are

modifying the spirit of the younger Negro men. Trained in modern schools of thought, they begin to show a wholesome attitude of fellowship and freedom for their women. The challenge to young Negro womanhood is to see clearly this trend and grasp the preferred comradeship with sincerity. In this matter of sex equality, Negro women have contributed few outstanding militants. Their feminist efforts are directed chiefly toward the realization of the equality of the races, the sex struggle assuming a subordinate place.

OBSESSED with difficulties that might well compel individualism, the Negro woman has engaged in a considerable amount of organized action to meet group needs. She has evolved a federation of her clubs, embracing between eight and ten thousand women, throughout the state of New York. Its chief function is to crystallize programs, prevent duplication of effort, and to sustain a member organization whose cause might otherwise fail. It is now firmly established, and is about to strive for conspicuous goals. In New York City, one association makes child welfare its name and special concern. Others, like the Utility Club, Utopia Neighborhood, Debutante's League, Sempre Fidelius, etc., raise money for old folks' homes, a shelter for delinquent girls and fresh air camps for children. The Colored Branch of the Y. W. C. A. and the womens' organizations in the many churches, as well as in the beneficial lodges and associations, care for the needs of their members.

On the other hand, the educational welfare of the coming generation, has become the chief concern of the national sororities of Negro college women. The first to be organized in the country, Alpha Kappa Alpha, has a systematized and continuous program of educational and vocational guidance for students of the high schools and colleges. The work of Lambda Chapter, which covers New York City and its suburbs, is outstanding. Its recent campaign gathered together nearly one hundred and fifty such students at a meeting to gain inspiration from the life-stories of successful Negro women in eight fields of endeavor. From the trained nurse, who began in the same schools as they, these girls drank in the tale of her rise to the executive position in the Harlem Health Information Bureau. A commercial artist showed how real talent had overcome the color line. The graduate physician was a living example of the modern opportunities in the newer fields of medicine open to women. The vocations as outlets for the creative instinct became attractive under the persuasion of the musician, the dressmaker and the decorator. Similarly, Alpha Beta Chapter of the national Delta Sigma Theta Sorority recently devoted a week to work along similar lines. In such ways as these are the progressive and privileged groups of Negro women expressing their community and race consciousness.

We find the Negro woman, figuratively, struck in the face daily by contempt from the world about her. Within her soul, she knows little of peace and happiness. Through it all, she is courageously standing erect, developing within herself the moral strength to rise above and conquer false attitudes. She is maintaining her natural beauty and charm and improving her mind and opportunity. She is measuring up to the needs and demands of her family, community and race, and radiating from Harlem a hope that is cherished by her sisters in less propitious circumstances throughout the land. The wind of the race's destiny stirs more briskly because of her striving.

Ambushed in the City

The Grim Side of Harlem

By WINTHROP D. LANE

AN unkempt woman, with hair graying, shoulders rounded and eyes rimmed with thick glasses, reads a newspaper on a subway car in New York City. She is colored. Her skirt is in rags, one toe shows through a shoe, an elbow pushes the lining of her sleeve into sight; perhaps she has just left her mop and pail in some downtown office building. Turning the pages hastily, she seems to be hunting for a particular place. At last she stops. Her forefinger runs up and down the columns. She is looking at the financial page. Finding an item, she gazes closely at it for a moment, and then throws the paper onto the seat beside her. She has a dejected look. Apparently she is through with the paper.

She has been looking for "the numbers." The numbers she wanted were the day's totals of bank exchanges and bank balances—announced each day by the Clearing House and published by the newspapers. On these she has been gambling. Suppose the exchanges were $793,482,450 and the balances $86,453,624. She is then interested in the number 936, because that is made up of the seventh and eighth digits, reading from the right, of the first, and the seventh digit of the second. She and many others are playing this game—a species of policy. If she has put her money, which may be only a few pennies, on 936 that day, she wins. Each day she looks forward to discovering what this combination is. It is the bright spot for her.

The stakes are high if she wins. She reaps 600 times what she wagers. If she wagers a nickel, she wins thirty dollars; if she wagers a quarter, she wins $150; a deposit of fifty cents will bring her $300. These stakes have lure; they are a king's stakes. They will make her rich for the moment. She does not consider the chances against her. She does not consider that she has never won and that only once did she ever hear of anybody winning. The bare possibility of capturing so much money makes her heart beat faster.

Since there are 999 numbers of three digits, or 1000 if we include 000, she seems to have about one chance in a thousand of winning. By the law of averages, she might play the same number daily for three years without a strike. The banker pays 600 times the sum wagered. He, therefore, seems to have a sure thing; barring lucky wins by large gamblers, he can't lose in the long run. That does not interest her, either.

All Harlem is ablaze with "the numbers." People play it everywhere, in tenements, on street corners, in the backs of shops. "Bankers" organize it, promote it, encourage it. They send their runners into flats and stores. You give the runner the money you are betting, write your number on a slip of paper, and wait. If the number you chose is the one that wins next day, you get your money. Runners round up new business, stake off territory and canvass all the people they can reach. A person living in an apartment

house may be the agent for that house. The names of these bankers are known in the neighborhood. One rides around in a $12,000 limousine and has a liveried chauffeur. Minor bankers abound; men and women, getting $200 capital, start in the "numbers" business. Recently, it is said, white men have been trying to wrest the control of the game from blacks; a Jew who formerly used his talents in the hooch business is spoken of as the leader in this effort.

"Always out first with the bank clearing numbers" reads a placard advertising the New York Sun in Harlem. Inspiration for lucky numbers is got from every source. People get their numbers from dream books; fifteen or twenty cents will buy a dream book, and a dream about any topic listed in it has an appropriate number. Or two people exchange street addresses. "Ah'm gonna play it! Ah'm gonna play it!" says one, as he takes down the address of the other. They get their numbers from the numbers of hymns given out in church, from subway cars, from telephone numbers, from dates, from baseball scores, from the prices they pay for purchased articles, from the license tags of passing automobiles. By combining or rearranging these, or using them unchanged, they tempt fortune.

One trouble is, of course, that they don't always get what they win. Many a banker, finding that large sums have been won from him, avoids payment; his victim has no recourse, since the whole transaction is outside the law. The streets of Harlem are being walked by people looking for those who owe them money won at "the numbers." The New York Age, a colored weekly, published a story about one banker who skipped to Cuba with $100,000 taken from the Negroes of Harlem; it is common to win $12, $18 and $30 and not get it. This is only an exasperation of the extortion. The whole game, as it is staged, smells of exploitation.

GREAT number of Negroes have recently swarmed up from the South to swell the Negro colonies of Northern cities. Many of them are unfamiliar with city ways. They have become an invitation to the exploiter and the fakir—the gambling promoter, the necromancer, the fortune teller, the fake druggist, the quack doctor, and even more deliberate cheaters, such as the rent gouger. Living compactly in restricted areas, they supply a fertile field. Density of population is the fakir's paradise; it is the cheater's fairest opportunity for secrecy and success. There he can strike and hide, or be continuously lost in the moving mass of his fellow beings. And, credulous and child-like, the Negro peasant migrant has provided fresh opportunities in Northern cities for many forms of exploitation.

Black art flourishes in Harlem—and elsewhere in New York. Egyptian seers uncover hidden knowledge, Indian fortune-tellers reveal the future, sorcerers perform their mysteries. Feats of witchcraft are done daily. A towel for turban and a smart manner are enough to transform any

Harlem colored man into a dispenser of magic to his profit.

Come with me into any little stationery store on Lenox or Seventh Avenues—the two main business thoroughfares of the district—and peep into the dream and mystery books there offered for sale. Some of these can be bought, as said, for fifteen or twenty cents; others cost a dollar. Here is one called Albertus Magnus. It is described as the "approved, verified, sympathetic and natural Egyptian secrets, or White and Black Art for Man and Beast, revealing the Forbidden Knowledge and Mysteries of Ancient Philosophers." Another is Napoleon's own Oraculum and Book of Fate, containing the explanations of dreams and other mysteries consulted on every occasion by Napoleon himself.

Stop in front of a well-known drug store on Lenox Avenue. Here roots, herbs and barks are displayed in the window. "Devil's Shoestring" one of these is called; others are "Jim Shanks," "John Conqueror," "Rattlesnake Master," "Sacred Bark" and "Jesuits' Bark." In curled forms, in powders, in spirally bunches, in thick little knots, they lie there; they are sold as cures for various forms of illness. I was interested in knowing just what these were; so I asked the druggist. He showed me the United States Dispensatory. Some of the names in his window are local and folk names for plants growing in various parts of this country and elsewhere, and these plants are mentioned in the Dispensatory as being credited with cathartic, diaphoretic and other medicinal qualities. That is all very well; it does not mean that taking these roots and leaves home and boiling them and then drinking the water enables you to obtain the benefit of those qualities. The plants have other qualities which come out in the water as well as those you want, and you get the essence of the whole, which may have quite other effects than those you anticipate. Again, no one can tell whether these plants are really what they are represented to be or not. Their sale is under no supervision; they may be roots of saplings dug in the Bronx, or bark from cherry trees disguised.

In these matters the Negro is, in large measure, his own enemy. He is bringing his own simplicity to the help of those who would take advantage of him. No good can come from blinking the fact that the Negro is, by and large, the great exploitable race of the Western world. Many Negroes find it so easy to expect something wonderful to happen; eager for pleasure, they are sanguinely expectant that it awaits them around every corner. They have the child's love of phantasy, too; they would escape from the harsh realities of a world in which they are not treated very well.

In addition to all this, many of the uneducated majority have a deeply imbedded trust in the white man—a holdover from slavery. This lies at the root of much exploitation. The Negro comes to our Northern cities, and we think that he is ready to cope with the complexity of St. Louis, Chicago and New York City. He is not. To transplant him from Georgia to Lenox Avenue is not to change him on the train; often he is still the simple and innocent child of his Southern life.

I am not blithely cataloging the Negro here as the possessor of a "child-mind." That is the pet formula of pseudo-scientific race detractors. The Negro has sufficiently proved—and this number of Survey Graphic is only further proof—that, given opportunities, he can rise to any heights. The simplicity, innocence and child-like qualities of some Negroes are due in large part to lack of education and to the lack of certain kinds of experiences. They have not been invited to play an aggressive role, or even to create beautiful things. They have been kept under the thumb of the whites. Their innocence is the sort that you will find among rural whites and "green" foreign immigrants; it is "peasant-mindedness" in part.

Neither the facts, nor the explanations of the facts, however, justify members of his own race, or whites, in taking advantage of the simplicity that lies around them.

THERE are ways in which the Negro is more deliberately exploited in Harlem than in other Northern cities. He is subject to being fleeced in rent. This is not a rhetorical flourish. It is cold fact. I am not here referring merely to high rents, to "what the traffic will bear." I am referring to extortion.

The Negro is gouged. Because he is a Negro, because he can be taken advantage of, because his racial position makes it possible to gouge him, he is gouged.

Hear John R. Davies, judge in the Municipal Court in Harlem, who sees colored tenants pass in streams before him, seeking relief: "It is common for colored tenants in Harlem to pay twice as much as white tenants for the same apartments."

Hear Lillian Grant, acting chairman of the Mayor's Committee on Rent Profiteering, also white, who looks at the whole city and sees Harlem in the perspective of comparison: "Negroes pay exorbitant rents. Their situation is terrible."

Let us come to particulars. Sophie Ellerbee is a colored tenant worth knowing. She came into court the other day and told the judge that the white family preceding her in the apartment into which she had just moved had paid $50 a month; the corporation owning it was asking her to pay $75 now. This increase she thought excessive. Her attorney requested that the owner be brought into court and required to divulge its income, expenses and investment (as it could be compelled to do under the law), and thus to show whether the rent was justified. The jury awarded Mrs. Ellerbee a $20 reduction from the sum asked. When the verdict was announced, the attorney for the owner, who was a colored lawyer, moved to have it set aside.

"This rent is justified," he said. "The colored district is crowded. These Negroes cannot go anywhere else. If they attempt to move into houses formerly occupied by whites, they should pay what the landlords ask. It is the law of supply and demand."

The judge, Jacob Panken, flamed at him. Judge Panken had seen many colored tenants come into court with tales similar to that of Mrs. Ellerbee, and he said:

"I agree that the verdict should be set aside, but for the purpose of securing Mrs. Ellerbee a still greater reduction in rent. Your own client has admitted that it is making $10,000 a year on a $30,000 investment. That is excessive. This rent is too large. And you, as a colored attorney, ought to be ashamed of yourself. You as a lawyer are helping colored and white landlords to prey on your own."

As the attorney left the court, embarrassed, cries of "Shame!" came to him from the Negro spectators in the room.

Other colored tenants were in court the same day. Through the services of a white lawyer twenty-one of these secured reductions varying from $10 to $23 below the rents asked. "It is pretty good evidence that the landlord knows he is charging excessive rents if he accepts a reduction voluntarily, without going to trial," said the attorney. The calendar of the Municipal Court in Harlem is crowded with the cases of colored tenants seeking relief. The white lawyer who acts as attorney for the West Harlem Tenants' League, an organization befriending tenants in that neighborhood, had 15 cases set down for trial on one day, 41 on another, 37 on another and 32 on another.

The National Urban League is an organization of white and colored social workers and others. It is interested in the welfare of city Negroes. The New York branch of the league studied rents paid by both white and colored people in blocks accomodating both in the spring of 1924. "We found that Negroes paid from 40 to 60 per cent higher rents than white people did for the same class of apartments," said Mr. Hubert, secretary of the Harlem office.

Through the courts, under the emergency New York state rent laws, relief can be secured. It is the families that do not go to court that continue to pay the unduly high rents. Unfortunately these are the vast majority. For every Mrs. Ellerbee there are many other colored tenants who, through ignorance, inertia or the congestion of the court calendar, do not get relief. Obviously individual trials cannot be given every tenant who is charged too high rent in Harlem; the court of justice is not the remedy for an extensive economic practice.

Let us look for a moment at the growth of this situation. Fifteen years ago Harlem as it is today did not exist; the colored population then was much smaller than it is now. It has grown continuously, swollen by additions from without. As the colored area grew, it has pressed against contiguous white territories. Block after block gave way. Stubbornly each block yielded. White people did not want to see their neighborhoods turn black. First one street was set as the "dead line" (in the white parlance) of the Negro advance, and then another. Always there were outposts, colored families breaking over the bounds and invading territory hitherto exclusively white.

This situation is the paradise of the ruthless landlord, or rent charger. If you own an apartment house in Harlem, if you do not live in it, and if you want the largest profits you can get, you will open it to those tenants who will pay you most. These are the tenants who are most in need of it. The whites do not have to have it. They can go elsewhere— to other parts of the city, to the suburbs, or they can just keep ahead of the Negro invasion and move a few blocks away. The Negro cannot; he will not be given an apartment elsewhere, he cannot be easily accomodated. He can live only in a limited area, and that area grows only bit by bit. So he will pay what you ask—or, rather, he will agree to pay what you ask and then he will pay it if he can.

The profiteering is not all done by white landlords. There are men of both races who have a reputation for fairness. There are colored operators who have performed a public service to their race in addressing themselves to the extreme problem of shelter, but there are colored owners of houses who charge just as high rents as do white owners. Investigation shows that taking advantage of the colored people, or making money out of them, is not a white monopoly.

How, it will be asked, do Negroes find money to pay these rents? By strategy, and taking their own part. They do it by going without other things. They cut down on fun,

food and clothing, and stretch what money they have to cover the rent. But they have other tricks. One is the "rent party." This is a popular form of diversion in Harlem. It goes by the name of the "social parlor." A person invites friends in for the evening, to dance and have a good time, and charges them twenty-five cents a couple; that is one way of getting help to meet the monthly rent bill. Another is to take in lodgers. Lodgers are legion in Harlem. The State Housing Commission told of one apartment properly accomodating about ten persons that was occupied by forty-four. Harlem has gone to the extreme of the double shift. One room is not infrequently let out to two people, one of whom occupies it at night and the other during the day.

THE moment one begins to inquire about exploitation in Harlem, he hears about cabarets. In Harlem there are cabarets to which both white and colored people are admitted. There are cabarets where white and colored sit at the same table, dance together, talk together, drink together, leave together. Many flashy young people of both colors come to these and get riotously or near riotously merry; some less flashy people come; and some sober and sedate folk sit at the tables. All told there are about fifteen cabarets in Harlem. A few cater only to the well-behaved, others to the less well-behaved, and some to roughnecks. Two or three of the better places are now the resorts of downtown specialists in the latest places of interest.

No doubt people are fleeced a bit in paying for their entertainment, no doubt some people are swept along pretty rapidly on a current of erotic pleasure, a current of uncertain direction and ambiguous goal. But they come there of their own accord; they seek the cabaret. As an instrument of exploitation the cabaret does not touch many people. Its scope is the scope of a retreat for devotees.

Another subject often mentioned in connection with exploitation is prostitution. I am aware of no way of proving that the Negro is sexually more or less moral than other people. If there is any exceptional organized assault upon the continence of Negro women, I do not know of it.

LET us turn now to the gentle subject of hooch. Harlem is hooch-ridden. He is a bold man who will undertake to say what part of a city like New York, with its many congested foreign and native quarters, is the wettest. The wash of the booze sea has not left Harlem out; that district may well claim a deeper inundation than any other.

Those syndicates, or firms, or companies, or combinations, that set you up in business as a druggist, equipping you with the white jars and other colorful stock of a druggist's shelves, in order that behind your counters you may run a hooch dispensary, have lined Lenox and Seventh Avenues with such fake establishments. These sell rivers of bad booze to the colored residents of Harlem. There are excellent drug stores in Harlem, but these are drug stores only in name. They have small stocks and cannot fill prescriptions adequately. They specialize in synthetic gin and bad whiskey. Practically all of these places are owned by white people.

There are syndicates also that fit you out with the window displays and front rooms of delicatessen stores.

"A Negro clerk who works in a drug store on Lenox Avenue came running in to me the other day," a competent colored pharmacist in Harlem said (*Continued on page* 713)

The Church and the Negro Spirit

By GEORGE E. HAYNES

THE last Sunday of September, 1924, was a dramatic day in Harlem. The Salem Methodist Episcopal Church, a congregation of Negroes, took possession of the church building, parish house and parsonage of the Metropolitan Methodist Episcopal Church, a body of white communicants. The white congregation had assembled in large numbers for the last service they were to hold in their accustomed place of worship. Just a few blocks away there was an unusual attendance of the Negro congregation at the building—two converted apartment houses with the partition walls removed—they had used for fourteen years, beginning with the days when the church was a mission. At a designated hour, the Negro congregation marched quietly and in an orderly manner out of their old structure and up Seventh Avenue toward the Metropolitan Methodist Episcopal church house. The doors of the Metropolitan Church opened wide; the white pastor and his people arose to receive the Negro pastor and his people. There were Negro and white visitors from their common denomination to witness and participate in this historic event. The Negro pastor and the president of his board of trustees were welcomed to the pulpit by the white pastor and the president of his board. After appropriate songs and addresses, the keys of the church property were presented by the white trustees of the outgoing congregation to the Negro trustees of the incoming congregation. The benediction was pronounced amid expressions of joy and fellowship not unmixed with tears.

The taking over of church property by Negroes is a frequent occurrence in Harlem, as it is in the other rapidly growing Negro centers in the cities of the North. About eight years ago the Metropolitan Baptist Church bought from a white congregation an imposing stone building at Seventh Avenue and 128th Street and moved into it. Three years ago the Williams Institutional Church of the Colored Methodist Episcopal denomination purchased an excellent plant—once a flourishing Jewish synagogue—in 130th Street.

Such a transfer of white church property not infrequently accompanies a shifting of population. Within the past three years the Negro population of Harlem has pushed forward as the white population has moved westward across Eighth Avenue to St. Nicholas Park and up beyond 145th Street almost to the boundary of the Polo Grounds, and south of 125th Street, between Eighth and Lenox Avenues. During that time the fine building of a Swedish congregation west of Eighth Avenue has been taken over by a body of Negro Congregationalists, the Grace Congregational Church of Harlem. The imposing structure of a Lutheran Church at Edgecombe Avenue and 140th Street has been bought and occupied by the Calvary Independent Methodist Church. According to a recent announcement, the Mt. Olivet Baptist Church, one of the oldest and largest Negro congregations in the city, after worshipping for many years in a church house in 53rd Street, has purchased for $450,000 the beautiful Adventist Temple, built of white Indiana limestone, at 120th Street.

Quite as interesting as these acquisitions of existing edifices has been the success of Negro congregations in erecting new church structures in the face of the high cost of land and building construction in Manhattan. About fifteen years ago St. Philip's Protestant Episcopal Church sold its property in the Pennsylvania Station zone for a large sum and used a part of the proceeds to erect, under the supervision of a Negro architect, an attractive and very serviceable brick church building and parish house on lots extending from 133rd to 134th Streets. The Abyssinian Baptist Church sold its property in 40th Street and built, on 138th Street, a church building and community house at a cost of about $325,000. In plan and program, like many of the churches named here it is a thing of beauty and an instrument of service. "Mother Zion" Church, of the African Methodist Episcopal Zion connection, found about twenty years ago that its constituency was becoming too far removed from its location in Bleecker Street. A fine structure therefore was erected in 86th Street where its leaders thought a Negro neighborhood would develop, but the subway opened up and carried Negroes farther north. About twelve years ago "Mother Zion" moved again and erected a building in 136th Street. To accommodate its growing institutional activities a new addition to the structure is now completed on a plot which runs through to 137th Street. In a triangle near 138th Street, St. Mark's Methodist Episcopal Church, now in the mid-town district, is erecting an institutional structure to cost a half million dollars.

In the purchase of buildings from white congregations and in the erection of new structures, the development in Negro church equipment in New York is typical of what has happened on smaller scale in such cities as Baltimore, Chicago, Cleveland, Saint Louis. Also in a few smaller cities churches have made commendable efforts to meet the growing demands of these people. In Saint Louis during the observance of Race Relations Sunday this winter

St. Philip's P. E. Church

695

delegations from white congregations that had sold their structures to Negro congregations returned for services on that day to their former churches to worship with the present occupants. St. John's Congregational Church in Springfield, Mass., Bethel African Methodist Episcopal Church of Chicago, the Sharp Street Methodist Church of Baltimore, Olivet Baptist Church in Chicago, "the largest Protestant church in the world," with nearly 11,000 members, and the Second Baptist Church of Detroit are outstanding examples of a broad and vigorous institutional service.

THE Negro church is at once the most resourceful and the most characteristic organized force in the life of the Negroes of the Northern cities as it was in the Southern communities from which they come. Some of its main problems may be summarized in a four-fold statement:

1. To provide adequate buildings and other physical equipment for attracting and serving the rapidly increasing populations.
2. To give fellowship to newcomers who have been connected with the church of the same faith and order in their former homes.
3. To have adequate personnel and organization for rendering social service in the housing, health, recreational and other needs of a large proportion of the masses in the community.
4. To meet with understanding and wisdom the increasing throng of intelligent people, who know little of serfdom, and who feel the urge of their vigorous years in the turmoil of the city.

We have spoken of typical solutions of the first of these; let us now consider the others.

So recently have men of all races come to dwell in cities that their churches often have the organization and equipment typical of the small town and rural district. This is especially the case with the Negro church because only in the past sixty years have its constituents been moving with the population stream from the rural districts to urban centers. Only within the last twenty years have the numbers assumed large proportions in most of the communities that have grown up around the industrial plants of the Northern cities. As Negroes moved North they have

brought their church with them. Individuals and groups, mainly of Baptists and Methodists, have transferred their relationships from the little churches of their Southern communities to the "watch-care" or to full membership of churches of the "same faith and order" in Northern communities. In a few cases whole congregations from Southern communities have moved North together and brought their pastors with them. In other cases Negro churches in Northern cities, which before the heavy migration of the last ten years had small struggling congregations, have increased their membership to large numbers and have become powerful in resources. Many of them have able ministers who, like the physicians, lawyers, editors, and business men who followed in the wake of the wage-earners, have come from the South to answer the Northern call.

Back in the Southern communities the little rural church, conspicuous for its bell tower, rests among the trees beside the road. It is the natural meeting place of the people once or twice a month when the non-resident minister comes to preach, and when the weather does not make the roads unfit for travel. Often the people come as far as ten or fifteen miles. Frequently they bring baskets of food and remain all day. Between the enthusiastic and extended services and amid the social amenities of meal time, they exchange the gossip of the countryside, the wisdom and experience of the cropping season, and the prospects, hopes and fears of the future.

In the typical Southern town or small city one or two churches of each of the more popular denominations, particularly of Baptists and the four principal Methodist denominations, have a resident minister. The church building is better built than those of the churches in the open country and the services are held usually every Sunday with Sunday School for the children. The church enters considerably, too, into the leisure time and recreational life of the people by an occasional sociable or picnic, stereopticon exhibition, and, on rare occasions, a traveling moving picture show. Around the church revolve the interests of family life. The churches in the larger cities such as Atlanta, Memphis, Louisville or Richmond, in architectural design, physical facilities, and personnel compare reasonably with other favorable phases of Negro life. In Norfolk one of the lead-

"Mother Zion", A. M. E. Zion Church   Mt. Olivet Baptist Church   Abyssinian Baptist Church

ing Baptist churches, under the guidance of a young college-trained man, has a community program including extension classes for boys and girls, day nursery, playground and other social features.

From these communities of the South—rural districts, towns and cities—thousands of Negroes have moved to Northern cities. With the rapid increase of colored populations in the Northern cities, church facilities have not been adequate either in seating space for the assembly of worshippers, in arrangements for religious education, still in its infancy among white groups, or in sufficient personnel to give the service of social ministry to the thousands that come. For example, in 1920 the estimated seating capacity of Negro churches in Greater New York was about 24,000. In 1924 with the increase that has been made by taking over additional churches from white congregations and the erection of commodious buildings, the estimated seating capacity of twenty-seven Negro churches and sixteen missions. in Harlem alone is about 21,000. There are thirteen churches with estimated seating capacity from 500 to 2,500 each; the others range from 200 to 400.

The thirst of the people for the cooling water brooks of religion is shown in the way they crowd the buildings that are available. Examples are many. The seats of the large auditorium of the Abyssinian Baptist Church are filled when the hour of service arrives and often standing room is at a premium. St. Philip's Protestant Episcopal Church, with a service of high church type, is often crowded to the doors on Sunday morning. Mother Zion African Methodist Episcopal Church and Metropolitan Baptist Church often have larger numbers than they can comfortably seat. Frequently some of these churches have overflow services.

Besides the large self-supporting congregations with well-appointed buildings, there are nearly a score of "house-front" and "mission" churches. The "mission" churches are those that receive a part of their support from denominational missionary or extension societies which are stirred to action by the teeming unchurched masses of the district. These societies subsidize salaries of ministers, assist in the purchase of buildings or in other ways help to extend their denominational effort to evangelize and serve the people of this region. The "house-front" churches are started usually when some individual who has felt the call to the ministry has gathered about himself a little flock, or when several persons join together and ask a minister to lead them. The purchase of an equity in a private house is usually made. The double parlors on the first floor are used for church purposes while the upper floors serve as a residence for the minister or for other tenants.

THE organization, support and operation of Negro churches have become increasingly independent of white people. Negroes have thus had valuable experience and group training in standing upon their own legs and in going forward to achieve ends mapped out by themselves. The Negro churches are almost exclusively racial both in their membership and in their administration. Even congregations that belong to denominations made up of a majority of white communicants, such as the Protestant Episcopal, Methodist Episcopal and the Congregational Churches, are for all practical purposes autonomous, exercising great independence in government and being controlled only to a nominal extent by the general organization.

In no place, perhaps, is the independent, voluntary character of the Negro church better illustrated than in Harlem. One of the strongest Baptist churches in this area has been developed during the past fifteen years under the guidance of a minister of striking power, who once remarked that "a leader is a fellow who has some followers." In about ten years his preaching and work have enlarged a handful of members into a host. With money largely raised by themselves, they moved from a dingy brick basement to one of Harlem's best stone church edifices. St. Philip's Protestant Episcopal Church is widely known for its financial resources; it purchased, more than ten years ago, a number of apartment houses in 135th Street. Three of these churches have parish houses, three others have institutional equipment, and two others that are soon to come into the district have announced their plans for developing work along these lines.

With the growth of numbers there has been concentration of Negro communicants in distinctly Negro congregations, and the denominations made up altogether of members of the race have shown especially (Continued on page 708)

Metropolitan Baptist Church   *Williams Institutional C. M. E. Church*   *St. Philip's P. E. Church*

EDITORIALS

HARLEM is a new community. Its social work structure, slight as it is, is probably more effective for that reason; it has been built flexibly and not around a set of fixed ideas.

New as it is, however, Harlem inherited its physical framework. One of its best informed leaders remarks that the Negro in Harlem is like the poor relation who inherits a limousine: he can ill afford to keep it going. Harlem was built for families with incomes well above the average. The Negroes who find themselves masters of it have not, in the mass, attained to that standard. So the mere pressure to win and hold shelter imposes a tax on the wage-earner that leaves little margin for self-improvement, and less for cooperative social activity. Out of Harlem's pinched resources, again, have come surprising sums for church buying and building, as Mr. Haynes testifies. While several of these churches have distinguished themselves by providing institutional facilities and using them for needed social service, most of them have not, so that the wave of church-building has meant that the lion's share of the money Harlem has had to give away has gone into brick and stone.

Harlem's newness affects also the personal resources on which social work must draw. There is a leisure class in Harlem, but it is not a large one, and it is not yet widely diversified. Its money is new money, and much of it has been made, not in the ordinary turnover of varied trades and industries, but in the more picturesque enterprises—cabarets, the stage, sports, sumptuary establishments. Rich as Harlem is in personal good-will and neighborly helpfulness, it is not such money as this that makes good "prospects" for social work financing.

Nor is the community as a whole, in spite of its apparent cohesiveness, knit closely together. It has been recruited too quickly from elements too diverse. It has been hammered together by segregation, to be sure, but the unity that results is different in kind from that which grows slowly among people who live together and in a particular place by their own full choice. Harlem is probably no more factional or parochial than the typical American city of 150,000 or 200,000 souls, but it is not safe to argue from the accident of color that it is less so.

The leaders in Harlem social work are sensitive to these facts. They recognize the comparative inexperience of the Negro in organized social effort, and welcome the technical aid and advice of the maturer organizations of New York. Whether those organizations have been fully aware of their responsibility to the rapidly growing Negro community is a fair question. A recent conference on delinquency, for instance, revealed an almost total lack of attention to the underprivileged Negro boy. A thorough-going social survey of Harlem—had New York any cooperative body capable of making one—would no doubt uncover so many unmet and ill-met needs that the "downtown" agencies would be spurred to more adequate and more imaginative cooperation with those groups among the Negroes which are already struggling with their own difficult problems with growing initiative and self reliance.

Granting the handicaps to community organization, it is true that Harlem has exceptional resources in the service of professional volunteers—notably such physicians as those who compose the North Harlem Medical Association. Henry Street nurses testify to the unusually cordial cooperation of local doctors with their work; the eagerness with which the services of the New York Tuberculosis Committee were received and used, and the long association of Negro physicians with the local work of the Charity Organization Society, are cases in point. Negro dentists not only give their time for clinical service but have clubbed together to buy equipment for their clinic.

WHAT agencies has Harlem for social work? The list is a long one, and to answer the question fully here is clearly impossible. Only a handful can be mentioned. The work of the churches, for example, is presented elsewhere in this issue: here it may be said in passing that they are doing yeoman service in meeting one of Harlem's most pressing needs—that for day nursery care for the children of thousands of employed women, many of whom work the long hours of the domestic servant.

Harlem is fortunate above other communities of its size in having one generalized community agency. While the New York Urban League has a specific program of its own, its significance is that it links up the social and civic work to be done with the potential workers in the community. It pioneers in its own right, and it organizes lines of communication after it has shown the way. It has had a hand in the beginning of a number of enterprises which, once begun, it has left free to develop. It has recently formed a continuing committee of one hundred women representing the whole community. Subcommittees deal with special phases of the Urban League program, but the group as whole is in readiness for any call and limits itself by no fixed objectives. The staff of the League, which of course is Negro, has called together a luncheon conference of fourteen local executives from social, health and educational agencies who meet periodically for common counsel. It serves as a clearing-house for newcomers in New York, and for specialized workers. It functions, in other words, a little like a nascent community council.

The range of its own activities may be imagined from the article on another page by Mr. Johnson of the National Urban League. Like the national body, it is controlled by a board of white and Negro directors, with the Quaker tradition strong among them; like the national body, it devotes much attention to the special problems of the Negro in industry. It studies and promotes vocational opportunities; it seeks to adjust the Negro in industry to his employer and the unions; in some fields it does individual placement work. In housing it acts as a medium between tenants and owners; in recreation it has labored with but a remote hope of success—for public outdoor playgrounds, of which there is but one, and that on the western fringe, in all Harlem. In health it is centering its efforts now on the problem of convalescense, and on the annual health week. Some indication of its standing in Harlem may be seen in the fact that its income from local membership has increased more than sixfold in five years.

It is the Urban League, too, which has provided the nucleus for a central social service building. It shares the dwelling-house which it now owns (and which is soon to be enlarged) with the Henry Street Visiting Nurse service and with the Harlem Tuberculosis Committee of the New York Tuberculosis Association.

The Henry Street Nurses do their customary work, and place special emphasis on a prenatal clinic. The Tuberculosis Committee comes near to being a general public health agency. Its chairman, a Negro physician, is a member of the board of directors of the New York Tuberculosis Association. Its program, shaped by a group made up about equally of Negro physicians and laymen and white social workers, and in the hands of a Negro staff, is a broad and flexible interpretation of the anti-tuberculosis campaign. Beginning with health talks in the churches and schools, it has come to include school nutrition classes; summer institutes at which local physicians have an opportunity to study the best technique in the handling of tuberculosis—an opportunity which is the more valuable because even in New York the limitations on hospital experience hinder the training of Negroes in medicine; medical examinations; a health club for mothers; and a free dental clinic organized at the behest of local dentists, with a volunteer staff of thirteen. It served as the gathering point for the Harlem Health Conference and each year gives the executive service necessary for carrying on Health Week in behalf of this conference.

Other agencies too are building up their community contacts. For example, during the past year the district secretary of the Charity Organization Society has been released from casework in order to develop community-wide relationships. A special committee on Negro problems, organized some years ago on the initiative of Negroes, has by a gradual and natural process been merged with the district committee, which thus becomes interracial, and there has been growing local support for the Negro case-worker on the district staff. The A. I. C. P., and other city-wide organizations, render their usual services in Harlem under central office direction.

THE Young Men's and Young Women's Christian Associations, both directed and officered entirely by Negroes, both housed in handsome new buildings in central locations, provide two much-used social centers for Harlem. The Y. M. C. A. serves about a thousand members with a dormitory, games, religious, athletic and social group activities, an employment office, a swimming pool and gymnasium, and, this year for the first time, with a summer camp. Thanks to a productive plant it is very nearly self-supporting. By way of community service, it keeps a well-informed secretary on duty all night to direct and help newcomers in New York (sent often by the Negro red-caps at the stations); maintains a rooming-house directory; opens its pool one morning a week through the summer to all boys of the neighborhood; and was the first association in the city to institute "splash week," during which every boy in the local schools— white or black—who does not know how to swim is given free instruction.

The Young Women's Christian Association, with a nominal fee, has two thousand members. For the time being it is without dormitory facilities, but it too maintains an all-night service and refers girls and women to suitable rooms, not to mention more difficult social adjustments, and its cafeteria is much used by both men and women. Emphasis is placed on a wide range of trade training courses. The index of the educational department's booklet is intriguing: Bible, Bookkeeping, Business English, Charm School, Children's Sewing, Citizenship, Crochet Beading, Dennison Craft, Dressmaking and Designing, English, Eyebrow-Eyelash Culture, Facial Massage, Filing. . . . A valued community service is given by the association merely by opening its meeting-rooms to various outside groups—groups which have made themselves so much at home that they often schedule their meetings without consulting their host! And no one can doubt that the agreeably-furnished lobby where girls and their friends of both sexes are welcome adds greatly to the amenities of huddled Harlem.

THE branch of the New York Public Library which stands on the main cross thoroughfare of Harlem, 135th Street, seeks to be what the Carnegie Corporation would call an intelligence center. Its staff includes both white and Negro librarians. It has held exhibitions of Negro art and readings of Negro literature. On March 1 it will open a loan exhibition of the original portraits and drawings by Winold Reiss which are reproduced in this number, together with a number of others made at the same time, some of which will appear in future issues of The Survey.

The library is now beginning to build up a special students' collection of Negro literature. Although there is rich and varied material by and about Negroes, it is so widely scattered in homes, in bookshops, in great reference libraries where it is a small part of the whole, and in private collections that it is comparatively unknown to most white people and to a large proportion of Negroes themselves. The library will set apart a special floor where such a collection may be easily available, with a competent colored librarian in charge, and has already formed a permanent organization of men and women to lend it support and to preserve and stabilize its policies. Much of the material sought for this collection consists of rare, out-of-print or costly books. It is hoped that many such now lost to the public in garrets or secondhand shops will find their way to a collection so well-founded and so safeguarded for public use. Much material usually regarded as ephemeral will be considered an essential part:

photographs, broadsides, prints, newspaper articles, autographed letters, and the like. Survey readers who can help in gathering such material are invited to do so and should communicate with Ernestine Rose, branch librarian, 103 West 135th Street, New York.

THE Canadian Industrial Disputes Investigation Act was on January 20 declared *ultra vires,* or as we should say, unconstitutional, by the Lords of the Judicial Committee of the Privy Council. The purpose of the act was to enable the Dominion Government to appoint anywhere in Canada a board of conciliation and investigation to which the dispute between an employer and his employes might be referred. Among other things it made it unlawful for an employer to lock-out or for a workman to strike, on account of the dispute, prior to or during the reference, and imposed an obligation on employes and employers to give thirty day's notice of any intended change affecting wages and hours.

The powers of the Dominion Government, conferred upon it by the Imperial Parliament, are defined in the British North America Act. Under a section of this act, the Dominion Parliament has a general power to make laws for Canada as a whole; but these laws are not to relate to classes of subjects assigned to the provinces, unless their enactment falls under heads specifically enumerated in the act. Exceptions to this rule might arise in case of war and of emergencies affecting the entire dominion such as the outbreak and spread of epidemic disease. The Supreme Court of Ontario had upheld the Disputes Act on the ground that a strike might conceivably spread from province to province and so create a menace to the dominion as a whole. It rested its argument largely upon an earlier decision of the Judicial Committee of the Privy Council that it was within the competence of the Dominion Parliament to establish a uniform system for prohibiting the liquor traffic throughout Canada excepting under restrictive conditions. The Judicial Committee finds that this decision is not applicable to the case of the Industrial Disputes Act, on the ground that· at the period of the passing of the Canada Temperance Act an emergency affecting Canada as a whole must be assumed to have existed, whereas neither in 1907 when the Disputes Act was passed nor since that time has a strike or lockout constituted such an emergency.

The final court of appeal in the British Empire therefore finds that in passing the Industrial Disputes Investigation Act, the Dominion Parliament exceeded its powers and after eighteen years of the law's operation declares it invalid.

IN a report which celebrated its semi-centennial, the Board of Health of Michigan tells of the remote days of the seventies and eighties when people had hardly heard of germs. One visitor, gazing through a microscope, asked how long those germs were, and learned with visible relief that 20,000 of them, laid in a row, would measure approximately one inch. "Oh," she said, "I'm not afraid of them little fellers." Within the past three months, however, some of them little fellers, and the belief of the public in their unseen powers, has laid low an industry which involves millions of dollars annually. As some hundreds of cases of typhoid fever, with scores of deaths, have been numbered in New York, Chicago and other cities which draw their supplies of oysters from the Atlantic beds, such a state of public panic has been created that oystermen from the Chesapeake northward are out of work; their season is almost over and their oysters have had no sale. Though some branches of the oyster industry have persisted in an unfortunate policy of shilly-shally, pointing accusing fingers at lettuce or celery as the source of the epidemic, the bulk of the group of producers have accepted sensibly the inescapable inference that there has been some pollution of oysters somewhere. They are ready to do almost anything to restore public confidence, but what? A Vigilance Committee of the producers centering in New York pledge their word of honor that only oysters of the most impeccable quality are admitted to the New York markets; other groups are crying for government investigation and certification. The Secretary of Commerce has asked Congress to appropriate $25,000 for a survey into the oyster industry to remove conditions which might cause typhoid or other disease, to be administered in all probability by the United States Public Health Service, which conducted a series of similar studies before the war. Whether the oyster industry succeeds in cleaning its own house, or we shall be obliged to bring in the government broom, it, and any other industry which observe its pitiful and generally undeserved plight, have had an impressive lesson in the sensitiveness of the popular mind to the germ theory, in the economies of prevention over cure and in the fact that an industry, like a chain, is judged by its weakest link.

THE dismissal of the notorious suit to test the constitutionality of California's minimum wage law (see The Survey, Feb. 15, 1925) leaves the question of the constitutionality of the law, so far as the California state courts are concerned, where it was before.

In Wisconsin Federal Judge Claude Z. Luse has made permanent the preliminary injunction restraining the Industrial Commission from enforcing the provisions of the minimum wage law relative to adult women workers in the plant of the Folding Furniture Works. In his ruling Judge Luse stated that "this case involves no attack upon that part of the minimum wage law which applies to the wages of minors. This court is bound to apply the principle of the Adkins case to the one at bar, and it is therefore held that the Wisconsin Act, so far as it affects the plaintiff in employing adult women is invalid."

In view of the fact that the members of the Industrial Welfare Commission of California, as defendants in the suit against the state minimum wage law, while accepting the decision of the United States Supreme Court in the Adkins case, leaned heavily upon the contention that that decision did not properly apply in the differing environment and circumstances surrounding the state's minimum wage laws, this ruling of Judge Luse in the Folding Furniture case gives occasion for serious apprehension. Doubt with respect to the future status of minimum wage legislation is increased by the similar action of the Supreme Court of Porto Rico. Because of the decision of the United States Supreme Court that the minimum wage law of the District of Columbia was not a health measure and was unconstitutional, the Supreme Court of Porto Rico has reversed its earlier favorable decision and has declared the Minimum Wage Act of 1919 unconstitutional.

WHEN the American delegation entered gallantly into the opium affray at Geneva it had three main propositions: to "pull up the poppy," that is, to limit the production of raw opium; to abolish the smoking of opium in the East through a ten years' period of progressive restriction; and to establish a Central Board of Control to list and check the amount of opium needed in each country for manufacture for home use or export, and control shipments from one country to another. The poppy is not to be pulled up, at least for the present; the abolition of opium smoking is shoved off almost indefinitely; but the Central Board of Control has been salvaged out of the confusion of crossed interests, and apparently the United States and Germany are to be asked to appoint representatives to sit with the Council of the League in the election of its members.

The first opium conference, which was convened last November, met to consider the question of opium smoking in the East. The tangible result of that conference is the convention abolishing the "farm system," with an attached protocol. This convention removes opium from the field of private sale and profit, and makes its distribution a government monopoly—an essential stage in the process of government regulation. The protocol, embodying a British suggestion, would limit smoking opium through a period of fifteen years, to start *after* an impartial commission has decided that the time is ripe for it—that is, in effect, when smuggling has been stopped, when China has established internal control which will afford some check on the appalling recrudescence of opium growing in her provinces, and when the force of public opinion in the other eastern states will permit more drastic regulation than their representatives now declare possible. The policy of registering and rationing opium addicts was affirmed as a declaration of principle. In the meantime all the states are to use all possible means to check the practice. This is a disappointing application of the principle in Article 6 of the Opium Convention that "The Contracting Powers shall take measures for the gradual and effective suppression of the manufacture of, internal trade in, and use of, prepared opium."

The second conference, of powers which produce opium and other products from which narcotic drugs are manufactured, has set up the Central Board of Control practically according to the American plan. This board is to consist of eight persons, not government employes, chosen to inspire general confidence by reason of their technical competence, impartiality and disinterestedness. It will receive estimates from the various governments stating in advance their probable requirements of opium for medical and scientific uses. Every three months it will receive and publish estimates of the current imports and exports of opium. The discrepancy between the amount necessary for medicinal purposes and the amount actually imported in each instance

will give a continuous indication of the quantities diverted to illegitimate uses. If an undue amount is shipped to any one point, the board can call the attention of the nations to the phenomenon, and request that shipments be suspended pending investigation. It has no administrative power except publicity. What the effect—or whether there will be an effect—of this new machinery can be determined only by actual trial of it. It certainly will show where the raw opium is going, and how much of the manufactured product is accounted for in legitimate export or home use; moreover it offers the inspiring precedent of an international body met to consider the world's supply and distribution of one raw material on the basis of national needs. Supported by vigorous public opinion that principle might go far.

ASIDE from their administrative achievements, the two conferences have accomplished a piece of public education of enormous magnitude, though many of their revelations have been negative. They have shown the tremendous complexities which beset the carrying out of any straightforward policy in the control of the world's supply of opium. Before that can be assured, China must put down her civil wars; Persia and Turkey, which produce opium for export, say that they must have loans and other help to enable them to change the custom of centuries and adapt other crops to the regions where opium now is grown; Jugo-Slavia must provide for her opium farmers; India, which alone eats opium, must discontinue the practice by domestic legislation, or yield the principle, hitherto guarded jealously, that her habits are subject to international agreement; the colonies of the western powers in the Orient must find a substitute for the opium revenue and some method other than the keeping of opium dens, to attract Chinese coolie labor; and a network of smuggling, spread over the East, the Philippines, linked even to the Occident, must be broken. Ideally the logical method to cut under all these difficulties would have been to stop excess cultivation of the poppy, and nip opium in the bud. Since the largest producer, China, has apparently no power to enforce such policy on her subjects, and the other countries have at present no intention or desire to do so (if the ability) the actual achievement of the conferences—the Central Board— must be accepted as important in its potentialities, and as a present tool for focussing and bringing into action that part of the world's public opinion which believes that opium must and shall go.

JUST a year afer The Survey's Giant Power number went to press, its forecasts of the social consequences reasonably to be anticipated from the rapid extension of large scale electrical development are sustained and reenforced by the scholarly and illuminating report of Pennsylvania's Giant Power Survey Board. The authenticity of The Survey's forecasts was largely due to the generous cooperation of Morris Llewellyn Cooke, director of the work of the Board whose findings and recommendations

Governor Pinchot laid before Pennsylvania's General Assembly on February 17.

On the basis of intensive research carried on under his direction during the past pear by an expert corps of engineers and economists, Mr. Cooke reaffirms our conclusion that electrical development, and especially the art of transmitting current in large volume over great distances practically without loss, has brought us to the threshold of momentous changes in our industrial, home and farm management, and transportation technique which will vitally affect conditions of life in both urban and rural areas. These changes are already in process on a gigantic scale. It is only a matter of months before electric generating and distributing companies will be interconnected from Chicago to the Gulf, from the Atlantic Coast to the Great Plains, from the state of Washington to and across the Mexican border. The quantity of electric energy now used for heat, light and power is such that in view of the present trend toward tying together the generating, transmitting and distribution systems, unprecedented economies are within reach. "This," says Mr. Cooke, "makes possible not only a widespread distribution but a revolutionary increase in the use of electricity in factory and in home, on the farm and in transportation."

These social advantages will not accrue to the great masses of our people unless they bring to bear upon the electrical industry the control of an enlightened public opinion. "No one," says Governor Pinchot in his message of transmittal, "who studies the electrical developments already achieved and those planned for the immediate future can doubt that a unified electrical monopoly extending into every part of this nation is inevitable in the very near future." It is impossible, he affirms, to imagine the force and intimacy with which such a monopoly will touch and affect, for good or evil, the life of every cititzen. "The time is fully in sight when every household operation from heating and cooking to sweeping and sewing will be performed by the aid of electrical power; when every article on the average man's breakfast table, every item of clothing, every piece of his furniture, every tool of his trade, will have been manufactured or transported by electric power; when the home, the farm and the factory will be electrically lighted, heated and operated; when from morning to night, from the cradle to the grave, electric service will enter at every moment and from every direction into the daily life of every man, woman and child in America." The question before us, he adds, is not whether there shall be such a monopoly, but whether we as a people shall control it or shall permit it to control us—whether we shall respect the human wastes and tragedies which were the by-products of the steam revolution, or whether by taking counsel of that experience we shall make the new giant more the servant than the master of our common life.

The report of Pennsylvania's Giant Power Survey Board is not only a great state paper but such a treasure house of information arranged and simply interpreted for the use of the laymen as has never before been available on the supremely important subject with which it deals, and which is of direct concern to men and women in every branch of social activity—industry, education, health and family casework. Readers who were interested in The Survey's Giant Power number will be glad to know that a limited number of copies are available upon application to the Giant Power Survey Board in Harrisburg.

The Negro in Print
A Selected List of Magazines and Books By and About Negroes

THE whole trend of literature about the Negro has turned from the controversial to the informational within the last ten years, and a culling of the most outstanding recent literature has been made for Survey readers. Except for purposes of historical record, whole libraries of controversial "problem literature" are now obsolete, and the primary requirements of the new situation are a fresh start and an open mind. In the general literature of the subject there are now available comprehensive and well-documented histories of the Negro, both in relation to America and to the African origins, with a marked tendency to take the whole question out of the context of debate and controversy and set it in terms of factual evidence in an accurate historical background and perspective. Even in relation to Southern conditions, the economic and sociological interpretation has eventually prevailed, and bias and special pleading are fading out of the literature. The following list is selected for general reading.

I—General Reading

A Social History of the American Negro, by *Benjamin Brawley*. Macmillan. Price $4.00.

The Negro in our History, by *Carter G. Woodson*. Third Edition. Associated Publishers. Price $2.50.

The Negro, by *W. E. B. Du Bois*. (Home University Library) Henry Holt. Price $1.00.

The Gift of Black Folk, by *W. E. B. Du Bois*. The Stratford Co.

The Negro Faces America, by *Herbert J. Seligmann*. Harper & Co. Price $2.50.

The Negro from Africa to America, by *W. D. Weatherford*. Doran. Price $5.00.

Christianity and the Race Problem, by *J. H. Oldham*, Doran. Price $1.75.

Race Adjustment, by *Kelly Miller*. Neale Publishing Co.

The Everlasting Stain, by *Kelly Miller*. Associated Publishing Co. $2.50.

More representative still of the modern scientific attitude and approach, is the marked growth of special studies of the Negro, not only of the academic type, and of the practical scientific study, but also of the reliable popular compendium of detailed information, the latter especially in connection with details of current developments within the Negro group. Quite noteworthy are the increasing evidences of liberalism of view on the part of Southern investigators and of the tendency to go to the Negro himself for that information which can only come reliably from inside the group life. A list has been made of the best available sources of detailed scientific and sociological information.

II—Sociological and Special Studies

A Century of Negro Migration, by *Carter G. Woodson*. Associated Publishing Co. Price $2.00.

Negro Migration, by *Thomas J. Woofter*. W. D. Gray Co.

The Education of the Negro Prior to 1861, by *Carter G. Woodson*. Associated Publishing Co.

The Negro in Chicago, Chicago Inter-Racial Commission, University of Chicago Press.

Darker Phases of the South, by *Frank J. Tannenbaum*. Putnam. Price $2.00.

The Southern Oligarchy, by *William H. Skaggs*. Devin-Adair Co. Price $5.00.

WHY HAVE LYNCHINGS
DECREASED
FROM 60 A YEAR TO 16 IN 1924?

THE NATIONAL ASSOCIATION FOR THE ADVANCEMENT OF COLORED
PEOPLE OFFERS IN EVIDENCE THE FACTS BELOW:

1. The N.A.A.C.P., beginning 1916, has SPENT MORE THAN $50,000 in the first and only organized, persistent, intensive campaign of fact and education against lynching in America.

2. The N.A.A.C.P. has HELD MORE THAN 4,000 PUBLIC MEETINGS and has distributed MILLIONS OF PIECES OF LITERATURE.

3. The N.A.A.C.P. has INVESTIGATED 44 LYNCHINGS ON THE SPOT, often at risk of life of the investigators, and has spread the facts obtained throughout the civilized world.

4. The N.A.A.C.P. FORCED THE DYER ANTI-LYNCHING BILL THROUGH THE HOUSE OF REPRESENTATIVES by a vote of 230 to 119, making that measure a national issue.

5. The N.A.A.C.P. published "Thirty Years of Lynching," a 105-page book, the ONLY AUTHENTIC RECORD OF LYNCHING IN AMERICA.

6. The N.A.A.C.P. HELD THE FIRST NATIONAL ANTI-LYNCHING CONFERENCE in New York, in 1919. Among those attending were Charles Evans Hughes, Governor O'Neill of Alabama, and Moorfield Storey. This Conference issued an ADDRESS TO THE NATION signed by 4 attorneys-general, 7 governors, 20 leading Southerners, and others.

7. The N.A.A.C.P. SPENT $6,980 in reaching 5 million people through "THE SHAME OF AMERICA," a full-page advertisement in leading dailies throughout the country, setting forth the plain facts about lynching.

8. The N.A.A.C.P. sent a MEMORIAL TO THE SENATE urging enactment of the Dyer Bill, the signers including 24 STATE GOVERNORS, 39 MAYORS, 88 BISHOPS AND CHURCHMEN, 29 COLLEGE PRESIDENTS AND PROFESSORS, 30 PROMINENT EDITORS, and many other influential persons.

9. COMMENT OF THE JUDICIARY COMMITTEE OF THE HOUSE OF REPRESENTATIVES (1924): "We believe that the decrease (in lynching) is due to the publicity given this crime, and the fear of a law by the United States, providing for punishment for those who participate and are responsible for lynchings. The American people generally have been for the first time told the truth regarding lynchings, and that they are not caused by the commission of heinous crimes, except in a small part of the total number lynched."

BUT LYNCHING IS NOT YET ABOLISHED—THE DYER BILL MUST PASS

IN ADDITION

THE NEGRO PRESS IN THE UNITED STATES, by *Frederick Detweiler.* University of Chicago Press.
THE VOICE OF THE NEGRO, by *Robert E. Kerlin.* Dutton Price $2.50.
SELECTED ARTICLES ON THE NEGRO PROBLEM, by *Julia E. Johnsen.* H. W. Wilson Co. Price $2.25.
THE NEGRO YEAR BOOK, edited by *Monroe Work.* Tuskegee Institute. Price $1.00.
CHRISTIANITY, ISLAM AND AFRICA, by *E. W. Blyden.*
RACES, NATIONS AND CLASSES, by *H. A. Miller.*
THE NEGRO IN THE NEW WORLD, by *Sir H. H. Johnston.* Macmillan. $6.00.
AFRICAN QUESTIONS AT THE PARIS PEACE CONFERENCE, by *G. L. Beers.* Macmillan. $6.00.
THE CLASH OF COLOR: A STUDY IN THE PROBLEM OF RACE, by *Basil Matthews.* Doran. Price $1.25.
THE BLACK MAN'S BURDEN, by *E. D. Morel.* London 1920.

III—Magazines

THE CRISIS, published by the *National Association for the Advancement of Colored People,* 70 Fifth Ave., New York City. $1.50 per year. This Association publishes pamphlets on various phases of Negro life.
THE MESSENGER, published monthly at 2305 Seventh Ave., New York City. $1.50 per year.
OPPORTUNITY, published monthly by the *National Urban League,* 127 E. 23rd St., New York City. $1.50 per year.
JOURNAL OF NEGRO HISTORY, publibshed quarterly by *The Association for the Study of Negro Life and History, Inc.,* Lancaster, Pa., and Washington, D. C.
THE HOWARD REVIEW: A Research Journal. Howard University Press Washington, D. C.

In general literature, the treatment of Negro life has taken a turn that can only be called revolutionary, so definitely and suddenly has literature broken with the traditional attitudes of previous decades. In drama and fiction the younger realists have gone in for detailed and serious studies of Negro life that have scrapped the old stereotypes and penetrated the true environment and psychology of the Negro. The older school only went skin-deep into Negro life: this new school with increasing penetration goes to the heart of the life it attempts to portray. Another school takes the aesthetic approach and just as startlingly reveals, both in the African Negro and the American scene, elements of strange exotic charm, individuality and beauty.

IV—The Negro in General Literature
Fiction

BIRTHRIGHT, by *T. S. Stribling.* Century. Price $1.90.
BLACK AND WHITE, by *H. A. Shands.* Harcourt, Brace. Price $1.90.
NIGGER, by *Clement Wood.* Dutton. Price $2.00.
HOLIDAY, by *Waldo Frank.* Boni & Liveright. Price $2.00.
PRANCING NIGGER, by *Ronald Firbank.* Brentano's. Price $2.00.
GREEN THURSDAY, by *Julia Peterkin.* Knopf. Price $2.50.
BLACK CAMEOS, by *R. E. Kennedy,* A. & C. Boni. Price $2.50.
WITH AESOP ALONG THE BLACK BORDER, by *A. E. Gonzales.*

Drama

GRANNY BOLLING, by *Paul Greene.* Theatre Arts Magazine.
WHITE DRESSES, by *Paul Greene.* Theatre Arts Magazine.
GRANNY MAUMEE AND OTHER PLAYS OF THE NEGRO THEATRE, by *Ridgeley Torrence.*
THE EMPEROR JONES, by *Eugene O'Neill.* Boni & Liveright. Price $2.00.
ALL GOD'S CHILLUN GOT WINGS, by *Eugene O'Neill.* Boni & Liveright. Price $2.00.

African Fiction

EBONY AND IVORY, by *Llewelyn Powys.* American Library Service. Price $2.00.
BLACK LAUGHTER, by *Llewelyn Powys.* Harcourt, Brace. Price $2.50.

AFRICAN CLEARINGS, by *Jean K. Mackenzie.* Houghton, Mifflin. Price $2.50.

THE QUAINT COMPANIONS, by *Leonard Merrick.* Dutton. Price $1.90.

GOD'S STEPCHILDREN, by *Sarah G. Millin.* Boni & Liveright. Price $2.00.

THE LONG WALK OF SAMBA DIOUF, by *Jerome and Jean Tharaud.* Duffield. Price $1.75.

Negro Culture

AFRO-AMERICAN FOLKSONGS, by *H. E. Krehbiel.*

SONGS AND TALKS FROM THE DARK CONTINENT, by *Natalie Burlin Curtis.* Schirmer. Price $4.00.

NEGRO CULTURE IN WEST AFRICA, by *George W. Ellis.* Neale Publishing Co. Price $2.00.

PRIMITIVE NEGRO SCULPTURE, by *Paul Guillaume and T. Munro.* (on press) Barnes Foundation.

African Art Issue of OPPORTUNITY, May 1924.

Sharing increasing contact with the general world of letters, and speaking with a new cultural emphasis and breadth, Negro authors are collaborating in giving an artistically conceived version of Negro life and feeling to the world.

V—Negro Belles Lettres

Poetry

AMERICAN NEGRO POETRY, compiled by *James Weldon Johnson.* Harcourt, Brace & Co. Price $1.75.

AN ANTHOLOGY OF AMERICAN NEGRO VERSE, compiled by *N. I. White and C. A. Jackson.* Trinity College Press, Durham, N. C. Price $2.00.

FIFTY YEARS AND AFTER, by *James Weldon Johnson.* Cornhill. Price $1.25.

THE HOUSE OF FALLING LEAVES, by *Wm. Stanley Braithwaite.* Luce. Price $1.00.

SANDY GEE AND OTHER POEMS, by *Wm. Stanley Braithwaite.*

THE HEART OF A WOMAN & OTHER POEMS, by *Georgia Douglas Johnson.* Cornhill. Price $1.25.

BRONZE, by *Georgia Douglas Johnson.*

HARLEM SHADOWS, by *Claude McKaye.* Harcourt, Brace & Co. Price $1.35.

THE COLLECTED POEMS OF PAUL LAURENCE DUNBAR. Dodd Mead & Co. Price $2.50.

Drama

RACHEL, by *Angelina Grimke.*

Fiction

SPORT OF THE GODS, by *Paul Laurence Dunbar.* Dodd Mead. Price $1.50.

THE UNCALLED, by *Paul Laurence Dunbar.*

THE MARROW OF TRADITION, by *Charles W. Chesnutt.* Houghton Mifflin. Price $1.50.

THE HOUSE BEHIND THE CEDARS, by *Charles W. Chesnutt.* Houghton Mifflin. Price $1.50.

THE WIFE OF HIS YOUTH AND OTHER STORIES, by *Charles W. Chesnutt.* Houghton Mifflin. Price $1.50.

THE CONJURE WOMAN, by *Charles W. Chesnutt.* Houghton Mifflin. Price $1.25.

THE QUEST OF THE SILVER FLEECE, by *W. E. B. Du Bois.* McClurg. Price $1.20.

BATOUALA, by *René Maran.* Seltzer. Price $1.25.

CANE, by *Jean Toomer.* Boni & Liveright.

THERE IS CONFUSION, by *Jessie Fauset.* Boni & Liveright. Price $2.00.

THE FIRE IN THE FLINT, by *Walter F. White.* Knopf. Price $2.50.

General

THE SOULS OF BLACK FOLK, by *W. E. B. Du Bois.* McClurg. Price $1.35.

DARKWATER, by *W. E. B. Du Bois.* Harcourt, Brace. Price $2.25.

THE POETIC YEAR, by *Wm. Stanley Braithwaite.* Small, Maynard. Price $2.00.

UP FROM SLAVERY, by *Booker T. Washington.* Houghton Mifflin.

AUTOBIOGRAPHY, *Frederick Douglass.* A. L.

(In answering advertisements please mention THE SURVEY. *It helps us, it identifies you.)*

THE CHURCH AND THE NEGRO SPIRIT
(*Continued from page 697*)

the vigor and power of numbers. In the independent Negro denominations there are more than 35,000 churches with over four million members enrolled and church property valued at over seventy million dollars. In the mixed religious bodies there are over 6,000 Negro churches, nearly three quarter million Negro members enrolled and over seventeen millions in church property.*

There is a strong racial tie between Negro churches, both of the independent group and of mixed denominations. Recently churches of the several denominations of Harlem joined forces in a league, affiliated with the New York Church Federation and employed an executive secretary. Denominational differences are no problem with these churches as there are frequent visits of delegations from one congregation to another and frequent ministerial fellowship and exchange of pulpits.

The Negro ministry has been making gradual gains in intelligence and social vision. The facilities for training of Negro religious leaders, however, are not commensurate with the provision for training in other lines. A recent survey of theological education showed how inadequate are the curriculum and the personnel of institutions for theological training of Negro youth. In New York, of course, all avenues of religious and theological education are open to Negro leaders, but most of the ministers lived during their years of training in sections where such facilities were not open to them. Negroes trained in social work have been on the scene in small numbers the past twelve or fifteen years, but social plans and programs are yet uncertain and have not fully engaged the churches. The Negro churches of Harlem, however, are developing along these lines. Six churches have trained staff assistants for religious education and social service. The great demand is for trained helpers for ministers to foster programs in these churches which will meet the larger needs of worship, religious education and social service.

A WHITE visitor to the morning services of a popular Harlem church remarked, "These people are taking their religion with intense earnestness. A white congregation is usually so restrained in their services that they seem to measure the transaction they are carrying on with God." The spirit of the Negro people is shown in the fleeting hours of their amusement and play, in the furtive expression of their appreciation of things beautiful, and in outpourings of personality and emotion as they gather in their places of worship, and as they render the many personal services the one to the other in the routine of daily life. Free self-expression in these directions is often limited in America by economic and social discriminations. Emotional experience and the personal experience of service, however, find large objective opportunity through the Negro church. The churches of the Negro people are channels of their spiritual life blood. They are less restricted, probably, than any other group organization. Especially in the South, from which the majority of the Negroes in New York, Philadelphia, Chicago and

* See Negro Yearbook, 1921-22, pp. 202-3.

other Northern cities have come in the last twenty years, the church is the most effective community agency for emotional, intellectual and other group expression. "The pillars of the church" are usually the leaders of the community. The social and cultural life of the group is largely influenced by these leaders; and the new environment puts this leadership to new tests.

RESIDENCE in northern cities brings to Negroes several advantages, such as greater freedom of movement, freedom of speech and assembly, that give play to increased group expression and intra-group intercourse. Lack of restrictions on street cars and railroad trains removes irritation of mind and body. The greater attraction of the paved and lighted streets, the parks, playgrounds and water fronts offer allurements to the young folk. Greater access to libraries, moving picture shows, theatres, dance halls, and other means of self-expression set up keen competition with the churches.

The throngs of the present generation have come up through public and private schools which although inadequate have given them a point of view based on modern knowledge. Negro illiteracy has been reduced from 90 to 22 per cent in sixty years. Thousands have been awakened in rural communities through such means as visiting lectures and the war drives. They are no longer satisfied with the older types of church service. These must therefore be pitched upon a plane of intelligence with an emotional appeal which holds its own in competition with those other channels of knowledge and emotional enthusiasm.

Nearly all the Harlem churches are led by men who sense this situation. Athletic and social clubs for young people are promoted. Musical and literary organizations which meet both on weekdays and Sundays attract large numbers. The Sunday afternoon lyceum or forum is on the program of many churches. Week day religious instruction and vacation Bible schools have also been fostered. The regular religious services for the adult congregation in most instances are conducted with dignity and order, with intelligent sermons to meet the personal and group problems with which these people wrestle. These church forces have been the principal power against the evils of the district which are always present.

The Negro churches of Harlem are visible evidence of the struggle of an aspiring people to express the best of life within them. Either in structures purchased from white congregations or in those they themselves build, they are organizing and developing personnel and membership to conserve the spiritual and ethical values of the race. They are struggling, often against great odds, to provide an avenue of self-expression to a people that is seeking to serve and to walk humbly with God.

(In answering these advertisements please mention THE SURVEY. *It helps us, it identifies you.)*

THE BLACK MAN BRINGS HIS GIFTS

(*Continued from page 657*)

lurked beneath. And at last she took out a little thin
black book and read.

She read about this country not belonging to white folks
any more than it did to black folks and that the black folks
got here before the pilgrims. I couldn't help stepping on
Birdie's toes because she says her people came in on some
boat named after a flower so long ago she's forgot their
names. The black girl said that the story of the Negro
could be found on every page of the story of America. This
made me sick and I turned and glared right at her. But
she looked right through me and went on. She said Negroes
had been soldiers in all our wars, had nursed the babies,
cooked the food and sung and danced besides working so
hard that "working like a nigger" was about the hardest
work you could picture.

And she asked us if America could have been America
without Negroes.

She had me up a tree, I must admit. And I reckon
the rest felt as I did—all except that editor.

The chairman looked at us with owl-like eyes; then
he shoved a paper at me and read it aloud as he did:

"*Timeo Nigros et dona ferentes*"

Nobody knows what he meant and nobody gave him the
satisfaction of asking.

WELL, we just sat and stared until she left. Then
we went on talking but we didn't touch the real
question; and that was, could we have America's Making
without Mrs. Cadwalader Lee and with the Negroes?

We couldn't make up our minds and before we had
courage to say so openly we went smash on religion.

We might possibly have had some sort of an America's
Making pageant if we hadn't discussed religion. You see,
the editor who is downright malicious and hates the Federation of Women's Clubs because they start things, got us
all wrong by trying to get a definition of religion. He was
strong on meekness and humility and turning the other
cheek and that sort of thing and I know he didn't mean a
word of it.

"I suppose," said Birdie, "that you'll be saying that the
Negroes have given us all our religion because they're
cowards and allowed themselves to be slaves and take insult
today meekly."

"I must admit," said the preacher, "that if the meek
inherit the earth, the American Negro will get a large
share."

"But will the meek inherit the earth?" I asked.

"I think so," said the chairman calmly.

Birdie jumped up and reached for her cloak. "I believe
you're a Jew and a pacifist," she said.

"I am both," he answered.

"And I suppose," said I, getting my hat on straight, "that
when somebody slaps you over, you turn the other cheek."

"I did," said he.

"Well, you're a fool," I answered, reaching for my coat.

And Birdie yelled, 'And what did they do to you after
you turned the other cheek? Answer me that."

"They crucified me," said the chairman.

urban and industrial. The Negro Sanhedrin, the most recent attempt at race organization, seeks to understand the nature and extend of race prejudice, and to work on the basis of this understanding. If it should turn out that race prejudice cannot be overcome by direct attack and opposition, it may possibly be circumvented by building independently where independence is necessary, and by cooperation where cooperation is possible. It would at least garner the harvest of prejudice to the best advantage of the race. The Negro Sanhedrin seeks to find the common denominator of racial ills, and would federate into one effective effort the scattered energies which are so largely wasted by friction and cross purpose. As a matter of fact, the race as a whole had never hitherto seriously essayed collective handling of the racial situation as a whole. There have been innumerable attempts at dealing with special features along local, religious, political and economic lines. But the integration of the race mind and the focalization of endeavor still await the fuller unfoldment of the workings of some such comprehensive movement as the Negro Sanhedrin. The twelve millions scattered throughout the length and breadth of the land are treated by a single formula so far as the white race is concerned. And yet the Negro has had to rely upon local and scattered effort to offset the solid line of racial exclusiveness with which he is confronted. He must seek concerted action to confront difficulties that are nation-wide and race-deep.

Every minority and suppressed group seeks self-expression. Woodrow Wilson let off the lid of a new Pandora's box when he so eloquently preached this doctrine as the shibboleth of the war. The Negro seeks self-determination also. In Harlem he seeks political self-expression. He wants men of his own race to represent him in the city council, in the state legislature and in the national Congress. Wherever a political area is numerically dominated by members of the race, they will naturally seek a voice in political councils. Here again segregation is basic. If the Negro were thinly scattered throughout greater New York, he would be politically negligible. In Chicago, in the recent election, Negro candidates were successful for state Senate, Assembly and the municipal Bench, and the whole race rejoices. What is it that unites twelve million Negroes in jubilation over such successes but the uniting force of race prejudice?

Business is the last place in which prejudice shows itself, and it is in this field that its harvest is least manifest. Scattered throughout Harlem on practically every street corner are Jewish stores catering to the vast Negro constituency. The Jew makes the most acceptable merchant among Negroes because he knows how to reduce race prejudice to a minimum. In Harlem, as in every other large city, the Negro proprietor conducts mainly sumptuary establishments such as eating-houses, barber-shops, beauty parlors, pool rooms, and such places as cater immediately to the appetite or to the taste. The more substantial stores which require a larger exercise of the imagination, such as those dealing in dry goods, shoes, furniture, hardware and groceries, are usually in the hands of whites. Race prejudice will sooner or later lead to race patronage in business as it has already

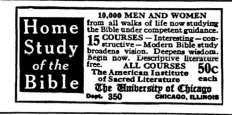

done in the professions; but it awaits the time when the Negro shall have developed the business aptitude to compete with the white dealer, who is shrewd enough to hold prejudice in restraint for the sake of trade.

The final outcome of race prejudice operating to establish and maintain Negro sections in New York and elsewhere must evidently be a self-sufficient Negro community, competent to cater to its own needs and necessities as well as to contribute its quota to the general industrial and economic life of the city as a whole. What then will be the form of race adjustment? Will the relationship of the two be characterized by amity or by enmity? We approach the issue with a mixed feeling of hopes and fears, but with our hopes triumphant over our fears. However bitter the fruit of the tree of prejudice may be, the Negro will eat thereof and thrive by the eating.

JAZZ AT HOME
(*Continued from page 667*)

For the Negro himself, jazz is both more and less dangerous than for the white—less in that, he is nervously more in tune with it; more, in that at his average level of economic development his amusement life is more open to the forces of social vice. The cabaret of better type provides a certain Bohemianism for the Negro intellectual, the artist and the well-to do. But the average thing is too much the substitute for the saloon and the wayside inn. The tired longshoreman, the porter, the housemaid and the poor elevator boy in search of recreation, seeking in jazz the tonic for weary nerves and muscles, are only too apt to find the bootlegger, the gambler and the demi-monde who have come there for victims and to escape the eyes of the police.

Yet in spite of its present vices and vulgarizations, its sex informalities, its morally anarchic spirit, jazz has a popular mission to perform. Joy, after all, has a physical basis. Those who laugh and dance and sing are better off even in their vices than those who do not. Moreover jazz with its mocking disregard for formality is a leveler and makes for democracy. The jazz spirit, being primitive, demands more frankness and sincerity. Just as it already has done in art and music, so eventually in human relations and social manners, it will no doubt have the effect of putting more reality in life by taking some of the needless artificiality out. . . . Naturalness finds the artificial in conduct ridiculous. "Cervantes smiled Spain's chivalry away," said Byron. And so this new spirit of joy and spontaneity may itself play the role of reformer. Where at present it vulgarizes, with more wholesome growth in the future, it may on the contrary truly democratize. At all events jazz is rejuvenation, a recharging of the batteries of civilization with primitive new vigor. It has come to stay, and they are wise, who instead of protesting against it, try to lift and divert it into nobler channels.

AMBUSHED IN THE CITY
(*Continued from page 694*)

to me. "He said: 'A friend of mine brought this prescription into my store. I can't fill it. You fill it for me. If he'd been a stranger, I'd have given him something. But I don't want to hand out to a friend that stuff we have on our shelves.' He didn't bother much with prescriptions, he confessed. Sometimes he put in substitute ingredients; sometimes he left out something that was called for. 'You leave your label off this and I'll put ours on' he said."

The Negro pharmacist continued:

"Some of these drug stores certainly are fakes. Why, they don't keep enough drugs on hand to fill simple prescriptions. Not long ago I sent three prescriptions out to fifteen of 'em— easy prescriptions; I just wanted to make a little experiment. I didn't bother with those drug stores over on Lenox Avenue— I knew what I'd be gettin' into there. I just stuck to Seventh Avenue.

"Well, you should have seen the collection that came back. One prescription called for a nerve sedative, a compound of chloral hydrate, tincture canabis and some other things. Two druggists put elixir of lactated pepsin—for indigestion!—into the prescription, instead of the elixir triple bromides I called for. And you should have seen those bottles! Some were half choked with gelatinous substances that had no business there; others had sediment. They were every color from yellow to dark brown. Why, those druggists just put in any old thing. Another prescription called for a seven-grain capsule. The capsules that came back weighed all the way from three grains to ten; the average was about four. They couldn't even get the quantity right! Those stores are a crime. 'Anything's good enough for niggers!' say the people who run them."

There are other forms of hooch joints—cigar stores, small restaurants, saloon-like shops, delicatessen stores and the like. The drinks they sell are very bad; it is commonly declared that the worst of the illegal booze is worked off on the Negro. These places have been exposed. Their addresses have been published time and again. The owner of The New York Age, Fred R. Moore, already referred to, is a fighting Negro. He is educated and intelligent. He believes in protecting his people from exploitation. Every week for months he has been publishing in his weekly a list of addresses; over it he puts the headline: Old and New Hooch Joints in Harlem. I know of no publication of a similar list of addresses elsewhere.

Sometimes Mr. Moore puts his list on the front page; it runs to about a hundred addresses. Here is part of the list on one street, taken from the issue of October 25, 1924: 404, 414, 419, 434, 448, 452, 481, 476, 477, 486, 488a—eleven within a single hundred numbers. Mr. Moore has never been the defendant in a libel action for characterizing these places as illegally engaged in selling liquor, and that fact is pretty good evidence that they are really what he calls them.

THE Negro in Harlem, like Negroes in many other places, is prey for poorly-trained white doctors and for unmistakable quacks. Some of these come to Harlem because they know that here quackery is easy; they fatten on the credulity of the Negro, and on his faith in the white man. Many of these doctors are prominent members of the community; a population of 200,000 spreads out before them, offering a lucrative field, and they take advantage of it.

Not long ago a white doctor in Harlem dismissed a colored patient, telling him that he had "spider cancer" at the base of his spine, and that it was incurable. Now, there is no such thing as spider cancer. The man had come to the doctor because he had hurt his back in a fall. The doctor applied dressing after dressing and plaster after plaster, and finally produced a creased, web-like spot on the man's back; it was this that he called "spider cancer." The poor fellow received proper treatment only when he went to a trained colored physician in the neighborhood.

"We know some of our white colleagues by their trails," said a colored physician, attached to the out-patient department of Harlem Hospital, to me. He was unwilling to be quoted if the names of these doctors were to be used, and so I have substituted letters for their names. "There's Doctor X, for instance. He is known by the plasters he leaves behind him. Whenever a patient has a pain, X puts a plaster over it. If you raise the shirt of a patient and find a plaster of mole skin adhesive there, you can say, 'Oh, I see you've been to Doctor X.' He always uses mole skin adhesive.

"Then there's Doctor Y. He uses pills, rotating them by color. 'What color did I give you last time?' he asks his patients, and then changes to another. It's easy to follow Doctor Y; just look at the mantlepiece and if his pills are there, you know what your patient has been up against.

"Doctor Z flops down on his knees and prays and prays with his patients. Though white, he knows his colored people, or a certain class of them. He will blare out in fine style his appeals to the Lord to help the treatment he has just given. I guess prayer is often necessary.

"Then there's Doctor A. 'What!' exclaimed Doctor A. 'Read medical books! I haven't read a medical book for ten years. I don't have to read 'em to practice on niggers!'

"They charge some of these colored people pretty high fees, too. The other day a white doctor charged $600 for drawing the water off a patient who had pleurisy—aspirating, it is called. This is ordinarily done by a physician in the course of a routine call. This doctor called it 'a major operation' and collected $600. They play on the Negro's ignorance of what is being done to him, and rob him."

ALL this, it can readily be imagined, has none too good an effect upon the Negro's health.

Any improvement that the race makes is made despite great obstacles. We all have heard that the Negro is not a healthy race. In a measure, this is true. Tuberculosis is the great enemy of the Negro. In the long run it kills one out of every six; few races show a greater tuberculosis deathrate. The incidence of rickets, a disease of malnutrition among children, is also high with the Negro. Chronic degenerative diseases, such as cerebral hemorrhage and organic diseases of the heart, are strong among Negroes. Cancer and diabetes carry off large numbers of them. The deathrate for the race as a whole is high, especially in cities.

In 1921 the deathrate among Negroes in the rural parts of registration states was 13.8 per 1,000; it was 10.8 for whites. In the cities it was 19.7 for Negroes, 11.8 for whites. Mortality among Negroes, 30 per cent higher than that among whites in the rural parts, was 67 per cent higher in the cities. In New York City the deathrate for Negroes in 1923 was 20.85, for whites 11.25. It looks as if the Negro were paying an unnecessarily heavy toll to the city by being unadapted to climatic conditions, or to prevailing industries, or to the housing available, or to all.

But what has the Negro been doing about this? He has been showing the world how a race can improve in health. His record is amazing. It is as if the Negro had said, "Come, we will be a bigger, better and physically more perfect race," and then had achieved it. Not long ago, Louis I. Dublin, statistician of the Metropolitan Life Insurance Company, published facts concerning health among the two million colored policyholders of that company; here is a group large enough to be representative and they live chiefly in towns and cities. From 1911 to 1923—twelve years—the deathrate for tuberculosis among these policyholders fell from 418 per 100,000 to 246, a startling improvement. In this same period the deathrate from typhoid was reduced 77.5 per cent. Who will say that the Negro is not improving in health? The four communicable diseases of childhood—measles, scarlet fever, whooping-cough and diphtheria—together show a decline of 33 per cent; there was a drop of more than 50 per cent in the mortality rates from diarrhea and enteritis among young colored children. The mortality rate for colored children under fifteen years was 10.1 per 1,000 in 1911; in 1923 it was only 5.5. "Colored mothers," writes Mr. Dublin, "have not been slow to learn how to care for and feed their babies in accordance with the best practice of the day.

Translate these figures into terms of life expectancy. In 1911 the Negro in this country—considering the Metropolitan figures as representative—was enjoying an average expectation of life of slightly more than forty-one years. In 1923 he was enjoying an expectation of nearly forty-seven years. In the short space of twelve years the Negro added six years to the length of time he had reason to expect to live, an astounding improvement.

The Negro's life expectancy to-day is just about that of the white people of the United States thirty or forty years ago; he is only a generation behind. He is where a number of European countries were just before the Great War. The mortality rate from tuberculosis is beginning to look like that among whites only twenty years ago, when the anti-tuberculosis campaign was begun. A race still living under primitive conditions in many places and often from hand to mouth has done this. "The Negro in America has proved himself thoroughly capable of profiting from the public health campaign," says Mr. Dublin.

All the more disheartening, then, are the difficulties to which attention has been called. The Negro in the Northern city lives in restricted areas of great congestion; he is elbowed and crowded by people of his own and the white color; he knows the evils of bad housing and often of bad sanitation and even squalor; he is set upon by quacks, tricked by fake druggists, fed every form of vile nostrum and vicious patent remedy concocted by man. "Anything is good enough for niggers" is the motto of too many white doctors, druggists, dentists, practitioners of all sorts who infest the colored districts and who have deliberately flocked thither as the colored population has grown.

The Negro has come to the Northern city and the exploiter, the conscienceless sucker of other people's welfare, has risen in his midst.

May it be as a result of these conditions that the improvement just noted has already suffered a set-back in some cities? In Chicago in 1923 the mortality rate was 27 per cent higher than in 1921; in Detroit it was 23 per cent higher. Has the Negro found that in health the Northern city is inhospitable? Have congestion and other difficulties reached a point at which they are beginning to take toll? The effect of the Northern city upon the Negro will bear watching.

Swift Memorial College

Swift Memorial College, Rogersville, Tennessee, is an institution for the Christian and higher education of Negro youth, and is under the auspices of the Presbyterian Church, U. S. A.

It is directly under the supervision of the National Board of Missions for Colored People, Pittsburgh, Pa.

It carries an English, Normal, Scientific, Teachers, and College Courses.

Its students have been recognized by the leading colleges and Universities of the U. S. A.

It is painstaking in the selection of its teachers, careful in the government of its students and thorough in instruction and training. No mistake will be made in going to Swift Memorial College.

All necessary information can be had by addressing,

W. H. FRANKLIN, PRESIDENT,

*Swift Memorial College,
Rogersville, Tenn.*

To the
NEW NEGRO

*Greetings
from*

WILEY COLLEGE
Marshall, Texas
M. W. Dogan, President

———

A Class "A" College for Future Leaders. Makes a Specialty of the Study of Race Problems

---

State of New Jersey
Manual Training and Industrial School

at

BORDENTOWN

Maintained for the vocational training of colored youth, with admission open to all residents of New Jersey.

Academic training for all students.

Stress is laid on all round development of students, physical and social as well as mental.

"Bordentown trains for life by giving the students a taste of life."

———

W. R. Valentine . . . . **Principal**

The
Atlanta School
of
Social Work

Trains Colored Social Workers for the South

Courses offered in
Social Case Work

Community Organization and Social Research

Field Work with Social Agencies

For further information address:
E. FRANKLIN FRAZIER, A. M.
36 Chestnut Street
Atlanta, Georgia

(In answering these advertisements please mention THE SURVEY. It helps us, it identifies you.)

717

tenders and teamsters decreased absolutely in the last decade. Aside from the clothing industry, the range of work remained about the same. Nearly 5,000 new women entered domestic service. The gross numbers of Negro men go into unskilled labor. There was an increase of only 57 male servants during the ten years and just 301 janitors. The solid concentration in personal service is being broken, and the workers scattered, but the skilled trades in such centers as New York still remain virtually locked to Negroes. The increases—where they occur—are striking, but this can be attributed to the low base from which these increases must be computed.

One may look to the character of New York's industries for another peculiar handicap. While offering a diversity of employment, the city has no such basic industries as may be found, for example, in the automobile plants of Detroit, or the iron and steel works and gigantic meat slaughtering industries of Chicago. In Chicago there is diversified employment, to be sure, but there is a significantly heavier concentration in the basic industries; more than that, there are gradations of work from unskilled to skilled. In certain plants skilled workers increased from 3.5 per cent of the Negro working population in 1910 to 13.5 per cent in 1920 in Chicago. In the slaughtering houses there are actually more semi-skilled Negro workers than laborers. The number of iron molders increased from 31 in 1910 to 520 in 1920 and this latter number represents 10 per cent of all the iron molders.

In the working age groups of New York there are more women than men. For every hundred Negro men there are 110 Negro women. This is abnormal and would be a distinct anomaly in an industrial center. The surplus women are doubtless the residue from the general wash and ebb of migrants who found a demand for their services. The city actually attracts more women than men. But surplus women bring on other problems, as the social agencies will testify. "Where women preponderate in large numbers there is proportionate increase in immorality because women are cheap." . . . The situation does not permit normal relations. What is most likely to happen, and does happen, is that women soon find it an added personal attraction to contribute to the support of a man. Demoralization may follow this—and does. Moreover, the proportion of Negro women at work in Manhattan (60.6) is twice that of any corresponding group, and one of the highest proportions registered anywhere.

The nature of the work of at least 40 per cent of the men suggests a relationship, even if indirectly, with the tensely active night life by which Harlem is known. The dull, unarduous routine of a porter's job or that of an elevator tender, does not provide enough stimulation to consume the normal supply of nervous energy. It is unthinkable that the restlessness which drove these migrants to New York from dull small towns would allow them to be content with the same dullness in the new environment, when so rich a supply of garish exitements is available.

IV

WITH all the "front" of pretending to live, the aspect of complacent wantlessness, it is clear that the Negroes are in a predicament. The moment holds tolerance but no great promise. Just as the wave of immigration once swept these Negroes out of old strongholds, a change of circumstances may disrupt them again. The slow moving black masses, with their assorted heritages and old loyalties, face the same stern barriers in the new environment. They are the black workers.

Entering gradually an era of industrial contact and competition with white workers of greater experience and numerical superiority, antagonisms loom up. Emotions have a way of re-enforcing themselves. The fierce economic fears of men in competition can supplement or be supplemented by the sentiments engendered by racial difference. Beneath the disastrous East St. Louis conflict was a boiling anger toward Southern Negroes coming in to "take white men's jobs." The antagonisms between the Negroes and the Irish in New York, which even now survive, were first provoked sixty years ago when these workers met and clashed over jobs. The hostile spirit was dominant in the draft riots of New York during the Civil War and flared again in the shameful battle of "San Juan Hill"· in the Columbus Hill District. These outbreaks were distinctly more economic than racial.

Herein lies one of the points of highest tension in race relations. Negro workers potentially menace organized labor and the leaders of the movement recognize this. But racial sentiments are not easily destroyed by abstract principles. The white workers have not, except in few instances, conquered the antagonisms founded on race to the extent of accepting the rights of Negro workers to privileges which they enjoy. While denying them admission to their crafts they grow furious over their dangerous borings from the outside. "The Negroes are scabs!" "They hold down the living standards of workers by cutting under!" "Negroes are professional strike breakers!" These sentiments are a good nucleus for elaboration into the most furious fears and hatreds.

It is believed variously that Negro workers are as a matter of policy opposed to unions or as a matter of ignorance incapable of appreciating them. From some unions they are definitely barred; some insist on separate Negro locals; some limit them to qualified membership; some accept them freely with white workers. The situation of the Negroes, on the surface, is to say the least compromising. Their shorter industrial experience and almost complete isolation from the educative influence of organized trade unions contribute to some of the inertia encountered in organizing them. Their traditional positions have been those of personal loyalty, and this has aided the habit of individual bargaining for jobs in industry. They have been, as was pointed out, under the comprehensive leadership of the church in practically all aspects of their lives including their labor. No effective new leadership has developed to supplant this old fealty. The attitude of white workers has sternly opposed the use of Negroes as apprentices through fear of subsequent competition in the skilled trades. This has limited the number of skilled Negroes trained on the job. But despite this denial, Negroes have gained skill.

This disposition violently to protest the employment of Negroes in certain lines because they are not members of the union and the equally violent protest against the admission of Negroes to the unions, created in the Negroes, desperate for work, an attitude of indifference to abstract pleas. In 1910 they were used to break the teamster's strike and six years later they were organized. In 1919 they were used in a strike of the building trades. Strained feelings resulted, but they were finally included in the unions of this trade. During the outlaw strike of the railway and steamship clerks, freight handlers, expressmen and station employes, they were used to replace the striking whites and were given preference over the men whose places they had taken. During the shopmen's strike they were promoted into new positions and thus made themselves eligible for skilled jobs as machinists. In fact, their most definite gains have been at the hands of employers and over the tactics of labor union exclusionists.

Where the crafts are freely open to them they have joined with the general movement of the workers. Of the 5,386 Negro longshoremen, about 5,000 are organized. Of the 735 Negro carpenters, 400 are members of the United Brotherhood of Carpenters and Joiners. Of the 2,275 semi-skilled clothing workers practically all are members of the International Ladies Garment Workers Union. The musicians are 50 per cent organized. The difficulty is that the great preponderance

(In answering these advertisements please mention THE SURVEY. *It helps us, it identifies you.)*

AMERICAN BIRTH CONTROL LEAGUE—President, Margaret Sanger, 104 Fifth Avenue, New York City. Objects: To educate American people in the various aspects of the dangers of un-controlled procreation; to establish centers where married persons may receive contraceptive advice from duly licensed physicians. Life membership $1.00; Birth Control Review (monthly magazine) $2.00 per year.

AMERICAN CHILD HEALTH ASSOCIATION—Headquarters, 532 17th St., N.W., Washington, D. C.; Administrative Offices, 370 7th Avenue, New York. Herbert Hoover, President; L. Emmett Holt, M.D.;* Livingston Farrand, M.D.; Thomas D. Wood, M.D.; Mrs. Maud Wood Park, 1st, 2nd, 3rd, 4th Vice-Presidents respectively; Corcoran Thom, Treasurer; Philip Van Ingen, M.D., Secretary; Edward M. Flesh, Comptroller. To promote health among children from conception to maturity—this to be accomplished through cooperation with parents, doctors, nurses, teachers, and other health workers; by dissemination of scientific information and teaching methods in schools, through conferences, addresses, pamphlets, publicity material, and a monthly magazine, "Child Health Magazine."

---

* Deceased.

AMERICAN COUNTRY LIFE ASSOCIATION—K. L. Butterfield, president; Henry Israel, executive secretary. Room 1849, Grand Central Terminal Bldg., New York City. Emphasizes the human aspect of country life. Annual membership $5.00 includes "Rural America" (monthly bulletin) and Annual Conference Proceedings.

AMERICAN FEDERATION OF ORGANIZATIONS FOR THE HARD OF HEARING—Promotes the cause of the hard of hearing; assists in forming organizations. Pres., Dr. Gordon Berry; Field Secretary, Miss Betty Wright, 1601 35th St. N.W., Washington, D. C.

AMERICAN HEART ASSOCIATION—Dr. Lewis A. Connor, president. Miss M. L. Woughter, acting executive secretary, 370 Seventh Avenue, New York. Organized for the purpose of promoting the prevention of heart disease and the care of those with damaged hearts in the United States and Canada.

AMERICAN HOME ECONOMICS ASSOCIATION—Leta Bane, executive secretary, Grace Dodge Hotel, Washington, D. C. Organized for betterment of conditions in home, school, institution and community. Publishes monthly Journal of Home Economics: office of editor, Grace Dodge Hotel, Washington, D. C.; of business manager, 1211 Cathedral St., Baltimore, Md.

AMERICAN PEACE SOCIETY—Founded 1828, labors for an international peace of justice. Its official organ is the Advocate of Peace, $2.00 a year. Arthur Deerin Call, secretary and editor, 612-614 Colorado Building, Washington, D. C.

AMERICAN SOCIETY FOR THE CONTROL OF CANCER—Frank J. Osborne, executive secretary; 370 Seventh Ave., New York. To disseminate knowledge concerning symptoms, diagnosis, treatment and prevention. Publication free on request. Annual membership dues, $5.00.

AMERICAN SOCIAL HYGIENE ASSOCIATION—370 Seventh Ave., New York. To promote a better understanding of the social hygiene movement; to advance sound sex education; to combat prostitution and sex delinquency; to aid public authorities in the campaign against the venereal diseases; to advise in organization of state and local social-hygiene programs. Annual membership dues $2.00 including monthly journal.

COMMUNITY SERVICE—315 Fourth Ave., New York City. A national civic movement for promoting citizenship through right use of leisure. It will, on request, help local communities work out leisure time programs. H. S. Braucher, secretary.

COUNCIL OF WOMEN FOR HOME MISSIONS—156 Fifth Avenue, New York. Organized in 1908: 20 constituent Protestant national women's mission boards. Florence E. Quinlan, exec. sec'y. Committee on Farm and Cannery Migrants, Summer Service for College Students, Laura H. Parker, exec. supervisor.

FEDERAL COUNCIL OF THE CHURCHES OF CHRIST IN AMERICA—Constituted by 28 Protestant communions. Rev. C. S. Macfarland and Rev. S. M. Cavert, Gen. Sec's; 105 E. 22d St., N.Y.C. Dept. of Research and Education, Rev. F. E. Johnson, Sec'y. Commissions: Church and Social Service, Rev. W. M. Tippy, Sec'y; International Justice and Goodwill: Rev. S. L. Gulick, Sec'y; Church and Race Relations: Dr. G. E. Haynes, Sec'y.

HAMPTON INSTITUTE—Trains Negro and Indian youth for community service. Advanced courses: agriculture, builders, business, home-economics, normal. Publishes "Southern Workman" and free material on Negro problems. J. E. Gregg, principal.

INTERNATIONAL MIGRATION SERVICE—To assemble data on international social problems and through work with individual cases to develop methods of international social service. Headquarters, London. Viscountess Gladstone, chairman; Professor Gilbert Murray, treasurer; Ruth Larned, executive. Address all inquiries to American bureau, 1 Madison Avenue, New York City. Director, Mary E. Hurlbutt.

JOINT COMMITTEE ON METHODS OF PREVENTING DE-LINQUENCY—Graham Romeyn Taylor, executive director, 50 East 42nd Street, New York. To promote the adoption of sound methods in this field, with particular reference to psychiatric clinics, visiting teacher work, and training for these and similar services; to conduct related studies, education and publication; and to interpret the work of the Commonwealth Fund Program for the Prevention of Delinquency.

NATIONAL BOARD OF THE YOUNG WOMEN'S CHRISTIAN ASSOCIATIONS—Mrs. Robert E. Speer, president; Miss Mabel Cratty, general secretary, 600 Lexington Avenue, New York City. This organization maintains a staff of executive and traveling secretaries to cover work in the United States in 1,034 local Y. W. C. A.'s on behalf of the industrial, business, student, foreign born, Indian, Colored and younger girls. It has 159 American secretaries at work in 49 centers in the Orient, Latin America and Europe.

NATIONAL CHILD LABOR COMMITTEE—Owen R. Lovejoy, general secretary, 215 Fourth Avenue, New York. Industrial, agricultural investigations. Works for improved laws and administration, children's codes. Studies child labor, health, schools, recreation, dependency, delinquency, etc. Annual membership, $2, $5, $10, $25 and $100 includes monthly publication, "The American Child."

NATIONAL CHILD WELFARE ASSOCIATION, INC. (est. 1913, incorp. 1914), 70 Fifth Ave., N. Y. C. (tel. Chelsea 8774). Promotes as its chief object the building of character in the children of America through the harmonious development of their bodies, minds, and spirits. Its method is, in co-operation with other organizations, to originate and disseminate educational material in the form of posters, books, bulletins, charts, slides, and insignia. Through its "Knighthood of Youth" it provides homes, schools and church schools with a method of character training through actual practice. Officers: Dr. John H. Finley, Pres.; Amos L. Frescott, Treas.; Charles F. Powlison, Gen. Sec'y.

THE NATIONAL COMMITTEE FOR MENTAL HYGIENE, INC.—Dr. William H. Welch, honorary president; Dr. Charles P. Emerson, president; Dr. Frankwood E. Williams, medical director; Dr. Clarence J. D'Alton, executive assistant; Clifford W. Beers, secretary; 370 Seventh Avenue, New York City. Pamphlets on mental hygiene, mental and nervous disorders, feeblemindedness, epilepsy, inebriety, delinquency, and other mental problems in human behavior, education, industry, psychiatric social service, etc. "Mental Hygiene," quarterly, $3.00 a year; "Mental Hygiene Bulletin," monthly, $ .50 a year.

NATIONAL COMMITTEE FOR THE PREVENTION OF BLINDNESS—Lewis H. Carris, managing director; Mrs. Winifred Hathaway, secretary; 130 East 22nd Street, New York. Objects: To furnish information, exhibits, lantern slides, lectures, personal service for local organizations and legislation, publish literature of movement—samples free, quantities at cost. Includes New York State Committee.

NATIONAL CONFERENCE OF SOCIAL WORK—Wm. J. Norton, president, Detroit, Michigan; W. H. Parker, Secretary, 25 East Ninth Street, Cincinnati, Ohio. The Conference is an organization to discuss the principles of humanitarian effort and to increase the efficiency of social service agencies. Each year it holds an annual meeting, publishes in permanent form the Proceedings of the meeting, and issues a quarterly Bulletin. The fifty-second annual meeting of the Conference will be held in Denver, Colorado, June 10th to 17th, 1925. Proceedings are sent free of charge to all members upon payment of a membership fee of five dollars.

NATIONAL COUNCIL OF JEWISH WOMEN—2109 Broadway, New York. Miss Rose Brenner, pres.; Mrs. Estelle M. Sternberger, ex. sec'y. Promotes civic cooperation, education, religion and social welfare in the United States, Canada, Cuba, Europe. Department of Immigrant Aid—799 Broadway. Miss Florina Lasker, chairman. For the protection and education of immigrant women and girls. Department of Farm and Rural Work—Mrs. Leo H. Herz, chairman, 5 Columbus Circle, New York City.

THE NATIONAL COUNCIL OF THE YOUNG MEN'S CHRISTIAN ASSOCIATIONS OF THE UNITED STATES OF AMERICA—347 Madison Avenue, New York City (Telephone, Vanderbilt 1200). Composed of 344 business and professional men, representing 1,540 Associations in 48 states, Hawaii, and the Canal Zone, and 388 Associations in 32 Foreign Lands. Officers: F. W. Ramsey, Cleveland, O., President; Adrian Lyon, Chairman of the General Board; John R. Mott, New York, General Secretary.

NATIONAL LEAGUE OF GIRLS' CLUBS—Mrs. Fannie M. Pollak, president; Mary L. Ely, Educational Secretary. Non-sectarian and self-governing organization of working women's clubs for recreation and promotion of program in Adult Education. Vacation Camps. 472 West 24th St., New York City.

NATIONAL ORGANIZATION FOR PUBLIC HEALTH NURSING—Member, National Health Council—Anne A. Stevens, R.N., director, 370 Seventh Avenue, New York. For development and standardization of public health nursing. Maintains library and educational service. Official Magazine, "Public Health Nurse."

NATIONAL PHYSICAL EDUCATION SERVICE—315 Fourth Ave., New York, N. Y. To obtain progressive legislation for physical education. Established at the request of a committee created by the United States Bureau of Education; 35 national organizations cooperating. Maintained by the Playground and Recreation Association of America.

(In answering these advertisements please mention THE SURVEY. It helps us, it identifies you.)

of Negro jobs is in lines which are not organized. The porters, laundresses (outside of laundries) and servants have no organization. The Negroes listed as painters are not in the painters' union, many of them being merely whitewashers. The tailors are in large part cleaners and pressers. The waiters, elevator tenders (except females) are poorly organized.

The end of the Negro's troubles, however, does not come with organization. There is still the question of employers, for it is a certain fact that preference is frequently given white workers when they can be secured, if high wages are to be paid. A vicious circle indeed! The editors of The Messenger have suggested a United Negro Trades Union built on the plan of the United Hebrew Trades and the Italian Chamber of Labor. The unions are lethargic; the Negroes skeptical, untrained and individualistic. Meanwhile they drift, a disordered mass, self-conscious, but with their aims unrationalized, into the face of new problems.

V

WITH the shift toward industry now beginning, and a subsequent new status already foreshadowed, some sounder economic policy is imperative. The traditional hold of domestic service vocations is already broken: witness the sudden halt in the increase of Negro male servants and elevator men. The enormous growth of certain New York industries has been out of proportion to the normal native production of workers. The immigration on which these formerly depended has been cut down and the prospects are that this curtailment will continue. For the first time, as a result of promotion, retirement and death, gaps are appearing which the limited recruits cannot fill. Note the clothing industry, one of the largest in New York. There is a persistent lament that the second generation of immigrants do not continue in the trade. Already Negro workers have been sought to supplement the deficiencies in the first generation recruits. This sort of thing will certainly be felt in other lines. The black masses are on the verge of induction from their unenviable status as servants to the forces of the industrial workers, a more arduous, but less dependent rank. They require a new leadership, training in the principles of collective action, a new orientation with their white fellow workers for the sake of future peace, a reorganization of the physical and mental habits which are a legacy of their old experiences, and deliberate training for the new work to come. It is this recreation of the worker that the Urban Leagues have tried to accomplish, accompanying this effort with a campaign against the barriers to the entrance of Negro workers into industry. Conceiving these workers as inherently capable of an infinite range of employment this organization insists merely upon an openness which permits opportunity, an objective experiment uncluttered by old theories of racial incompetence and racial dogmas.

The workers of the South and the West Indies who have come to this city with vagrant desires and impulses, their endowments of skill and strength, their repressions and the telltale marks of backward cultures, with all the human wastes of the process, have directed shafts of their native energy into the city's life and growth. They are becoming a part of it. The restive spirit which brought them to the city has been neither all absorbed nor wasted. Over two-thirds of all the businesses operated by Negroes in New York are conducted by migrant Negroes. They are in the schools—they are the radicals and this is hopeful. The city Negro—an unpredictable mixture of all possible temperaments—is yet in evolution.

But a common purpose is integrating these energies and once leashed to a purposeful objective, it is not improbable that in industry and in the life of the city the black workers will compensate in utility and progressiveness for what they lack in numbers and traditions.

CLASSIFIED ADVERTISEMENTS

RATES: Display advertisements, 25 cents per agate line, 14 lines to the inch. Want advertisements, 8 cents per word or initial, including the address or box number, for each insertion, minimum charge, $1.50. Discounts on three or more consecutive insertions. Cash with orders.

Address Advertising Department   **THE SURVEY**   112 East 19th Street New York City

---

WORKERS WANTED

SUPERVISING MATRON (white) for an institution of 300 children with an opportunity for working out the problem of the colored child along advanced lines. 5079 SURVEY.

WOMAN WORKER WANTED: Jewish, assistant and secretary to Superintendent small institution for unmarried mothers on Staten Island. Must have social service experience. 5034 SURVEY.

EMPLOYMENT office worker, college graduate with case work or employment experience preferred. Protestant, young, able to use typewriter. $1200.00-$1500.00. Apply to Carol W. Adams, 1545 Glenarm St., Denver, Colorado.

WANTED in a Philadelphia Hospital, a Social Case Worker, College Graduate with at least one year of Social Case Work Experience. Hospital Experience not necessary. 4996 SURVEY.

WANTED: Girls Club Leader, Eastern Settlement, State education, experience and references. 5063 SURVEY.

WANTED: Trained nurse and social worker to take charge of small mining community situated about forty miles from New York City. No. 5069 THE SURVEY.

SEVERAL financial secretaries for permanent positions are required by philanthropic institution. 5091 SURVEY.

WANTED: Family Case Worker for small Family Case Agency. Preferably one with experience and good theoretical training. Must speak Yiddish. 5096 SURVEY.

The Ad.

Wanted, for October 1st, home for little girl of four. Business mother travels part time. Desires complete care for child during absence from city. Child attends play school 9 to 12. Vicinity thirteenth street, west. 4890 Survey.

The Result

"I want you to know how effective the 'ad' proved which I placed in The Survey. I received only three answers but each one was from exactly the right sort of person. At the same time I advertised in the New York Times on Sunday. I received five times as many replies as from The Survey ad but not one of these answers was even worth looking into. These people entirely disregarded the points I made.
"4890 Survey."

WORKERS WANTED

NURSES, DOCTORS, TECHNICIANS of all kinds assisted in securing better places and better help. Hospitals, Schools and Industrial plants furnished with efficient nurses. We usually recommend only one applicant, never more than two or three. HUGHES PROFESSIONAL EXCHANGE, 603 Scarritt Building, Kansas City, Mo.

WANTED: Man to act as Boy's Supervisor and wife to act as babies caretaker. Children's Home located near city in country and modern congregate plan. Man should be active with boys and able to work with boys. Wife should be able to substitute in other lines such as ironing, seamstress and allied work if necessary. 5099 SURVEY.

COOPERATIVE PLACEMENT SERVICE. Social workers, secretaries, superintendents, matrons, housekeepers, dietitians, cafeteria managers. The Richards Bureau, 68 Barnes Street, Providence, R. I.

GRADUATE NURSES, dietitians, laboratory technicians for excellent hospital positions everywhere. Write for free book now. Aznoe's Central Registry for Nurses, 30 N. Michigan Ave., Chicago, Illinois.

WANTED: Refined married couple to take charge of cottage unit, thirty boys, small school near New York. Preferably one or both should be qualified for class room instruction, grammar grades. Apply by letter only. A. E. Wakeman, 72 Schermerhorn Street, Brooklyn, N. Y.

TEACHERS WANTED

TEACHERS wanted for public and private schools, colleges and universities. Education Service, Steger Building, Chicago; Southern Building, Washington; 1254 Amsterdam Ave., New York.

WOMAN TEACHER for lower primary grades; also young man teacher, unmarried, for manual training and elementary agriculture; at boys' training school of non-military type where home atmosphere is emphasized, situated in Ohio. Attractive compensation depending upon experience. Position open in September. 5094 SURVEY.

FOR THE HOME

Tea Room Management

In our new home-study course, "COOKING FOR PROFIT." Booklet on request.
Am. School of Home Economics. 849 E. 58th St., Chicago

SITUATIONS WANTED

EXECUTIVE with years of intensive experience organizing and conducting institutions and other works of social character in connection with dependent, delinquent and problem boys desires position as Superintendent of large Orphanage or Industrial School. Rural community and cottage plan preferred. References from those with national reputation as authorities. 5068 SURVEY.

Young couple, Jewish, thoroughly experienced SUPERINTENDENT and MATRON, who have satisfactorily filled previous positions eleven years, desire affiliation with Institution, highest references. 5088 SURVEY.

TRAINED AND EXPERIENCED social workers supplied for high-class positions. SOCIAL SERVICE DEPARTMENT, EXECUTIVE SERVICE CORPORATION, 1515 Pershing Square Building, N. Y. C.

YOUNG WOMAN, 30, Protestant, college graduate, desires travel Europe this summer as amanuensis to author, or governess-companion; German and French. 5087 SURVEY.

POSITION wanted by a trained and experienced social worker. 5098 SURVEY.

SCHOOL EXECUTIVE, 33, now public school superintendent Connecticut town, specialist educational and vocational guidance and social studies desires executive position or department headship in a New School. Begin September. 5060 SURVEY.

YOUNG MAN, experienced in institutional work for blind children wishes a position as superintendent or principal of a school for handicapped children. Prefers to build up a small school. 5092 SURVEY.

HOUSEMOTHER or superintendent in school or institution for boys or girls. Excellent qualifications. 4994 SURVEY.

JEWISH social worker, male, 38, fourteen years experience in executive capacity now employed, is seeking a new connection. Write to 5084 SURVEY.

EXECUTIVE Public Health Nurse desires position as Director of Health Center, Visiting Nurse Association, or County Health Work. 5082 SURVEY.

YOUNG MAN, 30, Jewish, with executive experience in public schools and private institutions desires work in executive or semi-executive capacity. Can assist in publicity as a speaker or writer. 5061 SURVEY.

EXPERIENCED New York man seeks position where his knowledge of publicity, motion pictures, exhibit and poster planning, editorial supervision and booklet writing may be used. Moderate salary. 5097 SURVEY.

COLLEGE trained, experienced, well recommended woman, seeks position with child-caring institution, in or near New York City. 5095 SURVEY.

SUPERINTENDENT of home for delinquent boys desires to make a change about May first. Good references. Age 49. Protestant, 5093 SURVEY.

(In answering advertisements please mention THE SURVEY. It helps us, it identifies you.)

MISCELLANEOUS

HAVE YOU SOMETHING TO WRITE, perhaps half written, which needs working over before it goes to publisher or printer? A report? An article? A book? If you are pressed for time, or have difficulty in expressing yourself, why not get an editor to help you? Understanding, experience, command of English, and a knowledge of editorial requirements are at your service. For further information address 5083 SURVEY.

TO OUR READERS: Contributions are solicited by a magazine published at a Sanatorium by the patients, and devoted to arts, letters and discussions. The sincere thanks of the readers can be the only compensation. Address "98.6," Cragmor Sanatorium, Colorado Springs, Colo.

RESEARCH: We assist in preparing special articles, papers, speeches, debates. Expert, scholarly service. AUTHOR'S RESEARCH BUREAU, 500 Fifth Avenue, New York.

BULLETIN BOARD

NATIONAL INTER-RACIAL CONFERENCE: Cincinnati. March 25-27. Secretary, Dr. George E. Haynes, Federal Council of Churches, 289 Fourth Avenue. New York City, and Dr. Will Alexander, Palmer Building, Atlanta, Georgia.

NEO-MALTHUSIAN AND BIRTH CONTROL CONFERENCE: New York City. March 25-31. Secretary, Mrs. Ann Kennedy, American Birth Control Society, 104 Fifth Ave., New York.

DELAWARE CONFERENCE OF SOCIAL WORK: Wilmington. March 26-27. President, Merle E. MacMahon, Children's Bureau, 9th and King St., Wilmington.

BETTER TIMES FIFTH ANNIVERSARY DINNER: New York City. April 2. Editor, George J. Hecht, 100 Gold Street, New York, N. Y.

NEW JERSEY STATE NURSES ASSOCIATION: Trenton. April 3. Secretary, Josephine Swenson, 12 Gordon Place, Rahway.

NATIONAL COMMITTEE ON PRISONS AND PRISON LABOR: New York City. April 13. Secretary, Julia K. Jaffray, 2 Rector Street, New York, N. Y.

NATIONAL LEAGUE OF WOMEN VOTERS. Richmond, Va. April 16-22. Secretary, Gladys Harrison, 532 17th Street, N. W., Washington. D. C.

CAMP FIRE GIRLS, ANNUAL CONFERENCE: Chicago. April 18-23. Local Executive, Mrs. William T. Grable, 504 Reaper Building, 72 West Washington Street, Chicago, Ill.

NORTH DAKOTA STATE NURSES ASSOCIATION: Bismarck. April 28-29. Secretary, Esther Teichmann, 811 Avenue C, Bismarck.

INTERNATIONAL COUNCIL OF WOMEN: Washington, D. C. May 4-14.

GIRL SCOUT CONVENTION: Boston. May 20-23. National Director, Mrs. Jane Deeter Rippin, 670 Lexington Ave., New York City.

CALIFORNIA CONFERENCE OF SOCIAL WORK: Sacramento. June 1-4. Secretary, Anita Eldridge, 55 New Montgomery St., San Francisco.

Y. M. C. A. SERVICE WITH BOYS, GENERAL ASSEMBLY: Estes Park, Colorado. June 4-12. Secretary, Ira E. Lute, 25 E. 16th Avenue, Denver, Colorado.

NATIONAL CONFERENCE OF SOCIAL WORK: Denver. June 10-17. Secretary, William Hammond Parker, 25 E. Ninth St., Cincinnati, Ohio.

NATIONAL TUBERCULOSIS ASSOCIATION: Minneapolis. June 15-20. Secretary. Dr. George M. Kober. 370 Seventh Ave., New York City.

NATIONAL ASSOCIATION FOR THE ADVANCEMENT OF COLORED PEOPLE: Denver. June 24-30. Secretary, James Weldon Johnson, 69 Fifth Avenue, New York, N. Y.

AMERICAN HOME ECONOMICS ASSOCIATION: San Francisco. August 1-8. Secretary, Lita Bane, 617 Mills Building, Washington, D. C.

SHOES

FOR THE LAME

THE Perfection Extension Shoe for any person with one short limb. Worn with any style of ready-made shoes with perfect ease and comfort. Write for booklet. Henry S. Lotz, Inc.. 125 East 28th St., New York City.

TRAVEL OPPORTUNITIES

EARN TRIP TO EUROPE: Organizers, Conductors, Chaperons, Needed. Economy Tour Europe next Summer. Y. W. and Y. M. C. A. and College Leadership. Social Workers, Y leaders and College Representatives wanted at once. 6 weeks Tour $390. Others $275-$550. Nine Countries. Small Group Divisions. Entire party limited 200. For appointment write, ALLEN TOURS. Boston, 17, Mass.

OFFICE SPACE

Approximately 1000 square feet of attractive space in high grade office building; Murray Hill section; particularly suitable for small welfare agency. 5075 SURVEY.

HOME SCHOOL

HOME SCHOOL for the runabout child. Individual care and instruction by college graduates. Partial scholarships for children whose parents are in educational work. The Bird House, Oldwick, N. J.

YOUR REAL ESTATE

Have you a Cottage, Camp or Bungalow to Rent or For Sale?

Have you Real Estate transactions of any kind pending?

Try the SURVEY'S Classified columns.

Special Real Estate advertising sections

April 1, May 1, June 1.

RATES
25c an agate line $3.50 an inch

Advertising Department

THE SURVEY

112 East 19th Street   New York City

HEALTH RESORT

THE BEECHES
Paris Hill   Maine

HEALTH RESORT for delicate, convalescent and nervous ladies seeking rest and pleasant recreation in Maine's delightful climate. Open June to November. Address letters to Station B., Poughkeepsie, N. Y., until June 1, care Blanche Dennes.

CURRENT PAMPHLETS

PERIODICALS

(In answering advertisements please mention THE SURVEY. It helps us, it identifies you.)

Here and Now

Don't read Survey Graphic over somebody's shoulder in a streetcar. It annoys him, it aggravates you to have only a glimpse of what is going on in social work and social thought. Here's the place and now is the time to have your own copy, monthly, fresh from the press, with articles in early issues by

Alain Locke
Robert R. Moton
James H. Dillard
Will W. Alexander
John Hope
Rossa B. Cooley
Gov. Alfred E. Smith
Francis K. Hackett
S. K. Radcliffe
Jacob Billikopf
Arthur Ruhl
Edward T. Devine
Patrick Geddes

And others

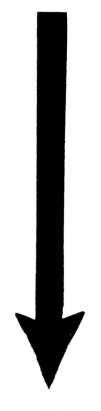

Survey Graphic, 112 East 19 Street, New York City

Gentlemen: Enter my subscription for Survey Graphic for 6 months' trial trip $1 (or full year $3) for which I enclose $......

Name ....

Address x